Default Semantics

MW00804281

Default Semantics

Foundations of a Compositional Theory of Acts of Communication

K. M. JASZCZOLT

OXFORD
UNIVERSITY PRESS

OXFORD
UNIVERSITY PRESS

Great Clarendon Street, Oxford OX2 6DP

Oxford University Press is a department of the University of Oxford.
It furthers the University's objective of excellence in research, scholarship,
and education by publishing worldwide in

Oxford New York

Auckland Cape Town Dar es Salaam Hong Kong Karachi Kuala Lumpur
Madrid Melbourne Mexico City Nairobi New Delhi Shanghai Taipei Toronto

With offices in

Argentina Austria Brazil Chile Czech Republic France Greece
Guatemala Hungary Italy Japan Poland Portugal Singapore
South Korea Switzerland Thailand Turkey Ukraine Vietnam

Oxford is a registered trade mark of Oxford University Press
in the UK and in certain other countries

Published in the United States
by Oxford University Press Inc., New York

© K. M. Jaszczolt 2005

The moral rights of the author have been asserted
Database right Oxford University Press (maker)

First published 2005
First published in paperback 2007

All rights reserved. No part of this publication may be reproduced,
stored in a retrieval system, or transmitted, in any form or by any means,
without the prior permission in writing of Oxford University Press,
or as expressly permitted by law, or under terms agreed with the appropriate
reprographics rights organization. Enquires concerning reproduction
outside the scope of the above should be sent to the Rights Department,
Oxford University Press, at the address above

You must not circulate this book in any other binding or cover
and you must impose this same condition on any acquirer

British Library Cataloguing in Publication Data
Data available

Library of Congress Cataloging in Publication Data
Data available

Typeset by SPI Publisher Services, Pondicherry, India
Printed in Great Britain on acid-free paper by Biddles Ltd., King's Lynn

ISBN 978–0–19–926198–7 (Hbk.)   978–0–19–922668–9 (Pbk.)

1 3 5 7 9 10 8 6 4 2

To Lidia Evelina,
who wants to write books when she grows up

Contents

Vance Joy's stories had drifted like groundsel seeds and taken root in the most unlikely places. They had rarely grown in the way he would have imagined, in that perfect green landscape of imagination, intersected with streams and redolent of orange blossom.

In certain climates they became like weeds, uncontrollable, not always beautiful, a blaze of rage or desire from horizon to horizon.

All these Harry had carried innocently, passing them on to his wife, his son, his daughter. Not having understood them, he transmitted them imperfectly and they came to mean quite different things.

Peter Carey, *Bliss*, London: Faber and Faber, 1981/2001, p. 19.

Preface

The content of what the speaker intends to communicate does not easily yield to theorizing. The representation of this content by a model hearer is probably as close as we can get to it in an attempt to account for the meaning of acts of communication. The most clear and adequate account of this meaning is always a formal one. And the most adequate formal account of discourse meaning is certainly a dynamic semantic account. Now, in order to bridge the gap between the intended meaning and meaning recovered by a model hearer in context, we need a theory of intentions. The most adequate framework for this task seems to be Gricean, and, of course, post-Gricean pragmatics.

A theory of meaning that combines a dynamic representation of discourse with an intentional explanation of processing has been long overdue. This book, I hope, will fill the gap. It is a theory of meaning of acts of communication and by extension a theory of meaning of discourses that assumes that the only interesting unit about which we can predicate meaning is an act of communication. This theory of meaning is also dynamic in the sense in which, to generalize, theories such as Dynamic Predicate Logic and Discourse Representation Theory are dynamic, and it is compositional in that compositionality is predicated of acts of communication.

The book assumes some basic familiarity with current semantic theory of the truth-conditional orientation, as well as some basic familiarity with Gricean, intention-based pragmatics. Information about the principles of the above orientations can be gained from textbooks such as Kearns (2000), Allan (2001), de Swart (1998), Kamp and Reyle (1993), Jaszczolt (2002a), and Levinson (1983). References in the text and notes give details of more specialised and more recent developments in the relevant areas and place the theory of Default Semantics in the context from which its theses get inspiration. Principles of dynamic semantics are briefly introduced—*ab initio*, I hope—in Chapter 3.

The book owes its appearance to many people. First, I would like to acknowledge my gratitude to the Leverhulme Trust for awarding me a research fellowship that freed me from all my teaching and administrative duties for the academic year 2003/4. I am also very grateful to Newnham College, Cambridge and the University of Cambridge for financially supporting my various research and conference trips during this period and to the Department of Linguistics for putting up with my absence. Freedom to think was much appreciated.

I am indebted to a great number of colleagues for their guidance in various ways: through discussions of my ideas and parts of the manuscript, and also through formal teaching and their enlightening publications. My particular thanks go to Henk Zeevat and Paul Dekker: to Henk for reading my work in draft form and discussing with me my various attempts to tame intensional contexts and compositionality, and to Paul for his excellent lectures on Dynamic Predicate Logic at ILLC, University of Amsterdam, which he kindly let me attend. Next, I am indebted to Stephen Schiffer for reading parts of the manuscript and pointing out to me various problems with my merger representation as it was in draft form. But for my brief visits to Amsterdam and New York, *Default Semantics* would have been much murkier. I also owe thanks to Stephen for teaching me a lot about compositionality through his various books and articles, including, of course, *The Things We Mean*. Further, I owe thanks to Thorstein Fretheim for impressing upon me the necessity of clarifying the scope of application of Default Semantics. Although the ultimate answer to this problem is still in the future, I hope I have at least addressed it thoroughly at this, still programmatic, stage of the theory. Other colleagues to whom I owe thanks for their comments and discussions at various stages of my work on the theory include Klaus von Heusinger, Hans Kamp, François Recanati, Anna Wierzbicka, and many others. Any remaining faults and infelicities are mine.

Some of the ideas have their origin in my earlier publications. I owe thanks to Elsevier Science for their permission to adapt appropriate sections of the following:

- *Discourse, Beliefs and Intentions: Semantic Defaults and Propositional Attitude Ascription*, 1999 (from chs. 1–3);
- *The Pragmatics of Propositional Attitude Reports*, 2000 ('Introduction');
- 'Against ambiguity and underspecification: Evidence from presupposition as anaphora', *Journal of Pragmatics* 34 (2002), 829–49.

I am also grateful to John Davey of Oxford University Press for his invitation to write this book. To Ken Turner, my co-editor of the book series CRiSPI (*Current Research in the Semantics/Pragmatics Interface*), my thanks for taking on more than his share of the editorial tasks while I was occupied with this project. Finally, I would like to thank my husband Charles Berthon and my daughter Lidia Berthon for making me remember that apart from writing this book, life includes family dinners, games of Monopoly and Scrabble, and other fun.

KMJ

Cambridge, July 2004

List of Abbreviations and Symbols

Abbreviations

Acc	Grice's acceptability operator
ACC	acceptability operator in DS
ACC_{Δ^n}	acceptability operator of the type of modality Δ and granularity n
ANCH	anchor in DRT
Att	attitude predicate in DRT
Bel	belief operator
C	DRS condition
CD	cognitive default
CPI 1	conscious pragmatic inference$_1$
CPI 2	conscious pragmatic inference$_2$
DI	Degrees of Intentions principle
DPL	Dynamic Predicate Logic
DRT	Discourse Representation Theory
DRS, D	Discourse Representation Structure
DS	Default Semantics
e	event
E	event point (Reichenbach)
fp	futurative progressive
GCI	generalized conversational implicature
iff	if and only if
I	assignment function
ILF	Interpreted Logical Form
M	model for a DRS
MOD	mode indicator in DRT
MoP, m	mode of presentation
MOR	Modified Occam's Razor principle
MR	merger representation
mt	measure of time
n	'now' (present moment)
p	proposition
P	predicate
^{P}(superscript)	partial representation
PI	Primary Intention principle
PoL	Parsimony of Levels principle
R	reference point (Reichenbach)
rf	regular future

s	1. state; 2. assignment
S	speech point (Reichenbach)
SCD 1	social-cultural default$_1$
SCD 2	social-cultural default$_2$
SDRT	Segmented Discourse Representation Theory
SOT	sequence of tense
t	time
tf	tenseless future
v	discourse referent
wrt	with respect to
WS	combination of word meaning and sentence structure

Symbols

*	ill-formed
$^?$(superscript)	unclear judgement of well-formedness
∃	existential quantifier of predicate logic
∀	universal quantifier of predicate logic
→	truth-functional implication
¬	truth-functional negation
&, ∧	truth-functional conjunction
∨	truth-functional disjunction
+ >	conversationally communicates
{ }	set
< >	intension
[ ],ν	semantic value
$_s⟦D⟧^M_{s'}$	dynamic value of *D* in *M* where *s* is the input assignment and *s'* the output assignment
⊨	tautology
<	temporal precedence
⊆	temporal inclusion
○	temporal overlap
Φ^*m	type of mode of presentation
⊤	symbol in predicate logic
≐	identity in the object language
;	sequencing operator
:: =	identity (for definiens and definiendum)
□	modal operator of alethic necessity
◇	modal operator of alethic possibility
| |	cardinality of a set
⊢ p	it is the case that *p*
!p	let it be that *p*
ʊ	representation of eventuality

Introduction

Discourse is composed of utterances and when we want to analyse discourse processing, we have to attend to the properties of utterances. This is what Default Semantics sets out to do. It sets out to provide cognitive foundations of discourse interpretation. It does so in a broadly conceived truth-conditional framework, where truth conditions are appropriated to utterances. In other words, what will interest us are the properties of utterances as basic units of discourse. Speaker's assertions in the form of utterances can be true or false. This has to be clearly distinguished from the orientation in the study of meaning according to which *sentences* have truth conditions, and in order to capture the meaning of *utterances* we have to go *beyond* truth conditions. Our subject of investigation is the processing of discourses and the main *unit* of analysis is an *utterance*. The *object* of analysis is a *discourse*: a string of utterances that make up discourses.[1] For this purpose, utterances are understood as *acts of communication*: they consist of linguistic and non-linguistic material that is used by the speaker to convey intended meaning.

Default Semantics combines the subject matter of post-Gricean 'truth-conditional pragmatics'[2] with the formalism and 'semanticization' of meaning found in Discourse Representation Theory (henceforth: DRT).[3] In other words, it is assumed that pragmatic information can contribute to the truth-conditional representation of an utterance. This information can have the form of conscious inference, or it can have the form of default meanings, arrived at without a conscious process. Unlike DRT, which follows the principle that semantic representations go beyond truth-conditional content,[4] Default Semantics is constructed, so to speak, 'one level higher': truth conditions pertain to the overall representation of the speaker's utterance seen from the perspective of a model hearer. There is no going 'beyond' truth conditions in the hearer's representation of content of the speaker's act of communication. From DRT, we borrow the idea of dynamic semantics as context change implemented in a semantic representation, and the idea that meaning in discourse will, somehow or other, turn out to be compositional, that is it will turn out to be a function of the parts and the structure (e.g. van Eijck and Kamp 1997).[5] In short, Default Semantics combines two seemingly incompatible theses as its assumptions:

(i) that *truth value can be predicated of utterances (acts of communication),* that is that pragmatic input contributes to the truth conditions;

and

(ii) that the theory of meaning of utterances and discourses is a *compositional, semantic* theory.

The compositional, semantic theory is understood as a theory of representations of meaning that pertain to utterances (understood as acts of communication) and their strings (discourses). Such semantic representations are called *merger representations* in that they combine (merge) information from word meaning, sentence structure, conscious pragmatic inference, and various kinds of default interpretations distinguished in what follows. Merger representations reflect the fact that various sources of information contribute to the overall meaning of an utterance. Ascribing compositionality to the level of such merger representations allows for the combination of the truth-conditional pragmatics perspective with the 'semanticization' of this perspective by applying the reanalysed and extended mechanism of dynamic semantics.

The main proposal, in a nutshell, is this:

- The theory of discourse meaning (the meaning of utterances and their sequences) is truth-conditional and dynamic.
- Pragmatic information, such as the output of pragmatic inference or defaults, contributes to the truth-conditional content.
- The representation of the truth-conditional content is a merger of information from (i) word meaning and sentence structure, (ii) conscious pragmatic processes, and (iii) default meanings. It is called a *merger representation.*
- Default meanings are conceived of as (i) cognitive defaults, stemming from the properties of the human thinking process, and (ii) social-cultural defaults, stemming from the way society and culture are organized.
- This merger is represented by using the principles of dynamic semantics, in particular those of *Default Semantics.* Applying the dynamic approach to mergers makes it possible to represent the meaning of multi-utterance discourses.
- Default Semantics uses an adapted and extended formalism of DRT but applies it to the output of the merger of the sources of information (as specified in the third bullet point above), that is to merger representations.

- Merger representations are construed as, so to speak, 'abstracts over thoughts': they contain that part of the content of thought that contributes to the *truth-conditional meaning of utterances and discourses.*

In short, in the account developed in what follows, pragmatically derived meaning contributes to the truth-conditional content, in both simple and complex constructions. But unlike in truth-conditional pragmatics, in my account truth conditions are associated with the level that does not endanger the autonomy of semantics. There are different kinds of input to the merger representation but only the *merger* is compositional and has truth conditions in any interesting sense from the point of view of discourse processing. The proposed amendment is this. Normally, compositionality is sought at the level of sentence structure. This is not so in Default Semantics. Word meaning and sentence structure, which are distinguished as one of the sources of input to merger representations, need not constitute a compositional input for the Default Semantics theory to be compositional: it is only the merger representation that has to be compositional.

Default Semantics shares what is probably the main assumption with current post-Gricean orientations in semantic and pragmatic theory, such as neo-Gricean pragmatics, relevance theory, and optimality theory pragmatics: since linguistic meanings underdetermine the content (proposition) expressed, we have to search for a 'pragmatic mechanism of completion[6] which can be best represented as an optimization procedure' (Blutner and Zeevat 2004: 1). In Default Semantics, this optimization is achieved through the interaction of the four sources of meaning information that contribute to the merger representation: word meaning and sentence structure, conscious pragmatic inference, cognitive defaults, and social–cultural defaults.

Utterance processing is assumed to proceed along the lines of dynamic representational semantics such as DRT. Default Semantics assumes the relational semantics of representation structures of DRT. This semantics is an adaptation and extension of the semantics of DRT as introduced briefly in Chapter 3, mainly after van Eijck and Kamp (1997). Part I contains a proposal of a new way of looking at meaning—as a merger representation, akin to thought but more coarse-grained than the rich and detailed content of thought. The proposed programme is then applied to various types of expressions and sequences of expressions in Part II. The proposal must not be regarded as a complete semantic theory: it is a programme for a unified theory of discourse meaning. It is the *linguistic and philosophical arguments for the proposed formalization* that constitute the subject of this book, not the complete system of formal interpretation of the merger representations. The latter are worked out only for some types of constructions: for semantically problematic expressions and phenomena which the theory has been independently argued to be, in principle, capable of handling in a more cognitively plausible and methodologically parsimonious way than other extant approaches. Undoubtedly, the proposed formalization can be improved upon in the future: there are *always* better solutions ahead.

The content of the chapters is as follows. Part I contains the theoretical foundations of Default Semantics. It introduces merger representations against the background of current discussions on logical form, compositionality, semantic underdetermination, pragmatic enrichment, and related phenomena and processes. It also introduces the notion of default interpretation used in Default Semantics and presents it against the background of several other current approaches to meaning that make use of default interpretations. In particular, Chapter 1 assesses the rationale for various levels of meaning representation and concludes with a proposal of one merger representation to which various sources of information about utterance meaning contribute. Chapter 2 discusses the difference between conscious pragmatic inference and default interpretation and concludes with a proposal of so-called cognitive and social–cultural defaults. Chapter 3 addresses the issue of compositionality of meaning and offers a solution of compositionality on the level of (dynamic) merger representations rather than dynamic linguistic semantic representations. In other words, it eschews the compositionality problem by 'shifting' compositionality, so to speak, to the level of abstractions over thoughts, in the sense that merger representations are more coarse-grained equivalents of thoughts and, like thoughts, they gain their compositionality through supervenience on the physical, or, so to speak, on what there is in the world.

Part II contains selected applications of Default Semantics to various types of expressions in English and to various semantic phenomena. In each chapter, I present some sample representations (merger representations) that use an adapted and extended formalism of DRT in order to present formally a model of discourse processing developed in Part I. Where new devices, such as new operators, had to be added to the language of Discourse Representation Structures (DRSs), I introduce their formal semantics below. Similarly, where an element of the DRT language has been used in a new way, I signal its reanalysis and the rationale for it. The numerous departures from the standard language of DRT are also discussed alongside constructing merger representations. To repeat, these adaptations and additions to DRT are necessitated by the facts that (i) the language of DRT is used here to represent discourse processing, composed of processing whole acts of communication, rather than linguistic competence, and (ii) merger representations do not give priority to any of their four sources of meaning information. In other words, grammar-based triggering configurations need not always be distinguished; only merger representations must.

Chapter 4 contains a default-semantics analysis of utterances with definite descriptions, focusing on the role of merger representations in capturing referential and attributive interpretations, as well as interpretations that contain a referential mistake. To repeat, merger representations are 'abstracts over thoughts', that is representations that are only as much fine-grained as the truth-conditional content requires on the particular occasion. Since they are, so to speak, 'thought-like', referential mistakes can be easily accounted for: the referring expression used by the speaker can be 'overruled' by one of the other sources of meaning information that produce a merger representation. Chapter 5 extends the application to propositional attitude constructions, distinguishing a sub-species of the *de dicto* interpretation in which there is a mismatch between the referring expression in the *that*-clause and the entity referred to by the speaker. It also contains a significant addition to the language of mental representations that allows for handling intensional contexts. Chapter 6 concerns futurity and modality. It demonstrates how a unified account of (i) various temporal and modal uses of the English *will* and (ii) various ways of expressing futurity in English can be constructed using the principles of Default Semantics. For this purpose, a new operator is introduced to the language of merger representations that subsumes various degrees of modal detachment under the concept of a *degree of acceptability*, loosely modelled on Grice's acceptability operator. Chapter 8 reanalyses sentential connectives and concludes that when the purpose of the theory of meaning is construing a model of discourse interpretation, sentential connectives in English do not constitute a natural category, neither do utterances that contain them give rise to any useful generalizations as far as the construction of merger representations is concerned. In short, the sample merger representations constructed in this chapter demonstrate that sentential connectives are much less problematic when analysed within the assumptions of Default Semantics than the last thirty or so years of theorizing about them makes them appear. Chapter 9 presents some partial arguments in favour of the punctual, 'exactly' semantics of number terms. It also contains a discussion of the role of approximative readings vis-à-vis the 'exactly' semantics and a discussion of the non-committal, 'just n' interpretation. Finally, the concluding Chapter 10 addresses the question of the advantages of a model where formal devices of a dynamic semantic theory are applied to the truth-conditional content which is the output of all the sources of meaning information that can be consulted in the processing of discourse. In other words, it assesses the success of 'semanticizing truth-conditional pragmatics' in terms of a dynamic *semantic* theory (in this very wide sense of 'semantic') called Default Semantics. It also makes some informed predictions about the scope of application of Default Semantics.

Notes

1 On assigning truth conditions to assertions vs. sentences see Soames (2002: 228–9). Soames stresses speakers' 'ignorance' about the *semantic content* and their alertness to the content of the *assertion*.

2 Represented by Recanati, Carston, Bach, Neale, and others. See, for example, Recanati (2003, 2004) and Carston (forthcoming).

3 See mainly Kamp and Reyle (1993); van Eijck and Kamp (1997).

4 Kamp and Reyle (1993) adopt Kaplan's (1989) definition of content, now standard in DRT.

5 Cf.: 'experience of the past ten years has shown that often, once the phenomena have been properly understood and have been given a systematic description using means that are not strictly compositional, it is then possible to also find a way of accounting for those phenomena that *is* strictly compositional, as well as attractive in other ways. Whether attractive strictly compositional solutions will become available in all cases is yet to be seen.' van Eijck and Kamp (1997: 233).

6 'Completion' in a non-technical sense rather than Bach's (1994*a*) 'completion' vs. 'saturation'.

Part I
Foundations

1

Meaning Representation: Setting the Scene

1.1 The semantics/pragmatics merger

Processing other people's utterances is normally fast and efficient. So, it seems uncontroversial that the theory of utterance interpretation should reflect this speed and efficiency of interlocutors. And yet the theoretical accounts of utterance meaning are heavily burdened with allocating various aspects of this process to various postulated domains. The semantics/pragmatics, syntax/semantics, and on some accounts syntax/pragmatics interfaces engender ample discussions in the literature on utterance interpretation and give rise to postulates of various levels of utterance interpretation. The theory of Default Semantics reduces the role of interfaces in utterance processing by arguing that the interaction of the sources of meaning information takes place prior to forming a compositional representation. The aim is to propose a way of accounting for utterance meaning that mirrors the speed and efficiency encountered in conversational practice. Instead of postulating levels of utterance interpretation and then trying to find out if they have any equivalent in the process they are supposed to explain, I shall begin with an assumption that there is one level of meaning to which various types of information contribute. The relevant question to ask is, *Where does meaning come from?*, but not, *What levels of meaning representation can be distinguished?*. Instead of interfaces and levels, it is more adequate to perceive the representation of meaning as a merger of the relevant sources. Such a merger will retain the appropriate place in a theory of meaning, that is that of a representation of utterance meaning, at the same time better reflecting the process of utterance interpretation. A 'representation of utterance meaning' will refer here to a representation, formed by a model addressee (or other hearer) of the speaker's utterance understood as an act of communication. Forming such representations follows some general principles laid out in what follows. These principles are sufficiently interpersonal to act as a foundation of a theory of acts of communication.

Before going into the details of a merger representation, a brief overview of the extant orientations is needed in order to place Default Semantics in a wider perspective of current views on the matter. The traditional view holds that in addition to lexical and syntactic ambiguity as in (1) and (2) respectively, there is also a third type of ambiguity that can be called semantic.

(1)   Let's go to the *bank*.

(2)   *The beautiful girl's dress* attracted my attention.

For example, a sentence with a negation operator *not* such as (3) is semantically ambiguous between the narrow scope and wide scope negation as in (3a) and (3b) respectively.

(3)   The white unicorn is not hungry.
(3a)   There is a uniquely identifiable entity called a 'white unicorn' and it is not hungry.
(3b)   It is not the case that there is a uniquely identifiable entity called a 'white unicorn' that is hungry.

The ambiguity position, held among others by Bertrand Russell, has been successfully refuted and replaced with a unitary semantics stance. In Gricean pragmatics, such differences in meaning as that between (3a) and (3b) can be attributed to implicated information. The existence of a uniquely identifiable white unicorn is not, strictly speaking, expressed by uttering this sentence. Similarly, in (4), the information that writing an article happened before swimming is implicated.

(4)   I wrote an article and went swimming.

Grice postulated a unitary semantics, complemented with the process of conversational *implicature* that results in conversational *implicata*. However, this proposal suffered from an unwelcome consequence that the content of the sentence that intuitively was part of its core meaning, such as the temporality of *and* ('and then') in (4), had to be relegated to the status of an implicatum.[1] Hence, in post-Gricean research it has been suggested instead that semantics is *underspecified* as to these aspects of meaning. Or, to put it less technically, semantics *underdetermines* meaning. The semantics of the conceptual representation system is considered to be truth-conditional and it is different from the semantics in the narrow sense (linguistic semantics) which is the direct output of the syntactic processing of a sentence (Carston 1988, 1998*a*, 2002*a*). Pragmatic factors, summarized in Grice's maxims of conversation, or in their subsequent reworkings by Horn (e.g. 1984), Levinson (e.g. 1987, 1995, 2000), and Sperber and Wilson (e.g. 1986), 'intrude' into such a semantics of the conceptual representational system and produce a propositional representation. There are ample discussions in the literature of the inadequacy of the ambiguity view and the classical Gricean implicature, among others by Kempson, Sperber and Wilson, Carston, Recanati, Bach, Atlas, Horn, Levinson, and Jaszczolt.[2]

Now, according to some representatives of this post-Gricean debate, such differences in meaning belong to what is said rather to what is implicated.[3] According to others, the differences in meaning belong to a separate level of default interpretations. Default meanings are introduced in detail in Chapter 2 and are going to occupy us in the remainder of this book. For the moment, it suffices to say that they are salient interpretations arrived at without the help of the context of the particular situation in which the utterance was uttered.[4] They arise without a need for conscious pragmatic inference. This level of defaults has been conceived in a variety of ways:

(i) as default interpretations that are resolved by semantics, as in DRT (see Kamp and Reyle 1993 and Section 1.6) and its offshoots such as Segmented Discourse Representation Theory (henceforth SDRT; see Asher and Lascarides e.g. 1998*a*, 2003);

(ii) as default interpretations that are resolved by pragmatics, as in Bach's level of what is 'implicit in what is said' (implic*i*ture; see Bach 1994*a*, 1994*b*, 2001);

(iii) as fully-fledged social and cultural conventions for default meanings (called also presumptive meanings; see Levinson 1995, 2000). According to Levinson, default meanings arise along the lines summarized in the three heuristics: Quantity ('What isn't said, isn't'), Informativeness ('What is expressed simply is stereotypically exemplified'), and Manner ('What's said in an abnormal way isn't normal'), which are a development of Grice's maxims of conversation.[5]

The theory of Default Semantics cannot be identified with any of these standpoints, although it has some affinities with all three. First, it recognizes salient, default meanings and in this it differs from relevance theory (Sperber and Wilson, Carston) where utterance meaning is always processed in the context. Relevance theory does not recognize context-free default meanings. However, it has a construct of a 'default context', a default scenario in which inference takes place. In this respect the difference between my approach and that of relevance theory is that, in my approach, the default scenario comes 'free', without pragmatic inference. From (i)–(iii) above, Default Semantics shares many theoretical assumptions with (i). In DRT, meaning is represented as discourse structures that combine information from syntax and from the changing context. All the information that contributes to the meaning of the utterance is semanticized. DRSs contain discourse referents and conditions that come from sentence grammar. Sentences are said to be frequently under-specified as to their precise meaning, and the surrounding discourse may resolve the direction in which the interpretation should proceed. Default Semantics differs from DRT in the role assigned to grammar. More precisely, it regards grammar as one of several sources of discourse conditions. The difference is this. DRT allows for semantic underspecification. To allow for underspecification means to recognize the privileged status of the *form* of the expression, and thus to claim that the logical form of the sentence which is the output of syntactic processing constitutes the 'core' of the meaning of the utterance, further enriched and filled in from some other sources of infor-mation. These sources can be conceived of in a broader or narrower sense. They normally include the situational context and salient, presumed mean-ings. In DRT, this contextualization is still rather minimal, confined to the fact that progressing discourse provides missing anaphoric links and other refer-ence resolution, and resolves presuppositions and ambiguities such as the collective and distributive reading of number terms. Default Semantics is more radical. It shows that in a dynamic approach to meaning, semantic underspecification is not indispensable. A more economical alternative can work along the following lines. Dynamic representations are probably the most satisfactory representations of meaning in that they have the potential for mirroring the speed and efficiency of utterance processing. They are considered to be mental representations of meaning and hence mirroring this efficiency and speed are their necessary prerequisites. So, let us ask the important question again: where does meaning come from? Dynamic seman-tic theories answer correctly that meaning comes from concepts and the way in which they are combined in sentences, but also from the changing context.[6] In other words, they try to preserve the compositionality of meaning, at the same time enriching the semantics to comprise all other relevant information that can influence what was said by the speaker. The representation that is underspecified, or a representation that allows for an ambiguity of readings, becomes complete after the addition of information from the surrounding discourse.

Now, if there are multiple sources of information about meaning, then it seems justified to entertain the possibility that grammar is not a privileged one among them but instead all sources 'conspire', to produce a *compositional* representation of utterance meaning. This assumption is a driving force for Default Semantics. In this approach, the truth conditions that interest us are the truth conditions of the *utterance* taken to be the one that the speaker intended to communicate rather than the truth conditions of the sentence alone. Compositionality is, so to speak, shifted one-level up and becomes a property of the meaning of utterances, where the latter are understood as acts of communication. This pragmatic approach to truth conditions is discussed at length in Chapter 3. For example, if the speaker says (5), the truth conditions that interest us pertain to the meaning representation to the effect that the speaker has not eaten the appropriate meal for the part of the day in which the utterance was issued, rather than the meaning representation to the effect that there is no time prior to the time of the utterance at which the speaker ate.

(5)   I haven't eaten.

The formalism of DRT should be able to provide such truth conditions.

At first sight, this standpoint is closely related to what can be called, in a sweeping generalization, the post-Gricean view on the semantics/pragmatics boundary: pragmatic input contributes to the truth-conditional content (Carston 1988, Recanati 1989*b*). Recanati (2004), for example, founds his analysis of meaning on the truth-conditional content of utterances. This content is for him an aspect of speaker's meaning.[7] He calls this standpoint *contextualism*:

By 'Contextualism' I mean the view according to which it is speech acts, not sentences, which have a determinate content and are truth-evaluable. (Recanati 2004: 154)

Default Semantics accepts contextualism with respect to truth-conditional content but does not endorse the view that contextualism commits us to speaker's meaning being 'pragmatic through and through' (Recanati 2004: 4). In Default Semantics, compositionality is a property of the meaning of acts of communication and one can at least try to entertain the possibility of a formal theory of meaning of acts of communication. In this sense, Default Semantics is a compositional semantic theory of acts of communication.

It seems that the formalism of DRT, suitably amended and extended, should be applicable to a view that is founded on such pragmatics-rich truth conditions. Just as we 'shift' compositionality to utterances (understood as whole acts of communication),[8] so do we attempt to apply an amended and extended formalism of DRT at that level. Although the semantics of DRT goes 'beyond' truth conditions understood as the truth conditions pertaining to the logical form which is itself the output of sentence grammar, the 'semanticization' of what is 'beyond' these truth conditions is easily translatable as 'pragmaticization' of truth conditions. In other words, DRT and truth-conditional pragmatics are not incompatible. The result of pragmatic inference and, on some approaches, also conversational defaults contribute to truth-conditions *à la* truth-conditional pragmatics, but this pragmatic contribution can then be conceived of as part of the semantic theory. Default Semantics is precisely such a semantic theory of acts of communication in that its truth-conditional representations are representations of acts of communication, formalizable by using the extended language of DRT. To repeat, this formalism is used 'one level higher', that is for acts of communication. As in truth-conditional pragmatics, there is no need to go beyond truth conditions. In fact, the 'beyond' is even further reduced than in Recanati's theory because acts of communication (that we call utterances) are whole, linguistic and non-linguistic, acts combined. For example, if the speaker makes a referential mistake and calls Joe Smith 'Jim Brown', it may still be Joe Smith that figures in the semantic representation. But this is not the place to go into the detailed content of representations of acts of communication. The content of merger representations is given in the applications throughout Part II.[9]

This inter-paradigm approach built upon both truth-conditional pragmatics and DRT retains what is best in both: a pragmatic contribution to truth conditions from the first, and a compositional, formal semantic account of the resultant representation from the other. Predictably, this approach requires some adjustments on the part of the DRT language. This is so because, unlike Default Semantics, DRT advocates a heavy reliance on sentence grammar. Default Semantics begins with a stance that this privileged status of the output of syntactic processing should not be assumed on trust. This is so for the same reason for which modules in utterance processing should not be postulated ad hoc: they then become theoretical constructs that facilitate the discourse about understanding utterances but are otherwise of dubious cognitive status. One may equally well envisage a dynamic semantic theory that would adhere to the principle of having one level of representation to which *all* sources of meaning information contribute, without making assumptions as to the ordering of these sources but discerning the sources in a way that reflects the intuitions of the interlocutors. In the process of utterance interpretation, one cannot pre-theoretically assume that the hearer processes the sentence form by using lexical concepts as one discrete source, and, say, background knowledge as another. Let us start with the more theory-free idea that all sources of information contribute to meaning 'on an equal footing', that is by a 'conspiracy', an interaction whose mechanism is for the moment beyond our interest. This is a radical change in the point of view that results in a much simpler paradigm: there is no underspecification, there is no ambiguity either, and there is a rich semantics that is a merger of contributions to meaning, whatever their provenance. So, in short, the alternative to the above views proposed here is that there is no middle level of meaning, no semantic underspecification, no ambiguity, but instead a merger of meaning components. In Default Semantics, unlike in DRT, logical form has no privileged status. In such an approach to meaning construction, there is no semantics/pragmatics boundary, and the ambiguity/underspecification dilemma proves to be a wrongly posed problem.

Default Semantics can thus be classified as option (iv) and added to the list presented earlier in this section: the meaning representation is a merger of information from various sources where all the sources are treated equally; there is no priority given to the output of grammar and hence, by definition, there cannot be any 'intrusion' of pragmatically derived content into a logical form. The unit of analysis is an utterance conceived of as an act of communication. The result of these assumptions is that the merger representation for (5) repeated below can be, say, (6). Sentence structure is not 'intruded into': it can also be overridden.

(5)   I haven't eaten.

(6)   Kasia is hungry.

This admission of (6) as the compositional meaning of the act of communication in (5) may seem difficult to accept at first glance as it goes against the established tradition that distinguishes the logical form of the sentence together with its developments as the propositional content of the utterance, adding implicatures as further propositions communicated by this utterance. Default Semantics is justified in being radically different in this respect. Its unit of analysis is envisaged somewhat differently: it is an act of communication that combines all linguistic and non-linguistic means of communicating the speaker's intentions. The output of semantic analysis is the merger of various sources of meaning that make up the act of communication. In this sense, we have a semantics—a compositional and truth-conditional one—of units that correspond to communicated thoughts. 'Correspond', because the unit of semantic analysis is more coarse-grained than thought, just as the output of semantic analysis (merger representation) is more coarse-grained than a putative representation of thought (whatever the latter may be). The output of semantic analysis is as fine-grained as is necessary for specifying the meaning of the act of communication, neither more nor less.

In short, in semanticizing all the contributions to the merger, Default Semantics resembles DRT and uses a reanalysed and extended formalism of DRT in constructing such merger representations.[10] The strongest argument in favour of such mergers comes from the relative statuses of utterances and underlying mental states. As will become evident in Chapter 2, mental states such as belief have a property of 'aboutness' that is, in a manner of speaking, as basic to them as compositionality is to the meaning of utterances. These properties of mental states and utterances contribute to the merger and their respective importance in meaning representation has to be duly recorded. If we shed the decades of talking about levels and interfaces and try to defend the merger, the next issue to resolve is the issue of the level on which compositionality of meaning should operate. In other words, if we no longer have a level of logical form that is separate from utterance meaning, then what is the use in retaining compositionality of meaning at the level of logical form? Instead, we apply the composition of meaning to the process of merging. The level at which compositionality is sought in Default Semantics is not unlike that entertained in Recanati's (2004) proposal:

> [T]he semantics of natural language is not insulationist.... [T]he meaning of the whole is *not* constructed in a purely bottom-up manner from the meanings of the parts. The meaning of the whole is influenced by top-down, pragmatic factors, and through the meaning of the whole the meanings of the parts are also affected. *So we need a more 'interactionist' or even 'Gestaltist' approach to compositionality.*[11] (Recanati 2004: 132)

The execution of this intuition is different though: Default Semantics is 'semantic through and through'. Arguably, formal semantics is the best way to remain compositional about meaning. I argue in Chapter 3 (Section 3.5.3) that a dynamic semantic theory of acts of communication is as far as we can go in the direction of pragmatics while remaining compositional. As will become evident in the applications of Default Semantics presented through-out Chapters 4–9, compositionality of the merger gives much better results than the compositionality of the logical form that has proved so problematic for a variety of constructions, to mention only all underdetermined senses including the classic propositional attitude constructions.[12]

A terminological caveat is due at this point. The terms 'underdetermina-tion' and 'underspecification' have been used in a variety of ways in the literature. In Default Semantics, underdetermination is a characteristic fea-ture of the sentence: the output of the processing of the sentence frequently underdetermines the meaning of the utterance. As such, underdetermination can be safely taken as a fact. In Examples (3), (4), and (5) above we have instances of such underdetermination. Underspecification is a more technical term that applies to the property of the semantic representation. Semantic representation is underspecified if it does not fully represent the meaning of the utterance. It is the level of such underspecified semantics that is denied in the merger approach of Default Semantics. Since the sources of meaning 'merge', there is no stage of utterance interpretation at which underspecification can arise. Underspecification is assessed in more detail in Section 1.2 where the methodological principles that govern this lack of underspecification are set out.

Moreover, it is necessary to distinguish the terms 'utterance meaning' and 'sentence meaning' as I have done so far. Namely, sentence meaning is the meaning of what is physically written or uttered. In Default Semantics, there is no need for such a unit in utterance processing. I refer to sentence meaning merely for explanatory reasons, in order to spell out the sources of the merger. Utterance meaning is what the speaker is taken by the addressee to mean by it. I shall reserve the expression 'speaker's meaning' for the wider notion of utterance meaning plus all the relevant inferences that can be drawn from it and which lie outside utterance meaning. In other words, I reserve 'speaker's meaning' for the utterance meaning plus its implicatures—with the proviso that utterance meaning, in Default Semantics, is not governed by the restrictions of the sentence structure and thus can be as in (6) for utterance (5). The expression 'what is said' will not be used in the theoretical sense, in spite of the discussions it has generated. 'What is said' has been used in the literature in such a variety of senses, statuses, and scopes[13] that exorcising it in the spirit of the proposed innocence is preferable to adding to the extant confusions. Finally, for the same theoretical reason to do with the merger, the term 'intrusion' into a level of representation proves redundant. If sources of meaning are treated on an equal footing (and it is demonstrated in detail throughout Chapters 2 and 3 that they should be so treated), then there is no 'intrusion', no 'core' into which 'satellites' can intrude. 'On an equal footing' means here that a random source of meaning information can take precedence over the other sources in a particular situation of discourse, as, for example, (5) and (6) demonstrate.

In this section I have introduced the view that the syntax/semantics, semantics/pragmatics, and syntax/pragmatics boundary disputes present utterance meaning in an overly complicated way. There is one level of meaning representation to which all relevant information contributes. There is no reason why we should treat the output of syntax as a privileged source of information. Frequently, there is a lot left to the inference from the context. Moreover, we also owe a great deal to the very properties of mental states that our utterances externalize. So, instead of a core provided by the output of grammar and intrusions from peripheral sources of meaning, we have a merger representation to which all information contributes on an equal footing. The principles supporting such a merger constitute the theory of Default Semantics and are spelled out in Sections 1.2, 2.2.2, and in Chapter 3.

1.2 Questioning underspecification

There has been considerable agreement in the literature that sentences such as (3), repeated below, are not ambiguous between the presupposing (see (3a) above) and non-presupposing (3b) reading. Instead, they are underdetermined as to their meaning.

(3)   The white unicorn is not hungry.

When a sentence has more than one reading and these readings cannot be traced back to two independent logical forms, then there is no ambiguity but rather some other type of interpretative difficulty, variously called sense-generality, underdetermination, indeterminacy, nondetermination, indefiniteness of reference, neutrality, unmarkedness, or lack of specification (see Zwicky and Sadock 1975: 2). Three decades later, underdetermination seems to have established itself as a general name for this phenomenon of openness to more than one propositional (truth-conditional) representation, facilitated by pragmatic inference to which such an incomplete meaning representation leads (see e.g. Atlas 1989; Horn 1992; Carston 2002a).[14] For example, a scalar term 'some' in (7) is not ambiguous, but instead (7) is underdetermined as to the interpretation in (7a) or (7b).

(7)   I have met some of her friends.
(7a)   I have met some if not all of her friends.   (lower-bounded reading)
(7b)   I have met some but not all of her friends.   (upper-bounded reading)

In Horn's (1992: 172) terms, 'what is *said* in an utterance is systematically underdetermined by what is *uttered*'.

Introducing underdetermination to semantic theory opened the way for more and more advanced proposals that obey methodological parsimony. In agreement with Occam's razor and in particular with Grice's (1978) Modified Occam's Razor (henceforth: MOR) that advocates not multiplying senses beyond necessity, theories of meaning came closer to representing the cognitive processes involved in understanding utterances. In other words, as was discussed in Section 1.1, since the processing of utterances is normally fast and efficient, the theory of this processing has to account for this speed and efficiency. If there is no stage of the interpretation of (3) at which the multiple readings are activated, no such ambiguity should be present in the theory either. The next step to take is to ask what levels *have* to be present in the theory.

Unlike the technical notion of underspecification, underdetermination is a fact of communication: sentences are frequently just guides to the full, intended proposition that has to be inferred. There is no methodological extravagance in acknowledging underdetermination: the fact that the physically uttered sentence is only a rough guide to the intended proposition does not yet mean that there is an underdetermined representation that is separate from some inferential completions. If we want to see utterance processing in terms of such representations, we need another concept, that of underspecification. And the latter is not as harmless as the first. It is heavily theoretically loaded and, as will become obvious shortly, it is quite redundant if we want to observe the methodological principle of parsimony and mirror the process of utterance interpretation.

The term 'underspecification' is normally used with reference to information carried by logical form and this is how I am going to use it here (see e.g. van Deemter and Peters 1996). For example, the logical form of (5), repeated below, is underspecified as to the interval which the statement concerns.

(5)   I haven't eaten.

In other words, the domain of quantification over time is not explicitly given. So, in underspecified semantics:

[t]he idea . . . is not to generate and test many possible interpretations but to first generate one 'underspecified' representation which in a sense represents all its complete specifications and then use whatever information is available to further specify the result. (Muskens 2000: 311)

If the aim is to generate logical forms of sentences, for example for the purpose of computational models of sentence processing, underspecified semantics is certainly justified. However, in a cognitively plausible account of utterance processing by human agents, this step is rather costly and contentious. It has been widely acknowledged that reasoning about the form of the sentence is not separate from reasoning about the content (see e.g. Muskens 2000). If so, separating them is justified in computational modelling of discourses (for example, as in Asher and Lascarides's 2003 SDRT) but when we try to adopt it in modelling the process of meaning construction by a hearer, it does not adapt so well to the purpose. The methodological principle to follow here is, if there is no evidence for separate levels of processing, do not postulate them. Such evidence would be constituted by modules in the mind that are responsible for sentence form, conceptual content, or deductive and other pragmatic inference. In fact, in the light of recent advances in syntax (Chomsky 1995, 2001, 2004) and pragmatics (Sperber and Wilson 2002), arguments for a strict separation are decisively weaker than those against.[15] In order to formulate this methodological principle in its general form, all we have to do is follow MOR and apply it to levels of representation of meaning. I have called this application a principle of Parsimony of Levels (PoL; Jaszczolt 1999*a*, 1999*b*):

PoL: Levels of senses are not to be multiplied beyond necessity.

So, underdetermination is a fact, while underspecification is to be introduced with extreme caution. It is not banished completely: if we ask *to what extent* sentences have to be disambiguated for logical reasoning to proceed (van Deemter 1998), we will observe that it is not absolutely necessary to arrive at the full, complete proposition in order to get by in conversation. Sometimes, the 'unfinished' representation suffices. In such cases, it is legitimate to talk about underspecified logical forms that constitute the final stage of processing of an utterance: the addressee may not be able to infer more, or may not need to infer more for the purpose at hand. This is where a model of utterance processing by human agent and a model of computational processing can meet: both allow for such underspecification to take place. Van Deemter (1998) proposes a logic for underspecified representations: the system tries to disambiguate a representation but it stops as soon as the representation becomes sufficiently specific to act in further reasoning. Defining 'ambiguity' as leaving interpretation options open, he calls this account an 'ambiguous logic'. Ambiguous logic gives further evidence for the claim that contextual and other information may be utilized at various stages of utterance processing and hence underspecification is also a matter of degree rather than constituting one unique stage as an output of grammar. But, most importantly, it shows that underspecification is a term that is grossly overused in semantic theory: when there is no evidence of this level, it should not be postulated.

Now, if underspecification is not banished completely but rather is confined to the cases where it can be discerned with psychological plausibility, then we have to decide exactly how and when it has to be discerned. According to some accounts, logical form is underspecified and can be completed or expanded quite freely, without the need to account for these inferential additions[16] in the syntactic representation (e.g. Recanati 2002*a*; Carston forthcoming). In other words, there need not be any empty slots in the logical form to fill in in order for such additions to take place. But, naturally, the simplest scenario would be to demonstrate that there are in fact such slots.

Then we would retain rich semantics, founded on a solid output of syntactic processing, and contain pragmatic inference within the bounds of the slots, as in the following proposal:

Here is the view of linguistic communication I find plausible. First, a speaker makes an utterance, and her linguistic intentions uniquely determine a certain syntactic structure, or 'logical form', as it is known in syntax. If her utterance is a successful linguistic assertion, the logical form is sentential. Successful interpretation involves assigning denotations to the constituents of the logical form, and combining them in accord with composition rules that do not vary with extra-linguistic context. (Stanley 2002: 149)

In other words, all the expansions of logical forms that give the minimal rather than the intended proposition, as well as the completions of logical forms where the latter are semantically incomplete, are, in fact, assigning values to constituents of the logical form, to the elements of the sentence itself. There are no 'unarticulated constituents' of the logical form; all the constituents can be traced to the logical form itself and all participate in the composition of sentence meaning: '[m]uch syntactic structure is unpronounced, but no less real for being unpronounced' (Stanley 2002: 152). Arguments on both sides are plentiful (Stanley 2000; Stanley and Szabo 2000; King and Stanley 2005 vs. e.g. Bach 2000; Carston 1988, 2002*a*, forthcoming; Recanati 1989*a*, 1993, 2002*a*, 2004; Levinson 2000). The starting point is not equal for both orientations, however: the onus of proof lies on the advocates of syntactic slots and there has not as yet been any successful proof provided.

Nevertheless, it seems possible to use the intuition of the rich semantics in a way that makes the differences between radical semantics and radical pragmatics (Recanati's 1993, 2002*a*, 2003, 2004 term is 'truth-conditional pragmatics') cease to look polarized. King and Stanley (2005: 113) set out to demonstrate that 'much more counts as genuinely semantic than skeptics about the scope of semantic content have maintained'. But in order to share this view it is not necessary to resort to slots in logical form. Semantic content, as an input to the truth-conditional interpretation, is also commonly conceived of in a dynamic way in which the outcome of the processing of the context, the information from default readings, and other possible sources of meaning all contribute to the semantic representation quite independently of the (static) logical form. So, one can be *semanticizing* meaning without ascribing all of it to syntax. The difference is not merely terminological: Stanley, Szabo, and King talk about a rich semantic content, not just semantic content that can be ascribed on the basis of the sentence alone. So, they want to have their cake and eat it: they want a rich semantic content, that is they want more than the sentence but at the same time they want to call it a sentence, a unit of syntax. One may wonder for what purpose they make this move. After all, semanticizing meaning (having rich semantics) can be achieved in more intuitively plausible ways in dynamic semantic theories. As will be argued in Chapter 3, we can retain compositionality if we apply it to a unit that combines information from syntax, context, defaults, properties of thoughts, and any other sources that have been or may in the future be discovered. In other words, we apply it to the merger that I introduced in Section 1.1. So, when King and Stanley (2005) point out that the syntactic slots theory endorses a correct view of speakers' intuitions about semantic content, it has to be remembered that the intuitions about semantic content can be preserved without such slots. One of the examples they discuss is that of indicative conditionals as in (8):

(8)   If you ate *some* of the cookies and no one else ate any, then there must still be some left. (from King and Stanley 2005: 155)

They claim that the reading 'some but not all' is 'genuinely semantic': it is not due to the intrusion of pragmatic inference but rather it is the result of the processing of focus. They mention focal stress as in (8). But the problem with focus is that it is not always marked in a special way, or, if it is, the marking can appear in a variety of forms. Focus can come from semantic contrast, it need not be intonational or be marked in any other way.[17] In order to account for conditionals in general, they assume the possible-worlds analysis that involves the similarity relation between worlds. They assume that the syntax of the conditionals triggers this search for similar worlds in the context. However, how this would give us the world with some but not all cookies being eaten, when no special focusing is present, is not clear. And focusing does not mean slots: it can affect truth conditions but it need not amount to slots; it is more likely to amount to the alternatives of the focused element that are invoked in the process of utterance processing.[18]

All in all, King and Stanley make an important point that before postulating truth-conditional pragmatics with free, not syntactically controlled enrichment (see e.g. Recanati 2002*a*), before discarding intuitions about semantic form, one has to investigate all semantic options. But they fail to investigate any further beyond the least plausible: syntax of some non-existent 'sentences'.

It has to be observed that, if one wants to follow the route of parsimony of levels of representation, it seems that one can go further than semantics and propose a dynamic syntactic representation where some sort of world knowledge, default knowledge, and other sources of information contribute to syntax directly. Dynamic Syntax is such a proposal. In Dynamic Syntax, representations are constructed incrementally and rely on various inputs. This is realized as a goal-directed tree growth:

[T]he essence of all explanations is the transition from one decorated [i.e. with annotations or requirements, KJ] partial structure to another. The dynamics of transition between the input and output structures is the heart of the explanation. On this view, the phenomenon of underspecification of expressions such as pronouns *vis-à-vis* their interpretation is *not some aberrant departure* within an otherwise regular formal language system.[19] The skeletal nature of their interpretation taken independently of context is, to the contrary, a reflex of the fact that a natural language parser is a set of principles for progressive and goal-directed processing of linguistic input. (Kempson, Meyer-Viol, and Gabbay 2001: 261)

The general assumptions of dynamic syntax are, broadly speaking, compatible with the merger I propose: instead of a rigid, static output of syntax, we have the growth of information in which factors external to words and their combinations play a part. The question remains, why should we adopt rich syntax if syntactic processing is easily discernible as a separate process of meaning construction? If, as all dynamic approaches agree, the sources of information about meaning are interleaved in processing discourse, why not commence with an assumption that all these outputs of the sources of information 'sum up', so to speak, somehow or other, but we do not yet know precisely how?[20] The merger representations of Default Semantics take this step and the privileged role of the structure is suppressed. For the moment, let us take it to be suppressed on methodological grounds and on the grounds of the lack of evidence. In Chapter 3 and in the applications of Default Semantics that follow, this impartial merger acquires further grounds for justification. It has to be borne in mind, however, that on a certain level of generalization this discussion is largely terminological: a dynamic theory of meaning that recognizes an interaction of various sources of meaning information is the core of both Dynamic Syntax and Default Semantics.

Finally, one has to bear in mind the fact that in various approaches under-specification can be applied to a variety of phenomena. For some, the under-specification of the logical form can account for all the missing conceptual elements of the speaker's utterance. For others, it accounts for only some systematic choices of readings. This distinction is quite independent of the syntactic slots/free enrichment controversy. A 'middle solution' is that of choice functions advocated by von Heusinger and Egli (e.g. 2000; von

Heusinger 2000*a*, 2000*b*). Choice functions indicate in the logical form that there are options of interpretation:

The epsilon operator is interpreted by a choice function Φ, which is a function that assigns to a non-empty set *s* one of its elements, as defined in [9] or alternatively in [10]. Intuitively, a choice function selects one element out of a set, and an epsilon term *εx Fx* refers to an *F* that is selected by a choice function Φ out of the set of *Fs*.

(9) $\Phi(s) \in s$ if $s \neq \emptyset$

(10)   *f* is a choice function (i.e. *CH(f)* holds) iff *P(f(P))*, where *P* is non empty. (von Heusinger and Egli 2000: 4)

For example, the specific reading of indefinite descriptions can be accounted for by choice functions as follows:

(11)   Every student read a book.
(11a)   CH(f) & $\forall x$ (Student (x) → Read (x, f(book))) (adapted from von Heusinger and Egli 2000: 5)

Although, as the authors admit, the scope of application of choice functions has not yet been established, it seems that this device is very useful in representing the underspecification of quantifying expressions and some other expressions, such as negation, where the choice of reading is readily formalizable. Choice functions allow for getting rid of cumbersome quantifier raising (von Stechow 2000), which, like any other LF movement, has no semantic motivation and has never been accepted in categorial surface grammars.[21] How it would deal with context-dependent instances of free enrichment is not yet certain.

The next unresolved issue concerns the status of a *representation*. In dynamic semantics, there is no agreement as to whether representations are needed at all. In Dynamic Predicate Logic (henceforth DPL; Groenendijk and Stokhof 1991), the syntax is the same as that in traditional predicate logic, but the interpretation rules are dynamic. Most importantly, conjunction and existential quantifier are interpreted in such a way that they are not restricted to syntactic scope. They can operate cross-sententially. By means of altering the interpretation rules, the additional level of semantic representation recognized in such dynamic approaches as DRT is disposed of. This is undoubtedly an ingenuous and highly parsimonious proposal from the methodological point of view. However, when the aim of the theory is primarily to reflect the cognitive reality of utterance processing rather than successfully to model natural language discourse from the formal point of view, representations are indispensable. I discuss this issue in more detail in Sections 1.6 and 3.1. Further evidence for the indispensability of representations is given in the applications of the merger representation pursued in

Chapters 4–9. If indeed syntax has no privileged status, if information from various sources merges in a single output and these sources are to be treated on an equal footing in the sense assumed above, then there is no need to push parsimony as far as the interpretations of DPL. In fact, DPL itself came to recognize anchoring to the world in order to account for anaphoric links. So, representationalism prevails.[22]

In what follows, I adopt the semanticization of meaning, but no underspecification of logical from. Logical form is what it is: the output of syntactic processing, and all attempts to make it what it is not, or embellish or complete it with information coming from elsewhere, succumb to the myth that gives the logical form a privileged place in utterance interpretation, that is treats it as the core source of meaning. The latter, however, is not an assumption that one must necessarily follow.

1.3 Questioning logical form

As is evident from the discussion in Section 1.2, logical form may not be an interesting concept for a theory of discourse as it does not necessarily constitute an independent stage in utterance processing. When it is conceived of as the output of syntactic processing that can be further enriched in order to represent the proposition meant by the speaker, it would have to be demonstrated that this output of syntactic processing is present as an independent level of meaning at some stage of utterance interpretation. When, on the other hand, it is conceived of as a (dispensable) level of semantic representation over and above the meaning content as in DPL, it easily collapses into a much richer level of a propositional, sometimes enriched, representation.[23] If the output of syntax is not the same as logical form, then the 'extras' can be added almost at will. From now on, I shall talk about the logical form in the first sense, that is as the output of syntactic processing.

On the basis of extant evidence and the assumption of methodological parsimony spelled out as PoL, it is more plausible not to make use of such a level. There is no evidence that interlocutors interpret, for example, the sentence in (12) as (12a), prior to enriching it to (12b).

(12)   It will take some time to forget this incident.
(12a)   It will take a certain interval or other to forget this incident.
(12b)   It will take a rather long time to forget this incident.

This does not mean that the concept of a logical form should be banished from semantic theory. It is an important concept in talking about the result of syntactic processing. However, one should not be too hasty in allowing it the status of a psychologically real stage in processing meaning, at least until we know exactly where to place it in the overall picture of representing the meanings of acts of communication. Even in syntactic theory, one must beware of giving any ontological and epistemological status to logical forms as such. Instead, they are ways of talking about the output of what is conceived to be a compositional process:

logical forms are not reified. The logical form of a sentence is not another sentence, a structure, or anything else. Talk of logical form is a *façon de parler*, proxy for talk of a complex feature of a sentence *s* of a language L determined by what all canonical proofs of T-sentences[24] for *s* in various interpretive truth theories for L share. The relation *sameness of logical form* is conceptually basic.... *[T]he expression 'x is the logical form of y' should be retired from serious discussion. The basic expression is 'x in L is the same in logical form as y in L'.* (Lepore and Ludwig 2002: 68)[25]

Alternatively, if we adopt Stanley, Szabo, and King's view discussed in Section 1.2 that logical form has slots for all the information necessary to get the truth conditions right—in other words, if we trace all such additions to the sentence to its syntactic representation—then logical form ceases to have any useful function in the theory. It collapses to some richer propositional representation. If there are slots for the required addition, then there is only one rich syntactic representation that at the same time yields the expected meaning of the utterance of the sentence.

Similarly, Larson and Ludlow's (1993; Ludlow 2000) Interpreted Logical Forms (henceforth ILFs) dispose of logical form per se as a unit in processing meaning. On this view, the truth conditions of a sentence are a function of not only the syntactic structure and the semantic values of the constituents, but also the particular *words* used in the sentence. This is so because ILFs are composites of linguistic forms and extralinguistic objects. This is particularly useful in accounting for propositional attitude reports where the coreference of two referential expressions does not guarantee their substitutivity. In other words, (14) may be false although (13) is true, in spite of the fact that 'Yr Wyddfa' and 'Snowdon' are names of one and the same mountain.

(13)   Ralph: 'Yr Wyddfa is the highest mountain in Wales.'

(14)   Ralph believes that Snowdon is the highest mountain in Wales.[26]

As in the syntactic account of Stanley et al., the basic unit is an enriched logical form, a logical form that does not satisfy extensional compositionality. In other words, Larson and Ludlow resort to objects that are external to the output of the composition of structure and meanings arrived at through extensions. And if so, their ILF collapses to a rich propositional representation. If we take away the privileged status of syntax, we obtain a merger of the output of various sources of meaning—the step taken in Default Semantics.

There are various other semantic theories on the market that play with the notion of logical form in an attempt to account for intensional contexts such as (14). They either have to abandon extensional compositionality, or else abandon semantic innocence and assume that expressions have different meaning in different contexts. For example, in the hidden-indexical theory (e.g. Schiffer 1992; Crimmins 1992) 'Snowdon' in (14) refers to a mental representation of the mountain by the speaker which can be different from the representation held by Ralph while uttering/thinking 'Yr Wyddfa'.[27] Hidden indexicals are unpronounced but they are said to be real constituents of the logical form. In fact, Stanley et al.'s syntactic account comes with the most radical version of hidden indexicals: all nouns have a hidden indexical that takes care of the restriction of the domain of reference/quantification.[28]

All in all, despite the differences between the available orientations, it appears that bare logical form is at best a theoretical construct devised for explanatory purposes rather than a viable stage in processing meaning. And, even in its role as such a construct, it requires an admixture of the output of other sources of meaning. If so, it seems advisable on methodological grounds to take the last remaining step and assess this output of various sources on an equal footing, as a merger whose real structure we are only beginning to discover.

The merger representation in which the human processor does not discern different sources of information has been acquiring steady support in theories of speaker's meaning that stress the fact that enrichment is not a conscious process of 'enriching' some representation to arrive at another representation. In other words, there has been good evidence and even better theorizing against what Recanati (2003, 2004) calls the availability condition. This condition states that the person who makes an inference is aware that the judgement arrived at is based on inference from some earlier judgement. In embellishing the logical form, such awareness is not necessary and it would not be theoretically advantageous to postulate it. All this provides a further supporting argument for the *semantic* merger view, in the default-semantics sense of 'semantics' as a truth-conditional, compositional theory of meaning of acts of communication.

1.4 Questioning *what is said*

While logical form is assigned the modest role of a theoretical construct on our preferred view, the notion of *what is said* is best banished altogether.

Instead, a rich, merged representation reflects the meaning with which a sentence, a sub-sentential expression, or a multi-sentence string was used in a discourse. So, in effect, the merger representation is what is said in the sense of the meaning situated in context. However, it is not what is said by the sentence: it is not necessarily based on the content of the sentence. As was argued in Section 1.3, talk about 'what is said by the sentence' alone is redundant in semantic theory. So, all in all, it is senseless to use the notion of what is said without further qualifications as to (i) in what unit: sentence, utterance, discourse;[29] (ii) by what/whom: by the unit considered or by the speaker; and (iii) from whose perspective: the speaker's, the audience's, or the theoretician's.

Moreover, even if we resolve these qualifications, the very notion of saying invokes controversies and does not even seem to yield to experimental testing (Gibbs and Moise 1997; Nicolle and Clark 1999; but see also Noveck and Sperber 2004). It appears that, if we wanted a psychologically real notion of what is said, we would have to appeal to what was the most relevant information conveyed by the utterance according to the addressee: sometimes it may be just the content of the uttered sentence, at other times the enriched content, and at yet others an implicature.

The notion of an enriched logical form has been dubbed what is said (Recanati, e.g. 1989a, 2001); it has also been dubbed an *explicature* (Sperber and Wilson 1986; Carston 1988). The latter is unproblematic: it belongs to the particular theory and as such is clearly defined as a development of the logical form, with clear conditions for distinguishing it from implicatures. It is the former that gives rise to fruitless disputes which, although seemingly terminological, aspire to cognitive importance due to the intuitive importance of delimiting saying, as, perhaps, different for various reasons from stating, uttering, communicating, or conveying. Recanati's *what is said* is permeated with pragmatic components:

it is no longer possible to contrast 'what is said' with those aspects of the interpretation of utterances that are pragmatically rather than semantically determined; for what is said turns out to be, in a large measure, pragmatically determined. Besides the conversational implicatures, which are external to (and combine with) what is said, there are other nonconventional, pragmatic aspects of utterance meaning, which are constitutive of what is said. (Recanati 1989a: 98)

In other words, on Recanati's construal, in addition to sentence meaning, there is *what is said*, and in addition to these there is a more general notion of what is communicated: the latter includes the implicatures. According to Recanati, *what is said* is intuitively given: as he spells out in a later work

(Recanati 2003), *what is said* is not composed of a sentence meaning and conscious inferences from it. Instead, it is primitive as far as the processing of meaning goes. In Recanati (2004), it is *literal meaning*: 'literal' that allows for sense-enrichment or some sense-extension.[30]

Now, all is well if one shares this intuition of 'saying without really saying', that is saying something without physically uttering it. To those who do not share it, and among those are Paul Grice and Kent Bach, saying has to remain closer to uttering. Grice did not talk about enrichments of logical form; he merely signalled the need for reference assignment and disambiguation to be sorted out before what is said can be established. Bach (1994a, 2001) goes further and discusses the completion of incomplete *propositional radicals* (syntactically complete but semantically incomplete units to which truth conditions cannot be assigned) and the expansion of *minimal propositions* (propositions that are not meant literally). In doing so, he proposes that these completions and expansions are implicit in what is said, thereby blurring the boundary between what is said and what is implicated. Since such *implicitures* are 'built out of what is said' (Bach 1994a: 273), and since Bach objects to Grice's notion of *what is said* as too close to word meaning and sentence meaning, we have here a truly middle position: what is implicit in what is said is neither said, nor implicated, but something different altogether: an impli-cíture. Arguments from intuitive plausibility notwithstanding, this consti-tutes a further proliferation of entities: we have a middle level of meaning, which is taken to be a psychologically plausible construct for a theory of discourse processing. Occam's razor and PoL do not support it, and hence we shall try to do without it, as Section 1.5 shows.

Grice's *saying* something entails *meaning* it. So, metaphorical expressions are not cases of saying but rather 'making as if to say'. For Grice, saying means explicitly stating (Bach 1994a). The inconsistencies in this proposal are well acknowledged (Wilson and Sperber 2000): if the 'literal' was not 'said', then how can the metaphorical meaning be an implicature? Either *what is said* has to be redefined to encompass 'making as if to say', or metaphor is not an implicature.[31] If we freed the notion of saying from the requirement of meaning, we would have Recanati's rich *what is said* or, alternatively, we can go along with Bach and classify the possible situations as (i) saying something and meaning it; (ii) saying one thing and meaning another; (iii) saying one thing and meaning more than that; and (iv) saying something without meaning anything. If saying does not entail meaning, *what is said* need not be available to intuitions: '[t]o "preserve intuitions" in our theorizing about what is said would be like relying on the intuitions of unsophisticated moviegoers about the effects of editing on a film' (Bach 2001: 26–7).[32] This, surely, goes in the opposite direction to Recanati's saying as explicitly conveying by means of the sentence with its embellishments. In discussing the redundancy of the logical form in Section 1.3 we established the redundancy of such a minimal notion of *what is said* (see also Recanati 2001; Carston 2001; Vicente 2002 for further arguments).[33] We can now reject it by force of the same argument without further ado.

Be that as it may, it is certainly possible to defend the original Gricean notion of *what is said* as a technical construct, the object of study that is tangential to the issue of cognitive processing and hence impervious to arguments from psychological reality. As Saul (2002: 352) points out, Grice's original theory of implicature rests on an assumption that the audience (*and* the speaker) can be mistaken about what is said and what is implicated. What is said is not necessarily what is taken by the audience or the speaker to have been said. But if it is not, and if this concept of saying has nothing in common with utterance processing, then it seems that it is redundant for the reason that what is said by the speaker and what is taken by the audience to have been said are all there is. If we introduce a neutral, objectual *what is said*, as Saul argues Grice did, we are committing a methodological error with respect to Occam's razor and PoL. Also, surely, if Grice's saying entails meaning it, then dissociating saying from the speaker's awareness of saying it is senseless. First, one has to free saying from the entailment of meaning *à la* Bach, and when one has done so, the technical notion of saying is no longer the Gricean notion of saying. So, the argument fails.

All in all, I propose to retain the semantic innocence and treat *what is said* as it is treated in everyday parlance and not introduce it to semantic theory. What is said is not a level in utterance processing; it is not a theoretical unit either. It can be many things. And if it can be many things, let us respectfully exclude it from theorizing.

1.5 Questioning the middle level of meaning

Just as what is said can be many things, so the middle level of meaning cannot have an intuitively viable equivalent in common parlance. Speakers either state some content or they conversationally imply it. Just as *what is said* is to be banned from having a theoretical status in semantic theory, so will the middle level of meaning. Although intuitively nothing corresponds to the middle level, the middle level as a theoretical construct has been widely acknowledged. It is understood in a variety of ways. As was discussed in Section 1.4, for Bach the middle level is the level of expansions and completions of the output of syntax. It is the level of what is implicit *in what is said* but, confusingly, is not *part of what is said*. The arguments against the syntactic notion of *what is said* will thus by force apply to the level of impliciture and need not be rehearsed again. If there is no syntactic *what is said*, then there cannot be any implicit constituents of it.

A more detailed assessment is required of Levinson's middle level of meaning. Levinson (1995, 2000) proposes three levels of meaning: sentence meaning, utterance-type meaning, and utterance-token meaning. The middle level of utterance-type is the level that contains presumed, default interpretations:

This third layer is a level of systematic pragmatic inference based *not* on direct computations about speaker-intentions, but rather on *general expectations about how language is normally used*. These expectations give rise to presumptions, default inferences, about both content and force. (Levinson 1995: 93)

Levinson defends this level as a stage that is separate from semantics and pragmatics: it must not be incorporated in semantics, as DRT does, neither can it be reduced to context-dependent, nonce-inference in the manner of relevance theory. Instead, default inferences, called generalized conversational implicatures (henceforth, GCIs), 'sit midway, systematically influencing grammar and semantics on the one hand and speaker-meaning on the other' (Levinson 1995: 95). The strongest support for this intuition of the middle level is that there are salient, default meanings, such as that of (15) given in (15a).

(15)   *If* you help me with these logical formulae, I will explain implicature to you.

(15a)   *If and only if* you help me with these logical formulae, will I explain implicature to you.

This is called conditional perfection in that it strengthens the conditional in (15) to a biconditional in (15a). In Chapter 8, I question this principle of conditional perfection, but for the time being let us accept it on the strength of its intuitive appeal (and a long, virtually unchallenged, tradition). Or, to take a less systematic example, (16) is said to default to (16a).

(16)   The hospital employed a new *nurse*.

(16a)   The hospital employed a new *female nurse*.

If we consult our pretheoretical intuitions, it can hardly be contested that such default inferences go through. However, defaults do not necessitate the *level* of defaults which is argued by Levinson to be so indispensable:

it would seem incontrovertible that any theory of utterance interpretation would have to admit the contribution of a level at which sentences are systematically paired with preferred interpretations. (Levinson 2000: 27)

Once again, in agreement with the PoL principle and more generally with Occam's razor, if there is no evidence for a level of meaning, it should not be postulated.

There is also a more modest but still powerful argument against the level of GCIs that can merely be signalled here in general terms as its full power can only become clear after I have introduced types of defaults in Chapter 2. In short, according to the account in which there is more than one level of meaning, a level of meaning should be characterized by a uniformity of the source from which the meanings that pertain to this level are derived. For logical form, we have the output of grammar, that is the compositional analysis of structure as output. 'What is said' was banned because it can pertain to *any* level so labelled and has no uniform source. Now, the level of GCIs (and the level of Bach's impliciture, for that matter) are eclectic. Embellishments of what there physically is in a sentence can come from default presumptions about (i) the lexicon; (ii) the operations of the brain; or (iii) cultural and social conventions. On Bach's account, embellishments can also come from the situational context as what is implicit in what is said need not be presumed. In fact, this is also the case in Levinson's account to a lesser extent, as what is presumed depends heavily on the context: the context can prevent a GCI from arising or it can cancel it.[34] If embellishments are eclectic as far as their sources are concerned, then the 'level' they create cannot be but a waste basket.

The concept of the middle level is quite flexible. It can be bent further to accommodate regularities in discourse processing that are stated in some other ways such as, for example, Asher and Lascarides's (e.g. 1998*a*, 2003) rhetorical structure rules, which join the content of utterances in discourse. Asher and Lascarides's model works roughly as follows. The underspecified logical form is combined with those completions that are pragmatically preferred. Pragmatics is used to infer regularities called rhetorical relations. Preferred completions are arrived at by means of these rules, and hence by means of defaults. The need for such defaults is well justified: context is always changing, is incomplete, and regularities captured by rhetorical structure rules apply unless there is something in the situation or context that signals otherwise. Asher and Lascarides propose a systematic division between the logic of information content and the logic that 'glues' the contents of utterances, called the logic of information packaging and discourse update. The content of utterances is linked by rhetorical relations such as, for example, *Narration*: if sentence s_1 and sentence s_2 express events, then the event in s_2 normally follows that of s_1. Such relations contribute to compositional semantics and as such can be conceived of as a middle level of meaning, often arrived at without employing beliefs or intentions as is done in Gricean approaches. This is certainly an ingenuous way of capturing generalizations on both an intra- and an intersentential level, even more so because we do not need to envisage rule-triggered defaults as a separate level. 'Level' becomes only a manner of speaking about generalizations (rules) that pertain to rhetorical structure. For example, for (17) and (18), the model consists of the standard compositional semantics of these sentences, enriched with the semantics of the rhetorical relation of *Narration*, with the result that the event in (18) follows the event in (17).

(17)   Tom went into the shop.

(18)   He asked for a bottle of Chablis.

This relation is pragmatically inferred and is assigned by default. The processing of this discourse is explained as follows. First, there is the semantics of underspecified logical forms that is static (and extensional and first-order). Then, through accounting for pragmatically inferred relations, we have the semantics of the language of information content, which is dynamic (and at least first-order and modal). Finally, there is the glue language of information packaging that accounts for the origin and application of discourse relations, and its semantics is static (and propositional and modal). In other words, the logic of information packaging tells us how to infer discourse relations and how to enrich underspecified representations (see Asher and Lascarides 2003: 179). The elimination of the 'level' goes as follows. This is a model of competence for utterance interpretation and there is nothing to stop us from seeing the different logics of conversation (and the rules that contribute to one logic and are explained by the other) as disentangled threads of a web that we have earlier called a merger representation. In other words, pragmatically inferred information adds to the information in the underspecified logical forms, and it is desirable to talk about some of these pragmatic additions in terms of defaults provided by regularities of rhetorical structure. It is desirable from the point of view of the simplicity of the model, and, arguably, also in order to explain the cognitive process. However, these disentangled threads may well correspond to a web of cognitive processing that in reality is just a *tangled* web. In other words, the process of utterance interpretation is likely to resemble merger representations more closely than disentangled threads of layered representations. The main difference is that the SDRT account, being a competence model, is not engaged in the issue of the very *activity* of utterance processing and hence does not need to model this activity. The latter is precisely our task in Default Semantics.

All in all, sentence meaning, utterance-type meaning, and utterance-token meaning or their near-equivalents in other theories are good devices for spelling out the diversity of contributions to the total meaning of the utterance. However, they are poor, speculative candidates for psychologically real stages. If discerning the latter is at stake, then it seems safer, once again, to resort to a merger representation that is innocuous as far as the actual process of combination of information coming from different sources is concerned. Mergers of 'rich dynamic semantics'—a semantics of acts of communication—can now be given a try.

1.6 Representations in rich dynamic semantics

In this section I touch on the problem of whether representations are needed in semantics, and if so, how rich they should be. The discussion of representationalism will continue in more detail when we move to the assessment of compositionality in Chapter 3. I have suggested in the preceding sections that merger representations are preferred to discerning multiple levels of interpretation. They are preferred on the grounds of (i) the methodological parsimony of postulated levels, combined with (ii) the fact that such levels have only a hypothetical status. I have also briefly discussed various semantic, pragmatic, and in-between levels in theories of utterance interpretation and theories of discourse interpretation, the latter represented most notably by DRT and SDRT. It is evident that theories of the latter type have this advantage over the first that the scope of their application is discourse rather than an artificially isolated, proposition-based unit of an utterance. In constructing merger representations in Part II, I shall use the state-of the-art formal devices from dynamic approaches, and in particular DRT. As was signalled in Section 1.5 and will become evident in my discussion of types of defaults in Chapter 2, we shall not need any formal device to capture default meanings. Default interpretations will be the direct output of the merger and will be derived directly from the sources of meaning information distinguished by the theory.

Merger representations have to be dynamic, that is they have to account for context change. In order to do this, they have to combine semantic and pragmatic resources. But this combination need not necessarily mean an 'intrusion' of the output of pragmatic processing into a semantic representation. We shall follow methodological innocence in this respect and simply talk of a merger, until the properties of this merger can be further elucidated. Moreover, this merger has to incorporate information from defaults, understood as salient, unmarked interpretations, arrived at without pragmatic inference. I also tentatively propose that any non-default, context-specific information from nonce-inference contributes to this merger. I shall now assess these requirements one by one.

Dynamic theories of the semantics of natural language, dating back to the 1980s, allow, in principle, for the modelling of such mergers. They capture the fact that discourse interpretation proceeds incrementally. In other words, they account for the fact that the utterances (or other chunks of discourse) processed earlier in a discourse help the hearer in processing the subsequent chunks. The best examples with which to demonstrate this interrelation are pronouns, definite descriptions, or temporal expressions which require previous discourse for their interpretation. In (19), the interpretation of the second sentence relies on the interpretation of the first one for the resolution of the reference of the pronoun and the temporal adverbial. This correlation is clearly stated in a semi-formal notation in (19a), using some elements of the neo-Davidsonian analysis of events (Parsons 1990).

(19)   The Prime Minister went to America on Monday. Two days later he returned and gave a controversial speech at the House of Commons.

(19a) $\exists x \, \exists e \, \exists e' \, \exists e'' \, \exists t \, \exists t' \, \exists mt$ PrimeMinister (x) & $\forall y$ (PrimeMinister (y) $\rightarrow$ y $=$ x) & Going-to-America (e) & Subject (x, e) & Monday (t) & At (e, t) & Day (mt) & Time (t') & $t' = t + 2$ mt & Returning (e') & Subject (x, e') & $At(e', t')$ & Giving-a-Controversial-Speech-to-House-of-Commons (e'') & Subject (x, e'') & At (e'', t')[35]

'e' stands for a Davidsonian construct of an event, 't' for time, and 'mt' for measure of time. Example (19a) demonstrates the importance of considering chunks larger than a sentence as units. It shows that the reference assignment, once resolved, can be used again and again in interpreting the following sections of the discourse. DRSs capture this incremental process. Discourse referents such as *x* capture the coreference of the pronoun and the preceding definite description, while the discourse referents for time capture the temporal relations between events as in a partial DRS, illustrated in Fig. 1.1, where 't < n' stands for '*t* temporally precedes the time of utterance', and 'e ⊆ t' for 'the event *e* is temporally included in *t*'.

Before we assess the extent to which DRSs will have to be amended to serve the purpose of merger representations, let us for the moment take them as they are. DRSs are semantic representations that combine information from syntax and from the changing context. More importantly, they have the status of model mental representations and hence contain information for the purpose of modelling mental states and mental processing. By accounting for mental representations, DRSs with the same truth conditions can be

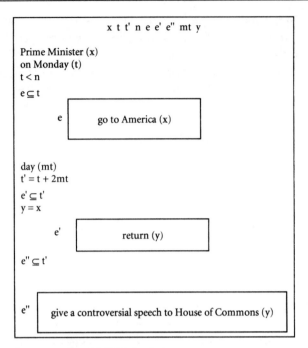

FIGURE 1.1 Partial DRS for (19).

different (see Kamp 1981, 1990; Kamp and Reyle 1993; Kamp 1996; van Eijck and Kamp 1997).To repeat, unlike in post-Gricean pragmatics, in DRT truth conditions are assigned to sentences. Semantics is *extended semantics* in that it goes beyond the truth conditions. We obtain representations of sentences which, later on, so to speak, help build up other representations. This may not be the 'most dynamic' view of meaning, but it is certainly one that allows for a greater accuracy in modelling speakers' mental states. In DPL (Groenendijk and Stokhof 1991, 2000), 'to know the meaning of a sentence is to know how it changes a context', that is, the 'meaning of a sentence is identified with its context-change potential' (Groenendijk and Stokhof 2000: 51; see also note 6 in Section 1.1). In other words, context is not *represented*, it is used directly as information to recover new information: 'the dynamics is an intrinsic feature of the meanings of expressions, and not of the process by which the representations are constructed.' (ibid.: 53):

The discourse representation structures themselves are not information, but representations of information. They are linguistic, not semantic objects. Sentences and discourses are interpreted indirectly via their representations. The interpretation of discourse representation structures takes the form of standard (static) definition of truth conditions. Hence, meaning as such is not a dynamic notion: the meaning of a representation, and hence of the (piece of) discourse that it represents, is identified with the set of models (possible worlds) in which the representation is true.

The dynamics of the interpretation process resides solely in the incremental build-up of the representations, and not in the interpretation of the representations themselves.[36] (Groenendijk and Stokhof 2000: 53)

As argued in Section 1.2, the fact that it is possible to provide a dynamic semantic interpretation of the language of first-order predicate logic does not yet mean that this is to be preferred. At first glance, by force of the PoL principle, it seems that representations should be discarded if incremental processing can be accounted for on the level of the interpretation of the formal language of modelling discourse. However, as the evidence from the application of DRT to anaphora resolution or propositional attitude reports and other intensional contexts suggests, modelling mental states requires representations. And the simplicity and parsimony of levels can only be compared if the aims and scope of theories are alike. In the case of DPL and DRT, they are not alike: in DPL, a dynamic interpretation of the formal language captures well the cross-sentential relations of coreference, but it does so at a cost. The interpretation is to be taken on trust. For example, the fact that conjunction in English is not unconditionally commutative is captured simply by assigning an interpretation to its predicate logic equivalent as in (20):

(20) $g\ [\Phi \wedge \Psi]\ h$ iff $g\ [\Phi]\ k\ [\Psi]\ h$

In words, 'the interpretation of $\Phi \wedge \Psi$ with input g may result in output h iff there is some k such that interpreting Φ in g may lead to k, and interpreting Ψ in k enables us to reach h' (Groenendijk and Stokhof 1991: 47). As a result of this incorporation of context change, conjunction is not commutative: $\Phi \wedge \Psi \neq \Psi \wedge \Phi$. To be commutative, the interpretations of Φ and Ψ would have to be the same in every model (see Groenendijk and Stokhof 1991: 63). The problem with (20) is this. One can devise a dynamic conjunction and introduce a new semantic interpretation of $\Phi \wedge \Psi$ by fiat, as in DPL, when the objective is to have a compositional, non-representational semantics. However, in a theory of discourse processing, we want to capture the fact that speakers of English reason in the following way: if sentence s_1 precedes sentence s_2 and they both refer to events, then the event in s_1 normally precedes the event in s_2, unless there is some indication that it is otherwise. The same rule applies to the use of *and* and the coordination of clauses as in (21):

(21)   We baked a lot of mince pies and ate them all before Christmas.

There are various ways of accounting for this rule of reasoning. Grice invoked principles of rational communicative behaviour translated into maxims of conversation. His neo-Gricean followers invoked default interpretations in the form of heuristics (Levinson 1995, 2000). Lascarides and Asher (e.g. 1993; Asher and Lascarides 2003) propose rules of rhetorical structure such as *Narration* (see also Section 1.5). Irrespective of the differences between these proposals, they have one feature in common: they purport to capture the principles of human reasoning, which is not an objective of DPL. DPL, with its dynamic interpretation of conjunction and existential quantifier, offers a language in which some selected types of expressions and phenomena that feature in natural discourse can be modelled. For our purposes, I shall preserve the level of representations, making it suitably parsimonious in the form of a merger, as was proposed in the previous sections. It is essential to emphasize that no evaluation of DPL vis-à-vis DRT ensues for my purposes: being representational is an assumed prerequisite for a cognitively plausible theory of discourse interpretation. The issue as to whether representations *can* be avoided is left until Section 3.2.

It also has to be stressed, again, that in merger representations I am using the extended and amended language of DRT without following the rules of meaning construction laid down by DRT. DRT assumes the level of under-specified semantics; its rules for constructing representations are also heavily based on syntactic processing, that is on the logical form of sentences. For example, temporality is accounted for by means of processing the grammat-ical markers of tense in the sentence, quite irrespectively of the use to which this form may be put. The use to which it is put cannot always be easily accounted for precisely because of the heavy reliance of discourse conditions on the output of grammar ('syntactic configuration'). The way merger rep-resentations deviate from this analysis is dictated by the fact that representa-tions in Default Semantics are mergers of the output of various sources and syntax is not assigned a privileged role there. The consequences for analysing temporality are presented in Chapter 6. Similarly, multiple readings of utter-ances, such as presupposing and non-presupposing readings, the referential and attributive readings of definite descriptions, or the restrictive and non-restrictive use of 'who' and 'which', are treated differently in DRT and in Default Semantics. In DRT, multiple DRSs can be constructed but there is at present no possibility of accounting for the relative salience of the readings that these DRSs represent. But when information from all the relevant vehicles of meaning is merged, it appears that there is no need to construct alternative DRSs. Instead, the ambiguity of reading is viewed as the existence of a salient reading, as well as other possible readings that can be triggered by the particular context. No selection of a representation, no cancelling of senses is required. In particular, even if the sentence is put to a use that is very different from that signalled by its logical form, this actual use can still be captured. For example, (22) has an obvious dispositional necessity reading that can be captured by the merger representation, while it cannot be easily handled by a syntax-based semantics:

(22)   Mary will sometimes go to the opera in her tracksuit.

This is the main difference between merger representations and DRSs of DRT. Such merger representations are proposed for various relevant types of expressions in the remainder of this book.

The sense in which merger representations are semantic should now be evident. Unlike in DPL, here 'semantics' is not an interpretation of a formal language. Instead, it is a meaning representation where meaning comes from various vehicles of information, as it obviously does in human interaction. For this reason, to do with capturing the gist of the process of discourse interpretation, I am not going to focus in what follows on the semantics/ pragmatics, syntax/semantics, or syntax/pragmatics interfaces. Once the assumption of a merger is in place, the interfaces do not belong to our theoretical discourse. They pose the problem of interpretation in the wrong way, focusing on what is only an intratheoretic issue of boundaries, rather than an issue about discourse processing.

1.7 Representations and conscious inference

Now, how can this idea of a merger in which all vehicles of information are treated on an equal footing be brought into line with the view that utterance interpretation consists of the processing of the sentence, complemented with inference about the speaker's intentions? These views are not incompatible. The question is, whether conscious inference from intentions has to be limited to those inferences that lie outside the merger. It has recently been suggested that it has to be so limited because such inferences are performed on the basis of what the speaker means by the utterance, and the meaning of an utterance seems to be arrived at by the hearer without any conscious process of inferencing. The reference of pronouns, the use of default meanings, and so forth are all arrived at without any evident conscious inferencing founded on some incomplete meaning representation. This view of direct communication has been worked out in the literature in Recanati's (2002a, 2003, 2004) proposal of direct communication, modelled on perception. On his account, the (pragmatically enriched) truth-conditional content of utterances is arrived at directly, like perceptual content. It is arrived at through the processing of the sentence plus the work performed by 'primary pragmatic processes' that are not available to intuition: they are direct, impenetrable, and different from the processes that lead to implicatures. The position he adopts, he calls 'anti-inferentialism':

For the anti-inferentialist, the step from 'the speaker intends to communicate that p' to 'p' is as automatic, as unreflective, as the step from 'the sentence says that p' to 'the speaker intends to communicate that p'. Normally, the hearer believes what he is told, or at least, he gets the information that p when he is told that p. ... Only when there is something wrong does the hearer suspend or inhibit the automatic transition which characterizes the normal cases of linguistic communication. On the anti-inferentialist view, then, communication is as direct as perception. (Recanati 2002a: 109)[37]

It is possible that this view of direct communication holds. But it is also possible that on some occasions the hearer consciously 'merges' information from various sources. This theorizing is still amenable to speculation based on partial arguments and some intuitive judgements. For this reason, we shall not, for the time being, a priori ban conscious pragmatic inference from contributing to utterance meaning. Naturally, this potential admission of conscious pragmatic inference opens up a new problem in that inference has to operate on some unit of meaning. Are we forced to reassess and readmit logical form, the output of grammar, as a semantically interesting unit? There is as yet no compelling reason to do so. At this introductory stage, we are merely stating what the possible players are in the game of 'meaning merging'. In other words, we delimit what can *possibly* and *plausibly* play a part. 'Merger' excludes, by definition, levels of meaning other than itself, while making no restrictions on the players. This is our starting point.

Furthermore, while Recanati claims that truth-conditional content so envisaged becomes a matter of pragmatics, my merger semanticizes all the sources of meaning. So, Recanati's direct communication is essentially compatible with my merger as a process, but not compatible with merger representation as a semantic representation. Recanati's truth-conditional content also differs from the content of merger representations. The latter, to repeat, is not constrained by the output of syntactic processing: we allow for the possibility of a merger in which the output of grammar is not embellished but instead overruled. Further particulars of this pragmatics-rich Default Semantics are proposed and defended in Chapter 3.

To compare and contrast the 'semanticization' and the 'pragmaticization' of meaning, let us look more closely at the latter. The *inferentialist* view advocates a module for handling pragmatic processing. Sperber (2000) proposes that the recognition of the speaker's intentions may rely on a biological trait called metarepresenting. Metarepresenting is a higher-order representation of an agent's thoughts, sentences, or utterances.[38] In other words, there is a metacommunicative module that handles comprehension. It is suggested that this module developed from a general mind-reading ability. While the idea of a comprehension module is certainly compatible with the idea of merger representations, in the sense that they can coexist, the actual mechanism is not. Discourse interpretation does not seem to be *predominantly* mind-reading. It is predominantly unreflective processing that relies on what is there in the discourse, on what is normally assumed when such discourse is encountered, and what can be added in this particular situation, without reading the speaker's intentions. As was argued above, in this respect discourse interpretation is thus largely anti-inferentialist.

An important caveat is in order here. The claim that interlocutors rely on a variety of 'shortcuts' rather than always processing the speaker's intentions does not mean that an account in terms of intentions would give wrong predictions. Surely, it would arrive at the same results as the anti-inferentialist account of Recanati's or my merger account. However, resorting to intentions when there is no evidence that the processor actually resorts to them seems unwarranted and costly. So, mergers resemble metarepresentations as to their status of a module, but differ from them in that they are not a sub-species of mind-reading. Sperber and Wilson (2002) try to reconcile default-based accounts with their inferential perspective by proposing that an inferential perspective is simply an unfolding of a psychological process summed up as a default for the purpose of discourse modelling. True as it may be of, say, SDRT, this cannot be easily squared with post-Gricean default-based views such as Recanati's, Levinson's, or my own. Defaults there are a legitimate, cognitively real component of utterance interpretation. In order to have a plausible account of communication *without* recognizing defaults, one has to resort to moves such as Sperber and Wilson's (2002) intuitive, unconscious, unreflective inference. Whether this is just a terminological difference remains to be seen as the discussion in the literature unfolds.

All in all, merger representations are closer in spirit to the anti-inferentialist orientation. Salient interpretations there are nothing else but examples of such direct communication. When the conjunction *and* defaults to 'and then', the addressee is not consciously using a rule, be it the rhetorical rule of *Narration* or a rationality principle of the Gricean or neo-Gricean type.[39] Neither is the addressee performing context-dependent inferring. Instead, the merger of the syntactic form p & q with the temporal sense happens automatically and unreflectively. However, this automatic and unreflective process is not just an automatic addition to the output of syntactic processing: the content of the utterance dictates whether it takes place. There is some evidence that content matters for such enrichment. For example, there have been experiments performed on the understanding of sentences such as (23) and (24), which are variations of the seminal 'donkey sentence' in (25):

(23)   Every boy that stands next to a girl holds her hand.

(24)   Every railway line that crosses a road goes over it.[40]

(25)   Every farmer who owns a donkey beats it. (from Geurts 2002: 135–6)

While (23) was predominantly judged to be true even if some boys held only the hand of one of the two girls standing next to him, (24) was predominantly judged to be false when the railway line went over only one of the two roads that it crossed. Naturally, similar results can be expected with the temporal interpretation of *and*. For example, in (26), *and* will not be temporal by default:

(26)   Tom won a prize in a singing competition and came first in the maths test.

So, instead of postulating defaults on the basis of the form alone and subsequently cancelling them in the process of interpretation, on the merger account defaults can simply not arise. This is so because all vehicles of information are treated on a par as contributors to the merger representation. This problem of default cancellation vis-à-vis default non-arising is discussed at length in Chapter 2. Similarly, in Chapter 2, I return to the distinction between (i) defaults that pertain to mental states and (ii) defaults that arise out of cultural and social practices, or merely from the significantly greater frequency of occurrence of certain interpretations. This typology is related to another loose end that we have just encountered, namely the question of the *unit* which gives rise to the default interpretation. Are defaults sentence-based, word- or expression-based, or is there even greater freedom of units which give rise to them? Cancellability vs. non-arising of such defaults is by no means tangential to this question.

Notes

1 In Grice's original parlance, the process of implicating (*implicature*) leads to an *implicatum*. In what follows, however, I shall use the term 'implicature' to refer to the outcome of the process, i.e. to the implicatum, in agreement with the current dominant tendency in post-Gricean literature.

2 See, e.g., Kempson 1975, 1977, 1979, 1986; Wilson 1975; Zwicky and Sadock 1975; Sadock 1984; Atlas 1977, 1979, 1989, 2005; Levinson 1988, 2000; Kempson and Cormack

1981; Sperber and Wilson 1986; Carston 1988, 1994, 1996, 1998*a*, 2002*a*, forthcoming; Recanati 1989*a*, 1989*b*, 1993, 1994, 2001, 2003, 2004; Bach 1994*a*, 1994*b*, 2001; Jaszczolt 1999*a*, 1999*b*, 2002*a*; Vicente 2002. This is only a small representative sample of this discussion that has remained cutting-edge until the present moment.

3 E.g. Sperber and Wilson 1986; Carston 1988, 1998*a*, 2001, 2002*a*; Recanati 1989*a*, 1993, 2001.

4 'Particular situation' has to be distinguished from 'situation type'. I discuss this issue in Chapter 2 while assessing the extent to which default meanings can be situation-independent.

5 In Levinson (2000: 35, 37, 38, respectively) called Q, I, and M heuristics.

6 The term 'dynamic semantics' has been used in a wide and narrow sense in the literature. In the latter, it is confined to the approaches taken by Heim, Barwise, and the Groenendijk and Stokhof 'Amsterdam school'. To use an expression that dates back to Irene Heim, only for these approaches is the meaning of an expression its *context change potential*. Geurts (1999) points out that these two types of approaches give rise to two different theories of presupposition projection: DRT supports the binding theory, that is the presupposition-as-anaphora view, whereas the 'truly dynamic' approach supports the satisfaction theory (see Geurts 1999: xi–xiii; Jaszczolt 2002*b*). However, for our purposes, we need 'dynamic' in the wide sense: both types of approaches are rightfully called 'dynamic' in that they incorporate the information from the changing context into the interpretation of sentences, which *ipso facto* becomes an interpretation of utterances as parts of discourses. See also van Eijck and Kamp 1997; Asher and Lascarides 2003; von Heusinger and Egli 2000.

7 Unlike in Default Semantics, where utterances are *acts of communication*. See Introduction.

8 See Introduction.

9 Referential mistakes are considered in Chapters 4 and 5.

10 See Jaszczolt 1999*a*, 1999*b*, 2000*a*, 2002*a*, 2002*b*.

11 My emphasis.

12 For the semantics and pragmatics of propositional attitude reports and an extensive bibliography, see Jaszczolt 1999*b*, 2000*a*, 2000*b*.

13 See e.g. Recanati (2004: 51) on 'what is said$_{min}$' and 'what is said$_{prag}$'.

14 For a detailed presentation of the ambiguity/underdetermination debates, see chapter 1 of Jaszczolt 1999*b*.

15 This argument works independently of the view the relevant linguists hold on the issue of the differences between the semantics of natural language and that of formal languages. See Chomsky (2002: 110).

16 Note, Recanati does not call them 'inferential' in that on his account such additions are performed on a 'sub-personal' level which should not be called inferential. See Recanati 2004, chapter 3.

17 See Gundel 1999 on contrastive focus.

18 See Rooth 1996; Jaszczolt 2002*b*.

19 My emphasis.

20 See also Ludlow's (2002) syntactic account of relative quantifier scope and negation, through structure-building. My questions concerning the psychological reality and, indeed, the rationale for a rich syntax apply also to Ludlow's account.

21 On the compatibility of choice functions with the minimalist programme see von Stechow 2000. See also Szabolcsi 1997 for a discussion of Beghelli and Stowell's functional projections in the LF that replace quantifier raising. The allowed readings, however, still have to be selected by context: syntax is separate from other sources of information and hence, crucially, is not *dynamic*.

22 See von Heusinger and Egli (2000: 5) for an assessment of the controversies in dynamic semantics, and Dekker 2000 on arguments for representationalism.

23 This can easily be inferred from Groenendijk and Stokhof (1991: 94).

24 From Tarski's Convention T, T-sentences are sentences of the form 'Φ is true in L iff p' in which a structural description of a sentence of L replaces Φ and a sentence in metalanguage, synonymous with it, replaces p. Then, Φ in L means that p. See e.g. Lepore and Ludwig (2002: 61).

25 My emphasis and explanatory note.

26 Propositional attitude reports are discussed in detail in Chapter 5. See also Jaszczolt 1999*b*, 2000*a*, 2000*b*.

27 For an excellent review of the problems with compositionality and semantic innocence in these and other semantic theories, see Clapp 2002.

28 For criticism see, e.g., Cappelen and Lepore 2002.

29 Recanati 2003*b*: ch. 4 points out this problem.

30 Including a 'literal figurative' category. See diagram in Recanati (2003*b*: 78).

31 The latter option is ingeniously offered in Carston 2002*a*.

32 What is particularly striking is that Bach tries to square this minimal, syntactic notion of what is said with his support for default reasoning. Default inferences rely on *implicit assumptions* (see Bach 2001: 25).

33 Vicente spells out the redundancy of minimal propositions in a way that my merger representations can espouse:

> Rather than assuming that the grammar outputs minimal but complete propositions which the inferential comprehension system has to get rid of, we can view the language system as yielding representations that come ready to interact with contextual assumptions. (Vicente 2002: 412)

While for her this interaction proceeds according to relevance theory and the underdetermined output of syntax, for me it is founded on the merger representations of Default Semantics.

34 See also Recanati 2003*a* on local, sub-sentential inferences.

35 See also Kamp 1990, discussion of his example 1.

36 My emphasis.

37 For an inferential perspective see, e.g., Carston 2002*b*.

38 See Wilson 2000; Sperber and Wilson 2002. For discussion see Happé and Loth 2002; Bloom 2002; Papafragou 2002.

39 See the discussion earlier in this section.

40 Arguably, one should also test the truth-conditional effect of the topic–focus articulation. However, the sentences that interest us are the ones with 'normal' intonation contour and with 'normal' word order. See Rooth 1996 and Hajičova et al. 1998.

2

Default Meanings

2.1 Varieties of defaults

It is hardly contentious that there is often a part to communicated meaning
that comes neither from the sentence, nor from inference. It just is there by
force of what we are like and how we function. Such assumed interpretations
are called default meanings, or presumed meanings. For example, (1) by
default means (1a) rather than (1b), and (2) by default means (2a).

(1)   The director of *The Pianist* is in trouble.
(1a)   Roman Polański is in trouble.
(1b)   The director of *The Pianist*, whoever he might be, is in trouble.

(2)   Roman committed a criminal offence and cannot enter the U.S.
(2a)   Roman committed a criminal offence and as a result cannot enter the
        U.S.

As long as we state this salience of some interpretations in a pretheoretical
way, it is a fact of conversation. But presenting these interpretations as non-
inferential, default interpretations makes the description intratheoretic and
vulnerable to counterarguments. Further, unpacking the notion of default
meaning also encounters some problems. The most important among them
are (i) the problem of defining the sense of 'default'; (ii) connected with it, the
problem of demonstrating whether any degree of context-dependent inference is allowed in default interpretations; and (iii) classifying such default
meanings as semantic, pragmatic, or independent, intermediate between the
two. I shall now briefly review some of the extant proposals before presenting
the solution in Default Semantics.

2.1.1 *Eclectic defaults*

Levinson's (1995, 2000) presumptive meanings, also called preferred interpretations, are given by the structure of the utterance, supposedly without
using any contextual clues. In the process of utterance interpretation, hearers
entertain hypotheses about meaning even before the meaningful unit (proposition conveyed by the utterance) is completed. Discourse interpretation

progresses incrementally, and hypotheses about meaning can also be entertained incrementally. For example, the quantifier *some xs* may give rise to a hypothesis 'not all *xs*' even before the utterance is completed. Default meanings arise across the range of phenomena, including scalar quantifiers as in (3), scalar adjectives as in (4), but also typical interpretations of collocations as in (5), (6), and even (7).

(3) I ate a few of the biscuits.   +> not all of them

(4) The coffee is warm.   +> not hot

(5) I used a coffee spoon.   +> a spoon for stirring coffee

(6) I used a silver spoon.   +> a spoon made of silver

(7) Peter's book is about a glass church. +> the book Peter wrote

('+>' stands for 'conversationally communicates'; see also examples in Levinson 2000: 185–6). Such default inferences are produced in the course of normal, rational communicative behaviour that is summarized in Levinson's three heuristics: 'What is said, isn't' (Q-heuristic); 'What is expressed simply is stereotypically exemplified' (I-heuristic); and 'What is said in an abnormal way isn't normal' (M-heuristic).[1] These heuristics summarize and consolidate the standpoint that the hearer does not always have to go through the process of recovering the speaker's intentions in order to arrive at the intended meaning. Instead, some meanings are instantaneous.

However, the three heuristics are only convenient generalizations. In fact, they are not even of an equal epistemological status. While I-implicatures[2] such as those in (5)–(7) arise simply as inferences to a stereotype, Q- and M-implicatures are less fundamental: they can only occur by comparison with what else might have been, but was not, uttered. So, even among the heuristics there are some priorities and unmarkedness. This signals that default meanings derived through different heuristics have a different status, and this fact should be reflected somehow or other in the set of the proposed heuristics. Before we pursue this question further, let us consider the set of examples (3) to (7) again. Levinson classifies such implicatures as generality narrowing that stems either out of the Q-heuristics (examples (3) and (4)) or the I-heuristics (examples (5)–(7)). And yet, a cursory glance at this set suffices to indicate that some of them appear to yield to obvious, uncontroversial salient interpretations while others do not. Examples (5) and (6) are undeniably interpreted with the expansions stated above. Arguably, they are the best candidates for default meanings if such are to be admitted. However, there is a strong sense of a lexical meaning there: 'coffee spoon' is a collocation that has almost the force of a compound, and so is 'silver spoon', as evidenced by

(5a) and (6a). When 'coffee spoon' and 'silver spoon' are accented in the usual, compound-like way, the explanations that follow (5) and (6) as in (5a) and (6a) respectively are indispensable.

(5a)   I used a coffee spoon, I mean a spoon used for scooping coffee beans.

(6a)   I used a silver spoon, I mean a spoon used for stirring liquid silver.

Sentence (3) does indeed normally carry the interpretation 'not all of the biscuits'. This interpretation takes place in virtue of the domain of quantification being specified by the preposition 'of': 'I ate a few biscuits' is less likely to carry the 'not all' sense. Example (4) is normally compatible with the proposition that the coffee is not hot. But this does not mean that this meaning is communicated whenever it is truly the case. 'Warm' means 'warm', full stop: drinking warm coffee may be a good thing when one is cold, and although the hearer would not deny that the coffee is most probably not hot, this is not a presumed, default meaning. Example (7) may not be a case for a default interpretation altogether. One has to know that the person who wrote the famous novel about constructing a glass church is called Peter in order to interpret the possessive as authorship. So, if there is a default, it is a default founded on some background knowledge and hence is a default that arises out of some processing of the context rather than automatically, instantly, prior to pragmatic inference. It is highly contentious to call it a generalized conversational implicature (GCI), in Grice's (1975) original sense of a context-free implicature. For the same reason, it is rather confusing on Levinson's part to call such cases GCIs. GCI seems to be a qualitatively different phenomenon.

So, what are default interpretations, if all our cases of generality narrowing are so contentious? Surely, there are defaults in anaphora resolution and other reference assignment, there are defaults in the unpacking of ellipsis, but all those seem to be governed by syntactic and semantic principles of some sort rather than being a subject for defaults in their own right.[3] If the criterion is to be that default meanings arise prior to any processing of the context, and thereby also without any processing of the speaker's intentions, then we do not have a uniform set of examples. If the criterion is to be that default meanings arise due to some refinement of word or sentence meaning due to the ways the world is, then our criterion is too general to capture what is going on in (3)–(7). Grammar, lexicon, and knowledge of contemporary fiction are the true sources of such interpretations. In fact, Levinson (2000: 368–70) makes this diversity look like a strength of his theory of generalized conversational implicature. His theory, he says, accounts for presumed meanings that arise at different levels of generalization, from (i) morphemes and (ii) words, through (iii) constraints on what is and is not lexicalized, to (iv) syntactic patterns into which pragmatic inference intrudes. All this meaning refinement can take place locally, before the meaning of the sentence is computed. While it is undoubtedly true that hearers make presumptions about the meanings of linguistic units of different granularity, from morphemes onwards, sweeping them all under the category of GCIs is at least unwarranted. First, they are not implicatures in a Gricean sense as they can arise locally, rather than post-propositionally. Next, in virtue of being local, these refinements are hardly presumed, unmarked meanings: they tend to be much stronger than that, especially those arising at the level of morphemes and words, as the 'silver spoon' and 'coffee spoon' examples testify.

We have come now to the core of the problem with Levinson's theory of presumptive meanings. Having made a virtue out of the multiplicity of levels at which defaults arise, he proceeds to postulating a middle level of meaning. Presumptive meanings, he says, do not reduce to semantics or pragmatics:

> that layer is constantly under attack by reductionists seeking to assimilate it either to the level of sentence-meaning or to the level of speaker-meaning; thus, for example, in the case of GCIs, Kamp, Peters, Kempson, van Kuppevelt, and others have all suggested that they should be in effect semanticized, whereas Sperber and Wilson and artificial intelligence local-pragmatics theorists have presumed that on the contrary they should be assimilated to matters of nonce inference at the level of speaker-intention. But GCIs are not going to reduce so easily in either direction, for they sit midway, systematically influencing grammar and semantics on the one hand and speaker-meaning on the other. (Levinson 2000: 25)

I have questioned the methodological principles underlying this middle level of meaning in Section 1.5. Now we can look at its *raison d'être* from the point of view of capturing different types of default interpretations. In this respect, this level is even more contentious. All it does is create an illusion of categorial unity beyond the eclectic collection of salient senses. In other words, the only obvious reason for the third level is to point out that the default interpretations that hearers arrive at are so diversified, arise on the basis of such categorially different grammatical units and at such different stages of utterance interpretation, that all we can do is to say that they are neither semantic, nor pragmatic, but a different kind of meaning altogether. If this is so, then it makes more sense to do away with the shaky integrity of the category of default meanings and look carefully at the differences among particular instances of such salient interpretations. Once we have done so, the need for the middle level is likely to disappear as a consequence of the disappearance of the eclectic category of presumed meanings. This is what I do in Sections 2.2 and 2.3 by distinguishing different categories of defaults.

2.1.2 *Rule-governed defaults*

In computational linguistics, defaults can be built into standard logic. Velt-man (1996), for example, provides a logical analysis of a generic sentence 'Ps normally are Qs' used for analysing modalities such as epistemic possibility *might*. He says,

It is just as valid to conclude 'Presumably x is B' from 'x is A' and 'A's are normally B' as it is to conclude 'x is B' from 'x is A' and the 'All A's are B'. One does not have to set one's mind to a different mode of reasoning to get the former. (Veltman 1996: 257)

The differences lie in the properties of the resulting logic: if there are default rules and default operators in the language, the logic becomes non-monotonic. Epistemic modalities are precisely such default rules.

More generally, for the contexts where the grammar of the sentence does not necessarily invite default reasoning, default interpretations have been recognized as the result of the application of some rules of discourse structure. Interlocutors are governed by the assumption that discourse is coherent. For the purpose of modelling discourse, this coherence can be captured as a set of rules that pertain to the meaningful links between utterances.[4] Segmented Discourse Representation Theory (SDRT), introduced briefly in Section 1.5, is probably the most comprehensive and best formalized of such proposals. To repeat, if sentences s_1 and s_2 represent events, then the event in s_1 is taken to precede the event in s_2 and the relation between them in *Narration*. Further, if s_2 is about a state, then the state is a *Background* to the event in s_1. Alternatively, an event in s_2 may provide an *Explanation* to the event in s_1, or the event in s_2 can be *Elaboration* to that in s_1 if it constitutes its part. The event in s_1 can also cause the event or state in s_2 and be subject to the relation of *Result*. Relations between rules are captured by axioms that prevent, for example, the relation from being *Elaboration* and *Narration*, or *Explanation* and *Narration*, at the same time (see e.g. Lascarides and Asher 1993: 464–5). On this approach, the logical representation of a discourse is constructed dynamically. There are logical forms of sentences, as well as relations between the eventualities that these logical forms concern. The relations are computed in the process called *defeasible reasoning*: logical forms are taken together with some other sources of information and the relations, such as temporal, causal, explanatory, etc., are computed as strong probabilities. The laws of defeasible logic are defeasible in the sense that they normally, but not always, obtain: *ceteris paribus*, the relation predicted by the law obtains, but in certain circumstances it may not. I discuss this idea in more detail in Section 2.5. As a result, there is normally no ambiguity of interpretation from the hearer's point of view: his or her world knowledge allows for an application of one or another rule to link the logical form of the sentences into a coherent discourse. This inference is non-monotonic: with the growth of information, the assumed relation may prove not to be the case.

The strong point of this approach is the modelling of the rhetorical relations *within the semantics*. More specifically, in the order of explanation, as well as in the order of modelled processing, there is a semantics of under-specified logical forms of sentences. This semantics is first-order, extensional, and static. Next, embellished with the necessary enrichments and comple-tions, there is the semantics of information content, which has to be modal, dynamic, and at least first-order (see Asher and Lascarides 2003: 188). The underspecified logical forms are combined with pragmatically preferred com-pletions to yield the information content. Naturally, such preferences require defaults because context is always changing and incomplete, and hence may not provide required information. Then, as was briefly discussed in Section 1.5, there is a semantics of information packaging, which is modal and static. The language of this packaging is called glue language in that it glues sentential logical forms together, defeasibly, by means of the operator '>' of A > B: 'if A, then normally B'. All this mechanism sums up to a dynamic semantic account of discourse meaning, proposed *not* as an explanatorily adequate theory of speakers' processing of utterances, but as a model of the human ability to perform such processing. It certainly works as a model of competence: it does not rely too heavily on speakers' intentions like post-Griceans do, neither does it resort to nonce-inference like relevance theory. It works well as a model of conversational competence devised for the purpose of computational modelling of meaningful relations between sentences in a larger text. The cognitive status of the proposed rules is hypothetical, but this fact is not detrimental to the theory in that the rules do what they are supposed to do: they generalize over what speakers and hearers, in some way or another, achieve in conversation. They are functional generalizations that enable a formal semantic account of discourse meaning. In a theory of utterance processing, however, it is this 'some way or another' that interests us. In other words, our aim is different: it is to account for the *practice* of utterance processing by a human agent. While the rhetorical rules are suc-cessful summaries over what humans do and they are well suited to explaining the truth-conditional effects of such relations between chunks of discourse, what they do is formalize competence. Default Semantics is thus not an alternative to SDRT.

The rules of Asher and Lascarides' competence model are numerous and ineradicable. To repeat, they also allow us to model discourse without re-course to speakers' intentions, except for the contexts whose intensionality necessitates such a move.[5] While this rids semantics of the most hazy entities of Gricean pragmatics, it also rids from it the possibility of misapplication as a theory of processing: intentions may be elusive, but they are real; rhetorical rules may be precise, but they are not the key to processing.

2.1.3 *Jumping to conclusions*

Defaults in reasoning have been vaguely proposed in a number of linguistic and philosophical accounts of meaning. Bach (1984) argued that in interpreting utterances, people use 'default reasoning', or 'jump to conclusions', because they 'know when to think twice'. Default reasoning is an 'inference to the first unchallenged alternative'. In other words, this reasoning is defeasible: we reason by default, unless we have evidence that we should not (see Bach 1984: 40). Bach (1987a, 1987b) allows for degrees of believing and intending and derives defaults from this gradation. Later he supports the idea by his proposal of standardization (Bach 1995: 683; 1998: 713) that means going beyond the literal meaning, facilitated by precedents of a similar use of the particular expression. Such standardization, distinguished from conventionalization, short-circuits the inference process: the speaker is not aware of performing an inference. However, this view has not been developed into a fully-fledged theory of default interpretations. In order for this proposal to have the force of a theory, it would have to contain a mechanism of processing of expressions that are liable to yielding default interpretations.

Notwithstanding its programmatic status, the proposal is noteworthy for its simplicity and intuitive plausibility. Hearers do jump to conclusions, and, more importantly, speakers assume that hearers will jump to conclusions, thereby overcoming the problem of the slow speed of speech production as compared with the speed of the recovery of meaning.[6] This jumping to conclusions is most effective when it proceeds along the path of preconceived beliefs in the form of defaults that do not require pragmatic inference. And this default reasoning is both intended and recognized as being intended. This notion of belief- and intention-based default is adopted in Default Semantics.

2.1.4 *Contents and sources of defaults*

As is evident from this sample of approaches, there is no consensus as to the meaning of conversational defaults, neither is there much evidence concerning their sources. Defaults stem out of heuristics of rational behaviour, be it Gricean, neo-Gricean, pertaining to the logic of information structuring, or some other defeasible logic. Defaults operate due to the structure and form of language, the way the world is, the way societies are organized, or the way the operations of our brain make us perceive and comprehend all these things. These sources and types are not necessarily mutually exclusive. While this is not the place to delve into the ontology of defaults, an epistemological stance is necessary. In other words, it will not suffice to assume and then support the assumption that utterance interpretation makes use of presumed meanings. Constructing such a category of defaults is unwarranted, as we have seen in the example of multifarious levels at which presumed meanings arise, as well as multifarious sources of information that lead to defaults. Such a category of defaults would be eclectic and contrary to the methodological requirement of a reliable definitional characteristic of category membership. And if there is evidence that 'default interpretation' as a clearly delineated semantic or pragmatic category is untenable, then defaults, whose indispensability is confirmed on independent grounds,[7] must belong to more than one class as far as the explanation of discourse interpretation is concerned—and hence also as far as the theory of cognition is concerned. This is achieved in Default Semantics by recognizing cognitive defaults, as opposed to social and cultural ones, as well as by relegating some apparent default interpretations to the status of either lexical, or, at the other end of the spectrum, nonce-inference meaning.

2.2 Cognitive defaults

2.2.1 *Defaults in semantics*

I proposed in Chapter 1 that, in accordance with the methodological principle of the Parsimony of Levels (PoL), it is preferable to adopt one level of meaning representation to which various sources of information contribute. I called this representation a merger representation. This is a semantic representation in the dynamic sense in that it combines information from (a) the discourse that is incrementally revealed to the hearer; (b) the changing context; *and* (c) changing intentions. Further discussion of the properties of this representation is the topic of Chapter 3. What is important at the moment is the tentative assumption that defaults must belong to this representation and hence they are semantic defaults. I have also established that it is preferable to begin with the stance that defaults allow for various kinds rather than constitute a uniform category. I shall now discuss a type of default that arises out of the properties of the mental states that underlie the process of linguistic communication. It will become evident that such defaults are the defaults in the strongest sense in that they pertain to the way humans think. Before discussing them, I present the philosophical background to the theory of cognition in which they are embedded.

2.2.2 *Intentionality of mental states*

Mental states, such as belief, fear, and doubt, are made public when they are externalized by some vehicle. The vehicle that interests us here is language. In other words, we are interested in the relation between linguistic utterances and the mental states that underlie them. But only some types of mental states are of interest to us. These are mental states that have content, are *about* something. For example, to believe or to fear is to *believe something* or to *fear something*. This property of mental states is called intentionality. In Latin, 'intendere' means to aim in a particular direction, to direct the thoughts to something, by analogy with aiming a bow at a target. Other examples of intentional mental states include desire, want, need, and expectation. Not all experiences are intentional: sensations, such as a state of elation or having an itch, are not. These are of no interest to us.

Intentionality has a long history in philosophy. Aristotle, Avicenna, and medieval doctrines of knowledge and experience lead indirectly to the highlight of intentionality research in the nineteenth- and early twentieth-century phenomenology in the works of, among others, Bolzano (1837), Brentano (1874) and Husserl (1900–01). Phenomenology is a study of conscious experience, the study of how things (phenomena) are presented in consciousness. Relevant intentional mental states are viewed dynamically, as mental *acts*. These acts give expressions their meaning, in a way in which an act of demonstration gives meaning to a demonstrative expression such as 'that'.[8]

Now, intentional acts can be about mental objects, real objects, or whole states of affairs (eventualities): states, events, or processes. I shall follow the later phenomenological tradition and assume that our mental acts are directed at real rather than mental objects, and at real eventualities. In Husserl's *Logical Investigations* (1900–01), such mental acts, called objectifying, meaning-giving acts, are components of meaning and sum up to a proposition. All such component acts are intentional. This was, for Husserl, a foundation of his grammar, later to be known as categorial grammar. Meaning is compositional in the following way. There are independent categories such as names and sentences, as well as dependent categories that combine with names in order to build up sentences.

Each act has its own appropriate, intentional, objective reference.... *Whatever the composition of an act out of partial acts [m]ay be, if it is an act at all, it must have a single objective correlate, to which we say it is 'directed'....* Its partial acts ... likewise point to objects, which will, in general, not be the same as the object of the whole act, though they may occasionally be the same.... The act, e.g., corresponding to the name 'the knife on the table' is plainly complex: the object of the whole act is a knife, of one of its part-acts, a table.... [T]he knife is the object *about* which we judge or make a statement, when we say that the knife is on the table; the knife is not, however, the primary or full object of the judgement, but only the object of its subject. The full and entire object corresponding to the whole judgement is the *state of affairs* judged: the same state of affairs is presented in a mere presentation, wished as a wish, asked after in a question, doubted in a doubt etc. (Husserl 1900–01: 114, emphasis in original)

So, *propositions, units of meaning, are built up through composing meaning out of elements which exhibit intentionality.* This is also the philosophical foundation of the merger representations of Dynamic Semantics. In this sense, merger representations are mergers of information from the sentence, from intentionality, and from other sources that contribute to the meaning of an utterance that are discussed in more detail later on in this chapter. A merger representation is the output of the process of composing meaning.

In contemporary research, intentionality is understood as a feature of brains, and thus only secondarily, epiphenomenally, as a feature of language.[9] Language is intentional insofar as it allows for expressing beliefs, desires, and other mental states (see Lyons 1995: 44).[10] For Fodor, 'intentional' means 'representational', having informational content (see e.g. Fodor 1994). Or, in an even wider sense, brain cells are intentional in being 'about other things':

Cells in the kidney or liver perform their assigned functional roles and do not represent any other cells or functions. But brain cells, at every level of the nervous system, represent entities or events occurring elsewhere in the organism. Brain cells are assigned by design to be *about* other things and other doings. They are born cartographers of the geography of an organism and of the events that take place within that geography. The oft-quoted mystery of the 'intentional' mind relative to the representation of external objects turns out to be no mystery at all. The philosophical despair that surrounds this 'intentionality' hurdle . . . —why mental states represent internal emotions or interactions with external objects—lifts with the consideration of the brain in a Darwinian context: evolution has crafted a brain that is in the business of directly representing the organism and indirectly representing whatever the organism interacts with. (Damasio 1999: 78–9)

The theory-internal and paradigm-internal definitions of intentionality are of no concern for our purposes. We can remain fairly non-committal. All that has to be assumed is that there are intentional mental states that underlie utterances. At this level of defining the subject matter we are thus in agreement with current intentionality research in the philosophy of language, such as Searle (1983, 1984, 1990a).[11]

Let us now see how merger representation can account for default interpretations. Linguistic expressions are intentional by force of the corresponding mental states being intentional. Utterances are intentional: they are about something, someone, or at the very least they are about a state, event, or process. Intentionality can be stronger or weaker. Sentence (8) can be *about* a person who is known, identifiable to the speaker, such as, for example, the writer Peter Carey, or about whoever happens to have written *Oscar and Lucinda*.

(8)   The author of *Oscar and Lucinda* is a very good writer.

In a special scenario, the speaker can also be referentially mistaken and think of, say, Roddy Doyle as the author of this novel. When we think of these three possible states of affairs corresponding to the three readings of this sentence in terms of the underlying beliefs of the speaker's, we can order them with respect to the strength of the intentionality of these beliefs. A belief about Peter Carey comes with the strongest intentionality. In other words, it is 'strongly about' an individual who is intersubjectively identifiable as the author of *Oscar and Lucinda*. A belief about Roddy Doyle has an intentionality that is 'dispersed', so to speak, between the individual who is intended by the sentence in the intersubjective sense (Peter Carey) and the individual who is intended by the speaker (Roddy Doyle). In this case intentionality does not 'reach' the correct object. Naturally, from the position of the speaker, intentionality is not any 'weaker' in this case of the referential mistake as compared with the correct referring in the first case. Dispersal and weakening of intentionality mean here that the object of belief remains a mental object, without achieving the status of a real-world referent.[12] The third scenario is that of referring to whoever wrote *Oscar and Lucinda*. Here the intentionality is even weaker: the speaker does not have any particular person in mind. So, intentionality is weaker here both in the subjective and intersubjective perspective—that is from the point of view of the speaker's beliefs, and from the point of view of the interpreter of the speaker's beliefs.

The strongest intentionality is the norm. It is not impeded by the subject's lack of knowledge, referential mistakes, and other intervening factors. This is then the *default intentionality*. In (8), the default intentionality corresponds to the referential reading of the definite description 'the author of *Oscar and Lucinda*' and to the speaker's belief concerning Peter Carey. The referential mistake reading and the final, attributive reading (about whoever wrote the novel) are cases of progressive weakening of intentionality. I have developed this analysis at length elsewhere and supported it with various syntactic, semantic, and philosophical arguments.[13] All that matters for the present purpose is that we have here a case of a default that can be traced to the intentionality of a mental state. I call this type of default a *cognitive default*.

2.2.3 *Degrees of intentions*

Next, it is necessary to translate this philosophical foundation of cognitive defaults into appropriate aspects of a semantic and pragmatic theory. In other words, default mental states correspond to default interpretations of utterances and what we ultimately want is a theory of meaning that would account for such default interpretations. In communication, the strongest intentionality of a mental state is reflected in the strongest referring by the corresponding act of communication (where there is one), at least in non-modal contexts.[14] It corresponds then to the strongest *intending*. According to Default Semantics, there are three kinds of intentions in communication: the communicative intention, the informative intention embedded in it, and referential intention.[15] Speakers communicate certain content (they communicate that they intend to inform about something), they inform the addressee about certain content, and they refer to objects and eventualities. This intending in communication, just as its mental equivalent of intentionality of mental states, can be stronger or weaker. And hence default interpretations can also be explained with reference to the strength of intentions in communication.

Now, as was established in Chapter 1, the semantic representation, called the merger representation, is the product of the uttered sentence (with its structure and individual concepts) and the speaker's intentions inferred by the model hearer. The intentions come in default and non-default strengths. In (8), the default reading corresponds to the strongest referential intention. In other words, it corresponds to the situation in which the speaker refers to Peter Carey. It also corresponds to the strongest intention to communicate and inform in that the communicated content and the informational content are the strongest in the intersubjective, observable sense.

At this stage we can introduce the second, after PoL, principle of Default Semantics, namely the principle of Degrees of Intentions (DI; from Jaszczolt 1999*a*, 1999*b*):

DI: Intentions allow for degrees.

They can be stronger or weaker. It also has to be observed that not all three types of intentions are always present. In particular, in the attributive reading of (8), the referential intention understood as referring to a particular, identifiable individual is not present. But we can 'construe' it as present without any harm to the argument. On a slightly different construal, where whole eventualities, as well as objects, are referred to, referential intention is present. It is merely weaker. There are various options to construe and define these types of intentions and the choice of a particular construal will not matter for my purposes. No matter how we construe them, we will always obtain degrees of strength of intending, be it the strength of the communicative, informative, or referential intention. Collapsing the communicative and informative intention to one, for example Bach and Harnish's (1979: 7) communicative-illocutionary intention that, *nota bene*, chronologically precedes Sperber and Wilson's distinction, will not make a difference either.[16] Moreover, on any of these construals, a generalization has to be accepted that the primary role of the act of communication is to refer to something: be it an object, person, or merely a whole eventuality. In Default Semantics, this is called the principle of Primary Intention (PI; from Jaszczolt 1999*a*, 1999*b*):

PI: The primary role of intention in communication is to secure the referent of the speaker's utterance.

DI and PI summarize how intentions work and how they lead to default and non-default interpretations. So, the merger representation, accepted as the one and only meaning representation in the theory, is in fact compatible with the Gricean, intention-based theory of meaning. By recognizing default interpretations, it is also *neo-Gricean* and can be contrasted with relevance theory that, also being intention-based, Gricean in spirit, advocates only context-dependent nonce-inference.

A caveat is needed here. Strengths of intentions are used for explanatory purposes and do not necessitate an assumption that the hearer *consciously processes* these intentions. Defaults are instantaneous and automatic. I develop this further in the following sections.

Examples of cognitive defaults are provided and discussed in Chapters 4–9 of this book. Suffice it to say that propositional attitude reports such as (9) are also susceptible to cognitive default interpretations.

(9)   Kasia believes that the best living novelist wrote *My Life as a Fake*.

Just as referential readings of definite descriptions come with the strongest intentionality of the underlying mental state, so the *de re* reading of a belief report (here, again, the belief report *about* Peter Carey) exhibits the strongest default intentionality, the strongest referential intention, and thus is the default. Other examples come from the modality of time expressions, default anaphoric links, and, to some extent, number terms. On the other hand, some types of expressions that are commonly regarded as yielding default readings are better classified as yielding other, non-cognitive types of defaults—or even no defaults at all but instead conscious inferences. Most commonly, these other defaults are cultural and social. They are discussed in the following section.

2.3 Cultural and social defaults

2.3.1 *Physical defaults?*

Salient interpretations, and more precisely interpretations that do not require conscious pragmatic inference, are very common in discourse. But many of them have nothing to do with the strength of intending. Utterances are interpreted in one way rather than another because the hearer tacitly knows, prior to situational embedding of the utterance, that normally this interpretation is the case. The hearer does not even need to process 'default intentions'. Inference about the intentions does not take place—or, more precisely, we need not hypothesize that it takes place. For example, in (10) and (11), the preposition 'in' is 'by default' interpreted differently: as (i) 'fully enclosed within the cup' and (ii) 'partly enclosed in the cup' respectively.

(10)   There is coffee in the cup.

(11)   There is a spoon in the cup.

We could, of course, produce a physicalist explanation to the effect that liquids have to be enclosed in a vessel and solid objects do not, or a func-tionalist explanation to the effect that coffee is for drinking while a spoon is for stirring drinks, or else a cognitivist explanation to the effect that humans normally experience scenarios in which these senses of 'in' are the case, respectively. Explanations can be multiplied but they are tangential to the issue at hand. What we want to know is whether such processing of 'in' in context is indeed the case. On the sense of 'default' adopted here, namely that default interpretations are interpretations that arise without any computation of intentions and other inference from contextual clues, any such processing of 'in' would testify to the non-default status of reading (i) of (10) and (ii) of (11). I shall follow the same methodological principle as the one used to postulate PoL and construct merger representations: if there is no evidence of such processing, it should be assumed that there is none. Only if such an assumption results in incorrect predictions are we justified in hypothesizing that some processing of the context is involved.

Now, in Levinson's theory of GCI, defaults can arise at various stages of utterance processing. In (10) and (11), they arise post-propositionally in that the relation between the object or substance and the container is revealed only at the end of the sentence. But this is accidental: in (12), the default of 'in' arises 'locally', in the noun phrase in the subject position.

(12)   Bad coffee in a china cup tastes better than good coffee in a paper tub.

However, postulating local defaults does not come free. If the default is local, then the remainder of the sentence may defeat and cancel it, and this is costly in processing. The hypothesis of local defaults cannot be accepted easily and I shall leave the issue of localism open until Section 2.4.2 when we can take it up in more depth.

What should the type of default in (10) and (11) be called? It is not cognitive as it does not arise out of the strength of intentionality and intending. It arises because this is what the world is like *and* because this is what we perceive it to be like. We could call it a *physical default*. But, is there a need to talk about defaults in (10)–(12)? In order to justify introducing default interpretations, the non-default senses have to be sufficiently salient to be worthy of consideration. In (10)–(12), they are not. So, in spite of the well-esteemed tradition of talking about defaults for spatial expressions, there is little reason to discuss them. Naturally, there are spatial expressions that allow for more than one salient reading. For example, 'under' in (13) can be interpreted as floating within the boundaries provided by the bridge, or moving forward until the bridge is reached.

(13)   The buoy floated under the bridge.

The literature on this topic is vast, especially in various strands of cognitive linguistics (e.g. Talmy 1985, 2000; Jackendoff 1990, 1991). Problems with spatial prepositions in a cross-linguistic perspective are also well researched (Levinson 2000; Levinson et al. 2003). However, the meanings here seem to depend clearly on the context. While (13) allows for both interpretations, perhaps with the slight intuitive preference for the first, (14) clearly prefers the second interpretation.

(14)   The boat floated under a waterfall.

If I am on the right track here, then spatial prepositions are interpreted one way or another depending on the entities to which they relate. In other words, the content of the sentence gives rise to some preferred (and default) interpretations. And, situational context may cause a different interpretation to arise instead. If this is so, then such defaults can be called cultural defaults in that it is the culture[17] in which we are immersed that gives us the required background to process 'floating' of buoys as 'floating in place', while 'floating' of boats is processed as moving forward. After all, if no grammatical aspectual marker is compulsory in (13) and (14), the decision concerning the type of movement has to be made on semantic grounds. Alternatively, the ambiguity of the reading of (14) can be ascribed to the verb 'float' being ambiguous between an activity and an accomplishment verb. Be that as it may, 'physical defaults' are not required.

2.3.2 *Social–cultural defaults*

Prepositions are a hard case and it may not be wise to make far-reaching generalizations prior to having extensive empirical data to work on, of the type provided in Levinson et al. (2003). But there are many other cultural defaults that are much more easily classified as such. I shall call them *social–cultural defaults* in that default interpretations caused by cultural stereotypes arise by the same mechanism as the ones caused by social stereotypes. In (15), the possessive interpretation is clearly dependent on cultural knowledge and, for interlocutors familiar with western European painting, the cultural default is 'the painting by Pablo Picasso' rather than, say, 'the painting that Pablo X bought'.

(15)   Pablo's painting is of a crying woman.

Similarly, stereotypical interpretations can be safely assumed as pre-inferential defaults. Ironically, these are known in the literature as 'inferences to a stereotype' (e.g. Levinson 2000). Instead of inference, we have here an instantaneous, automatic interpretation. In (16), it is unlikely that the hearer consciously goes through the step (16a) before enriching 'a nanny' to 'a female nanny'.

(16)   We advertised for a new nanny.   +> a female nanny
*(16a)   Nannies are normally female.

Instead, the hearer, as a member of a society in which (16a) holds, unreflectively comes up with the 'female nanny' interpretation.[18]

However, just as prepositions presented us with the doubt as to whether we need defaults there, so social–cultural defaults such as that in (16) give rise to fuzzy intuitions. After all, what the speaker uttered is that they had advertised for a nanny, of unspecified sex, age, social status, marital status, hair colour, skin colour, religion, sexual preferences, etc. How far do we want to go in postulating defaults? And, more importantly, what would the criterion for such a default representation of content be? There is no clear answer to this question and the only way to provide an answer would be to have access to the content of thought. So far, we have only theories and crude attempts at collecting experimental data, plagued by contentious experimental design.

But even if we had an answer to how fine-grained the content of thought is, we still have to admit a qualitative difference between (i) types of expressions in which clear alternative readings can be discerned, such as *de re* and *de dicto* readings of propositional attitude reports, referential and attributive readings of definite descriptions, or inclusive and exclusive readings of disjunction, and (ii) expressions which merely give rise to a more fine-grained picture of the situation than the sentence justifies. We can tentatively observe that social and cultural defaults seem to belong to the latter category. For example, in (15), even if there are some alternatives, they are only present in the form of general, very vague predictions, such as that there is some relation between Pablo and the painting, such as authorship, ownership, the picture he is looking at, the one he wrote an article about, and so on. This list is not formalizable as semantic alternatives—or as what has traditionally been called a semantic ambiguity. Any further specifications which are not the default have to be performed in the context, with the help of background knowledge.

This observation strongly suggests that social and cultural defaults are not as successfully formalizable as cognitive defaults which follow a pattern of gradual departures from the default that parallels the degree of intentionality of the corresponding mental state. The argument for considering them as default in the sense of the lack of contextual inference is also weaker here. While cognitive defaults are motivated by 'normal', undispersed intentionality, cultural and social defaults are only motivated by the methodological prerequisite not to postulate inferential processes beyond necessity. Combined with the fact that some such problematic defaults do not even come with salient, non-default alternative readings, there is little to recommend them. Even if they *are* cases of default interpretations, rather than being salient, context-driven inferences, they are still problematic in that they are hardly distinguishable from conscious, context-driven inferences. For example, while (15) is likely to be a trigger for defaults due to relying on deeply inculcated cultural knowledge, (7) is less likely to be so.

(15) Pablo's painting is of a crying woman.   +> the painting by Pablo Picasso

(7) Peter's book is about a glass church.   +> the book by Peter Carey

It is likely that, even if the hearer is well versed in Carey's novels, he or she still performs conscious inference. The boundary between such social–cultural defaults and social–cultural inferences can only be *assumed* as methodologically desirable and psychologically plausible. But any classification of interpretations as social–cultural defaults or conscious inferences based on social or cultural knowledge is still largely a matter of speculation.

Moreover, as is evident from the discussion of (16) and the granularity of the semantic representation (and as I argue further in Section 2.4), some social and cultural defaults lie outside semantics, that is outside the merger representations. In spite of the celebrated post-Gricean tradition that would have a lot of them contribute to the propositional representation and to the truth conditions if they are developments of the sentence structure, they are better regarded as often lying outside the truth-conditionally evaluable representation. Since, as we have seen in (16), their granularity is unknown and they do not come with clear semantic alternatives, we will have little to say about them in semantic theory and will have to leave them to sociolinguistics and anthropological linguistics for, at best, descriptive research. No formalizable semantic theory is, in principle, able to handle them and to go beyond acknowledging the fact that *sometimes* they can contribute to the truth conditions of the utterance.

The picture of meaning representation that is beginning to emerge is given in *Fig. 2.1. The asterisk indicates a tentative proposal. The level about which compositionality should be properly predicated is further reassessed in Chapter 3.

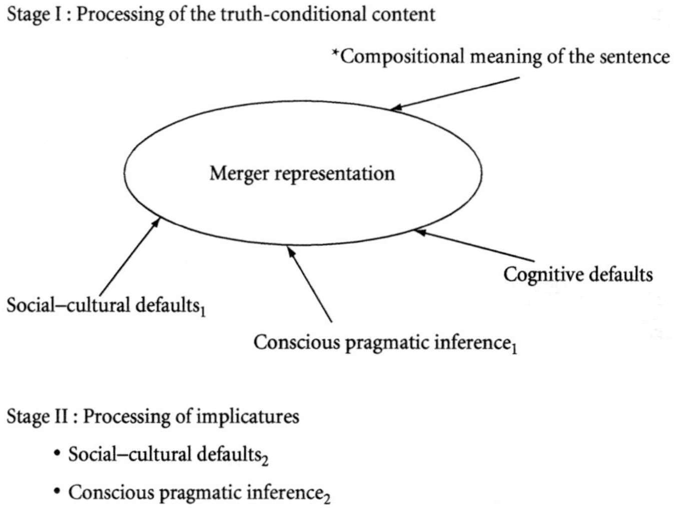

Stage I : Processing of the truth-conditional content

*Compositional meaning of the sentence

Merger representation

Cognitive defaults

Social–cultural defaults$_1$

Conscious pragmatic inference$_1$

Stage II : Processing of implicatures
- Social–cultural defaults$_2$
- Conscious pragmatic inference$_2$

*FIGURE 2.1   Utterance interpretation: first attempt

Social–cultural defaults indexed as '1' and '2' are not qualitatively different. Their distinguishing feature is their function. Social–cultural defaults$_1$ contribute to the semantic, truth-conditional content, while social–cultural defaults$_2$ contribute to implicatures. Implicatures are understood here, in principle, as in Carston (1988) and her followers: as propositions that are

functionally independent in reasoning (see also Carston 1998a, 2002a; Recanati 1989a), but with the proviso that, in Default Semantics, the truth-
conditional content of the act of communication is not restricted to the
development of the logical form of the uttered sentence: the output of
grammar can be overridden. Symmetrically, neither is *every* performed development of the logical form part of the truth-conditional content.[19] Sentence (15) is an example of a trigger for a social–cultural default$_1$, while (16) is
an example of a trigger for a social–cultural default$_2$. Analogously, conscious
pragmatic inference$_1$ produces an inferential addition to the semantic merger
representation and thus is truth-conditionally relevant, while conscious pragmatic inference$_2$ gives rise to implicatures—and hence to functionally separate thoughts.[20]

In Default Semantics, I will have little to say about social–cultural defaults.
To sum up, this is so, first, because investigating their sources lies outside
semantics proper—in sociolinguistics and anthropological linguistics, and
secondly, because the boundary between social–cultural defaults and conscious pragmatic inferences can only be properly established with sufficient
evidence from processing.

2.3.3 Lexical defaults?

Negative-raising is also a celebrated case of default interpretation in neo-
Gricean pragmatic literature. Negative-raising is a tendency for negation on
the main clause to be interpreted as negation on the subordinate clause. For
example, (17) normally communicates (17a).

(17)   I don't think Vernon Gregory murdered his classmates.
(17a)   I think Vernon Gregory didn't murder his classmates.

However, negative-raising seems to be restricted to certain verbs. (18) does not
normally communicate (18a). In fact, it seems to correspond to a wish that is
opposite to that underlying (18a), as in (18b).

(18)   I don't hope Vernon will be released from prison.
(18a)   I hope Vernon will not be released from prison.
(18b)   I wish against hope that Vernon be released from prison.

Surely, one could try to assimilate negative-raising to the category of cognitive
defaults by observing that the expression of the content of thought in (17a)
carries stronger intentionality than a denial of having a relevant mental
state in (17). But this is rather far-fetched, considering that we are not
comparing members of a gradable category: a thought about a certain
Vernon Gregory, that is a thought about an identifiable person (most likely,

Vernon Gregory Little, the main character of DBC Pierre's celebrated novel), is not directly comparable as to its degree of intentionality with the lack of any thought on that matter admitted by the speaker.[21]

Considering that negative-raising does not apply to all relevant verbs of attitude, all that remains is to classify interpretations such as that in (17a) as lexical preferences. In other words, some verbs have the property of undergoing negative-raising and this is a matter for lexical semantics. And if it is a matter for lexical semantics, it is also a matter for truth-conditional semantics in that defaults from the lexicon percolate upwards to affect the (pragmatics-rich) truth conditions. Such defaults are not very different from salient, preferred meanings of lexical items that have been standardly derived from homonymy, polysemy, or simply lexical ambiguity. It may seem that they are stronger in that they can arise as soon as the main clause is uttered, while 'bank', 'foot', or 'port' may have to wait for their interpretation a little further into the sentence. But this is not a generalizable property, as is evidenced by comparing (17) with (19) on the one hand, and (20) with (21) on the other.

(17)   I don't think Vernon Gregory murdered his classmates.

(19)   I don't think about this novel any more.

(20)   Port glasses are empty.

(21)   Port number one on this list is what I would like to visit.

Example (17), after the main clause has been uttered, could have still turned out to be (19), with no negative-raising. 'Port' in (20) is interpreted as soon as the word 'glasses' is uttered, while 'port' in (21) has to 'wait' a lot longer. Considering that little is known about activation versus underspecification of lexical meaning, and whatever is known has to be taken in conjunction with percolation of features (or, conceptual constituents) from the preceding context, the issue is best left as the case for lexical semantics and for a separate investigation.[22]

Default interpretations have also been predicated of sentential connectives. Levinson accounts for them by the I-principle: the conditional in (22) is 'perfected' to a biconditional in (22a); a conjunction communicates temporal or causal connectedness as in (23a) and (24a) respectively.

(22)   If you mow my lawn, I'll give you five dollars.
(22a)   If and only if you mow my lawn will I give you five dollars.

(23)   John took off his clothes and went to bed.
(23a)   John took off his clothes and then went to bed.

(24)   He broke his finger and couldn't play the piano.
(24a)   He broke his finger and as a result couldn't play the piano.

The I-implicature is not the end of the story, for the reasons discussed earlier in this chapter. Namely, it does not discriminate between different types of preferred interpretations as distinguished in *Fig. 2.1. In order to capture the default type, we could perhaps account for the enriched meaning of a conjunction and a conditional by appealing to the strength of the informative intention: the enriched propositions communicate more information. And, as we know from Section 2.2, we can go one step higher to the properties of mental states. The more informative the reading of the utterance, the stronger the intentionality. It follows that, by analogy with the analyses in Sections 2.2.1 and 2.2.2, the strongest intentionality is the default. By analogy with other defaults recognized in Default Semantics, the defaults will have to arise on a sub-sentential level, that is that of the sentential connective, and be realized, or not realized (albeit not 'cancelled' or 'overridden'), in particular contexts. This solution, however, will not work. If we tried to appeal to the amount of communicated content as if it meant the strength of the communicative and/ or informative intention, our approach would collapse all kinds of default interpretations back to one category because most additions to what is physically uttered would be more informative than what is uttered. So, perhaps we should look at the normal, default links between the eventualities combined by the connective and classify the interpretations in (22a), (23a), and (24a) as physical defaults? Perhaps, but by this token we are classifying relations between situations rather than senses of connectives. In addition, it is not at all obvious that sentential connectives undergo a uniform treatment and that they give rise to one type of default—if any. Their properties are further investigated in Chapter 8.

Number terms are also strong candidates for default interpretations. They have been regarded either as having the 'at least' semantics (Horn, e.g., 1976, 1984, 1985, 1992; Kempson and Cormack 1981; tentatively also Levinson 2000); as underspecified as to their 'exactly', 'at least', and 'at most' sense (e.g. Carston 1998b); or as having punctual, 'exactly' semantics (Koenig 1993; Geurts 1998a). Versions of punctual semantics seem to be emerging as the dominant orientation (see also Bultinck 2002[23]). It appears as if punctual semantics and the corresponding strongest referential intention suggested the cognitive default analysis: the 'exactly' sense is the cognitive default. Koenig (1993: 147) appeals here to the informativeness of interpretations. Greater informativeness is connected with the property of being a proper subset of a truth set: 'If the truth set of a sentence A is a proper subset of the truth set of a sentence B, A is more informative than B'. So, by saying 'three' the speaker conveys that it is not the case that the number is four, five, or more. There is only one step from such considerations of the strength of information to the explanation in terms of the strength of the referential intention. By saying 'three', the speaker refers to 'exactly three' (items, objects, entities, units...) and the associated referential intention, and *a fortiori*, the informative and communicative intentions in which this intention is progressively embedded, are the strongest. And so is the intentionality of the corresponding mental state. However, we have to beware of overgenerating. Although the explanation in terms of cognitive defaults works for number terms, it may not be necessary. We have to remember that the first thing to establish is whether there is a need to talk in terms of defaults in the particular type of expression. In the case of number terms, there does not seem to be. If, as all convincing evidence suggests, their semantics is punctual, then 'three' simply *means* 'exactly three', without invoking salient alternatives. And if it does not invoke them, we need no defaults. This punctual semantics for number terms is taken up further in Chapter 9. The issue is signalled here as another example that compels us to beware of overgeneration in applying the explanation by cognitive defaults.

The obvious question to ask is whether defaults that belong to the level of semantic representation stand up to evidence from language acquisition. Noveck (2001), among others, conducted some experiments in which he showed that children interpret scalar expressions logically: the logical meaning is the default. For example, 'might' is compatible with 'must', just as 'some' is compatible with 'all'. By the same token, 'three' would be compatible with 'four' or 'five' and hence have the semantics 'at least three'. Interpretations that incorporate scalar implicatures develop later. However, when we consider language acquisition in terms of a developing language system, this is no counterevidence at all: what is a semantic representation for children ceases to be a semantic representation for adults. There is no need to postulate inferential additions to the underspecified representation just on the grounds that children's semantic representations differ from those of adults. In Default Semantics, it is merely necessary to acknowledge that language development includes the development of the ability to represent content in terms of merger representations that include (i) pre-contextual cognitive defaults arrived at without conscious inference; (ii) social–cultural, background-based but not inference-based defaults; and (iii) conscious pragmatic inference.

2.4 Staying on the semantic track

2.4.1 *Defaults and truth conditions*

It is not my aim to provide a rigid classification of types of defaults, neither is it my aim to allocate types of expressions to types of defaults. The first task is not interesting, and the latter, as we have seen, is not attainable. This is so for reasons not unlike those behind the failure of the classifications of speech acts and classifying English verbs by illocutionary force. Rather, it is my aim to rethink the most common types of expressions that give rise to preferred, salient interpretations in a systematic way, susceptible to a formal explanation. For example, I will not now be interested in the content and scope of the category of social–cultural defaults such as (15) or (16) discussed above, in that their explanation clearly lies outside the domain of semantic theory. Moreover, as we have seen, at least some of the typical defaults of this kind arguably do not contribute to truth conditions. In (16), whether the nanny is to be male or female lies outside the meaning of the proposition. Last but not least, the boundary between social–cultural defaults and conscious pragmatic inference is not demonstrable, as (7) and (15) show.

Next, we also have to beware of easy overgeneration by explaining what is going on in conversation by appealing to social–cultural defaults. Not every interpretation that *can be explained* in terms of such defaults *is* a social–cultural default. In (25), reference assignment requires the resolution of the relationship between the mother and the baby.

(25)   The baby cried and the mother fed it.   +> the baby's mother

Since the default interpretation relies on the cultural and social knowledge that babies are normally nurtured by their own parents, we may be inclined to classify this sense of (25) as a case of a social–cultural default. But, surely, all that is needed is the resolution of the anaphoric link (in the sense of anaphora that subsumes presupposition), which proceeds according to the principle of the least effort in searching for an antecedent. This is, therefore, a case of a cognitive default and can be classified as *default for presupposition as anaphora*. Defaults for anaphora and presupposition are the topic of Chapter 7 and I will not discuss them further at this point. All that matters at the moment is the methodological directive to search for the simplest, plausible, generalizable, and formalizable explanation of what is going on in the process of utterance interpretation before resorting to social and cultural reasons. It matters because it is common practice to assume that discourse processing uses routes that are the simplest and require the least effort. This amounts to searching in the lexical and grammatical properties of expressions, as well as properties of mental states, steering clear of the properties of the social and cultural world. Following the reverse order would amount to taking a long and uncertain route when an easy, safe, and short path is available.[24]

Now, what does this confinement of semantics achieve for us as compared with widely accepted views such as truth-conditional pragmatics (e.g. Recanati 2003), post-pragmatic semantics (Levinson 1988), or truth-conditional semantics with the contribution of pragmatic processing (Carston 1988)? In fact, it is not very different from these approaches. We are still allowing for a pragmatic contribution to the truth-conditional representation by construing this representation as a merger (see *Fig. 2.1). We are not excluding truth-conditionally relevant nonce-inference such as that in (26):

(26)   You are not going to die.   +> from this wound

Utterance (26) can give rise to conscious pragmatic inference₁ of *Fig. 2.1. The main difference is that Default Semantics represents discourses as acts of communication and all the sources of information that contribute to the representation of meaning of such acts of communication are assumed to be, in principle, equally important. This means, to repeat, that the output of syntax can be overridden and the merger representation which results from interpreting (26) can sometimes be (26a) rather than, say, (26b).

(26a)   You should not worry.
(26b)   You are not going to die from this wound.

So, the distinction between the content of the merger representation and the content of implicatures does not match that between the explicature or what is said, construed as a development of the logical form, and implicatures. This issue was addressed at length in Chapter 1. Moreover, what we gain in comparison with other approaches is some order in default meanings. We cease to treat defaults as a uniform, semantically interesting category, and instead 'split' them, so to speak, into cognitive defaults on the one hand, and, on the other, social–cultural defaults that are not always semantic and only sometimes contribute to the truth conditions (as social–cultural defaults₁). In Chapters 4–9, I reanalyse some of the seminal categories of expressions that systematically give rise to default interpretations.

2.4.2 Questioning GCI

Levinson's I-inferences, that is pragmatic inferences that undergo the heuristic for a stereotypical interpretation of what is said simply and briefly, are not obvious candidates for default meanings, in spite of the author's effort to make them look so. They belong to the category of GCI in that any inference to the stereotype is context-independent. However, they are often local, sub-propositional. As such, they are a result of the interpretation *in context* of the expression that is the trigger of defaults. For example, the indefinite noun phrase 'a woman' in (27) may trigger the 'generalized implicature' such as 'not the speaker's wife, mother, sister, or any other close acquaintance or relation' even before the utterance is completed.

(27)   I saw a woman in a swimsuit in the opera yesterday.

In (28), this inference does not seem to take place.

(28)   There is a woman cellist in the Vienna Philharmonic. She is my sister.

Levinson (2000: 118) asks, 'in what sense are . . . I-inferences *generalized*'. Since they are the result of an interpretation of an utterance in context, they are, strictly speaking, just *defaults for that context*. 'A woman' triggers inference to 'not the speaker's wife, mother, or any other close relation' in some contexts but not in others. Levinson's GCIs can be local, sub-propositional, to a greater or lesser degree: they can arise at the level of words, phrases, and other subsentential expressions. Therefore, the notion of context has to be understood in the wide sense to comprise all that surrounds such a sub-propositional default trigger. In other words, in the incremental processing of an utterance, whatever comes after the point at which the default is triggered constitutes the context. Levinson's reasons for the category of GCI are as follows:

at a sufficient level of abstraction, it is quite clear that the kinds of inferences here collected—for example, conjunction-buttressing, negative-strengthening [e.g. from 'not like' to 'positively dislike'], preferred patterns of coreference [pronouns being anaphoric on the locally preceding fully referring expression]—do hold as preferred interpretations across contexts and indeed across languages. And at a slightly higher level of abstraction, the different types collected can be seen to share the property of maximizing the informational load by narrowing the interpretation to a specific subcase of what has been said. (Levinson 2000: 118)

Maximizing information by inference to a stereotype is certainly an unquestionable generalization of rational conversational behaviour.[25] However, a rationale for a unique category of a GCI does not follow from it. While some inferences are caused by the way our cognition works, others belong to the 'level of abstraction' of social and cultural patterns. While some are said to be word-based or local in some other way, others are sentence-based. Levinson's GCIs, or presumptive meanings, are therefore an eclectic category that comprises lexical and phrasal defaults on one end (local, pre-propositional, e.g. 'bread knife' as a knife for cutting bread, versus 'pocket knife' as a folding knife kept in a pocket) and sentential (post-propositional) defaults on the other. Sometimes, the level on which the default meaning arises cannot be clearly delimited. For example, 'secretary' defaults to 'female secretary' for administrative, assistant posts, but, alas, not for political functions of high prestige and responsibility. The fact that some of these meaning presumptions are driven by social conventions ('female secretary'), while others seem more deeply entrenched in our cognitive processes and have to do with the strength of intending ('if' $+>$ 'iff'),[26] only adds to the diversity of the class and fuels justified criticism (see e.g. Recanati 2003*a*).

As was demonstrated in this chapter, default interpretations of Default Semantics eschew this infelicity by distinguishing two separate construals of default interpretations: (i) cognitive defaults, triggered by the strength of intentionality of mental states and hence activated on the level of the merger representation (cf. a propositional representation, a DRS); and (ii) social-cultural defaults, activated by social and cultural conventions on any level on which it is appropriate for those defaults to arise: that of the propositional representation or that of implicatures.

2.4.3 *Questioning cancellation of defaults*

Levinson's GCIs are generated by default, without any conscious process of inference. They are generated when a trigger for such a default is uttered. So, they can be generated locally. However, at the same time, they are generated unless the context prevents them from arising. How can these two claims be held in tandem? If number terms by default render the 'exactly' interpretation, it is unclear how the context can prevent it from arising in (29).

(29)   Thirty five votes are needed to pass the motion.

Or, does the 'exactly' default arise locally after all? If it does arise, is it then *cancelled* after the verb form 'are needed' is processed? Or does it remain as the truth-conditionally relevant content until the whole proposition has been arrived at? Similarly, in (30), does the default referential reading of the definite description become cancelled once the futurity of the event is recovered?

(30)   The first child to be born in 2066 will be called William.

The discussion of the locality of such defaults is well under way in the current literature.[27] It is held rather in void in that it is restricted to arguments from the success of the hypotheses. What is emerging, however, is a semantic standpoint that defaults belong to the language structure, they are part and parcel of the computational power of grammar and as such they belong to semantics. If so, they have to be defeasible, that is cancellable in the context.

There can be no answer to the question of locality until there is reliable empirical evidence one way or the other. However, before rushing off to conduct experiments, there is a task for a theoretician. One has to start with a plausible, explanatorily adequate hypothesis. And the hypothesis of locality of defaults followed by cancellation is not without problems. First, and most importantly, cancellation is costly and we must not postulate it unless we have to. Rational conversational behaviour requires that hearers process utterances using the minimal effort to arrive at what is regarded as the intended interpretation. If they go through the process of default cancellation, then this can only be supported if in a considerable statistical majority of cases the default goes through. Considering the unpredictability of human conversation and life situations, this is rather unlikely. Statistical evidence would be of little help; so would a philosophical argument for or against determinism in life. Rather, it seems more appropriate to try to focus on the output of grammatical and lexical processing and assume that normally defaults are 'added' somehow or other to this output. Old-fashioned as it may sound, this construal eschews the danger of multiplying layers of interpretation and is, at the same time, in agreement with the construal of utterance processing we are building here. Merger representations of Default Semantics are fully compatible with such post-propositional defaults. The output of the sources of information provisionally distinguished in *Fig. 2.1 merges to produce a representation of the speaker's meaning as constructed by a model hearer. It seems that Grice was correct in assuming post-propositional GCIs. Where he was not correct was in assuming *one* uniform category of GCIs and, more importantly, regarding all of them as implicatures.

All in all, while I do not intend to solve here the cancellability–non-arising dilemma of default interpretations, I have argued that good methodological practice leads to retaining Gricean post-propositional GCIs, rethinking them as defaults, and repackaging them into various types. On this construal, the cancellation of defaults is avoided.

2.5 Limitations

While it is well acknowledged that default interpretations are common, the question remains as to whether they *have to* arise whenever they *can* arise. In other words, are there situations in which stereotypical meanings are not invoked although there is nothing in the context that would prevent them from being invoked? This question is closely related to the issue of ambiguity and underspecification discussed in Section 1.2. In computational modelling of discourse, it has been commonly assumed that agents can reason from incomplete premises. The hearer need not always complete the process of interpretation of an utterance before using this utterance as a premise for further reasoning. This assumption is founded on the methodological principle of parsimony: the effort put into interpretation has to be justified. Logical reasoning, performed by a human or machine agent, needs the discourse that is disambiguated/specified only to a certain degree; beyond that, the effort becomes vacuous (see van Deemter 1998 on 'ambiguous logic', the logic of underspecified representations). So, the merger representation need not always be completed. (By the way, neither do post-merger, social–cultural defaults$_2$ always have to be computed.) The fact that we can reason from underspecified premises does not, however, warrant an introduction of the level of underspecified semantic representation. Special cases do not warrant changing the rule and just as Occam's razor has to be preserved, so does Parsimony of Levels.

In addition to the possible non-arising of possible defaults, there is another limitation in explaining such salient meanings. If, as I have argued, it is desirable to 'stay on the semantic track' without straying into sociolinguistic and anthropological-linguistic descriptions, why not rearrange the players and fit all types of defaults into semantic theory, while banishing intentions and intentionality as ' "private" features of the participants' cognitive states' (Asher and Lascarides 2003: 76)? This is the move taken in SDRT. However, this move is engendered there by the assumption that the best way to account for meaning is to restrict one's modelling of discourse to features of linguistic utterances. So,

only if we restrict the theory's use of beliefs, intentions and other 'private' features of the participants' cognitive states—such as individual memory organisation or processing effort—will the theory be a *linguistic theory* with linguistic generalisations and explanations. (Asher and Lascarides 2003: 76)

To sum up our previous discussion of SDRT, this move makes the task of modelling linguistic meaning feasible. However, the presumed, salient interpretations have then to be captured by postulating a system of information packaging, with its own logic, which is fairly independent from the rest of modelling, that is from the logic of information content. Cognitive reality of processing that would be compatible with this system is, of course, at stake but modelling processing cannot (and need not) be a criterion of success there. What is gained by exorcising the mental, is lost in accounting for the process of discourse interpretation. We can't have it both ways. Since defeasible reasoning (reasoning to defaults in the absence of evidence to the contrary)[28] can be explained in either way, we are free to choose on the grounds of the theory's objectives: modelling language or modelling the interpretation process. Asher and Lascarides[29] maintain that whatever provides an explanation of linguistic meaning, also provides an explanation for objects of beliefs and other attitudes. If DRSs represent utterance meaning, then they also represent the content of beliefs. But we can go further than that and unveil the causal relation. In addition to the fact that language conveys cognitive states, it also inherits their properties. And if so, then whatever property relevant (intentional) mental states have, language expressions have them as well. DRSs then become reanalysed as our merger representations, combining the meaning from sentences, inference process, and defaults, including intentionality-based defaults. And, if we want a theory of human communication, we need a theory of discourse that does not ban such intentional explanations. To repeat, modelling of language itself as in SDRT can do without this requirement. Default Semantics cannot. A merger representation constructed by a model hearer is the backbone of the theory. The rest, like the ordering of the sources of defaults, is a matter for empirical testing for both orientations equally.[30]

Notes

1 This originated in Levinson 1987. For a similar reworking of Grice's original maxims of conversation, see Horn 1984, 1988. See also Chapter 1, note 4.

2 In Levinson's terminology.

3 I develop this further in Chapter 7 in the example of presupposition as anaphora.

4 E.g. Lascarides and Asher 1993; Lascarides and Oberlander 1993; Asher and Lascarides 1995, 1998a, 1998b, 2001, 2003; Lascarides and Copestake 1998; Lascarides, Copestake, and Briscoe 1996.

5 See Asher and Lascarides 2003: chapter 9.

6 See Levinson 1995, 2000 on the 'bottleneck of communication'.

7 Defaults are 'confirmed on independent grounds' because there is evidence from discourse processing that human agents use defeasible, default logic in the absence of contextual evidence. See e.g. Asher and Lascarides 2003; Lascarides and Asher 1993.

8 According to one contemporary view, demonstratives exemplify *procedural meaning*, i.e. they encode procedures for the recovery of the referent which then contributes to the truth-conditional content. See Blakemore 1987; Wilson and Sperber 1993.

9 Since language is one of the vehicles of thought, it inherits the intentionality of mental states. I do not, however, follow Searle in calling it 'double level of intentionality' or 'derived intentionality' (Searle 1983, 1984, 1990a). There is *one* intentionality that is a property of mental states and of the *vehicles* of these mental states that allow them to be shared among agents who possess them. For a detailed discussion see Jaszczolt 1999b: chapter 3.

10 In what follows, I shall use the term *mental state* in agreement with the current practice. No assumption about the membership of these two categories (*state* and *act*) is implied: I shall refer to attitudes such as belief, knowledge, or doubt.

11 See note 9.

12 I owe this point to a discussion with François Recanati.

13 E.g. Jaszczolt 1997, 1999b.

14 Modality has a definitional property of detachment from the content the modal sentence conveys. Therefore, default intentionality corresponds to this detachment. This issue is discussed in Chapter 6. Non-modal contexts subsume extensional as well as some intensional contexts such as attitude ascriptions. *De re* and *de dicto* readings of belief reports are also governed by this rule of the strength of intending. This issue is discussed in Chapter 7.

15 See Sperber and Wilson 1986; Bach 1992 for definitions and discussion.

16 For a detailed discussion of these three types of intentions see Jaszczolt 1999*b*: section 2.2.

17 In the wide sense.

18 See Recanati 2003*a* for a discussion of pre-inferential defaults, as well as local and post-propositional defaults.

19 See Chapter 1.

20 *Nota bene*, Recanati's (e.g. 2003*a*) primary and secondary pragmatic processes are not the same as conscious pragmatic inference 1 and 2. Primary pragmatic processes are unconscious and result in defaults.

21 Note that the reference assignment to Vernon Gregory as Vernon Gregory Little of DBC Pierre is almost certainly not a default itself. Rather, it is an effect of conscious pragmatic inference$_1$.

22 A lot of progress in this area has been made in computational linguistics. See e.g. Lascarides et al. 1996; Lascarides, Copestake, and Briscoe 1996; Asher and Lascarides 1995; Pustejovsky 1995.

23 Bultinck proposes an 'absolute value' of number terms, which eschews the problem of boundedness.

24 *Nota bene*, this assumption of the simplest explanation is compatible with our earlier assumption that all the contribution to merger representations can be treated 'on an equal footing'.

25 In a similar vein, Geurts (2000) considers an Informativeness Principle (IP) that says that stronger, more informative readings are preferred. He admits that this principle, stated in this general way, sometimes renders wrong predictions: the more informative reading is not always preferred. However, Geurts seems to underestimate somewhat the power of an informativeness-based explanation. I assess his arguments in Chapter 7 (section 7.4) while discussing presupposition and informativeness.

26 But see also Chapter 8.

27 Chierchia, Landman, Recanati. See Recanati 2003*a* for a critical overview.

28 See e.g. Lascarides and Asher (1993: 498); Asher and Lascarides (2001: 204).

29 After Asher, e.g. 1986. See Asher and Lascarides (2003: 378).

30 Cf. also: 'normally, discourse information about how a word should be interpreted—if there is any—wins over defaults from the lexicon'; Lascarides and Copestake (1998: 413).

3

Compositionality and Merger Representations

3.1. Compositional meaning

So far I have given some reasons for treating all types of information that contribute to meaning of utterances on an equal footing, in the sense that their output merges without giving priority to any of the types. I proposed that this output of all sources of information should be called a merger representation. In Chapter 1, the rationale for such a merger was established. In Chapter 2, I made an introductory attempt at identifying the factors that contribute to the merger (see *Fig. 2.1). The next question to ask is, how does compositionality fit in such a diversified representation? Or, in other words, what exactly is it, if anything, that is compositional? The simplest and most desirable answer would be that the lexicon and the structure of the sentence compose to form the meaning. On the construal proposed in this chapter, the output of syntactic processing (logical form) is not a unit in utterance processing of which compositionality can be predicated. As is well known from Frege's (1892) discussion of the principle of compositionality, not all sentences are compositional in this way and, if we wanted to preserve compositionality, meaning would have to be redefined as something different from reference. In addition to extensional contexts, there are contexts in which more than the extensions matters to the meaning. Such intensional contexts are, for example, belief reports. Jonathan may not consent to the report in (2), although he had previously uttered (1) and despite 'the author of *Jack Maggs*' and 'Peter Carey' being coreferential.

(1) Jonathan: Peter Carey is the best living novelist.

(2) Tom: Jonathan believes that the author of *Jack Maggs* is the best living novelist.

In other words, the principle of substitutivity of coreferential expressions does not hold here: the substitution does not always preserve the truth value in intensional contexts, that is it does not preserve it on all occasions of use.[1]

Substitution fails because Jonathan may think of Peter Carey under a particular *guise*, also known as the *mode of presentation*. For example, he may
know his novels *My Life as a Fake*, *The True History of the Kelly Gang*, and
Oscar and Lucinda, but be unaware that he also wrote *Jack Maggs* and some
other works. So, in addition to the extension (identity of the referent), the
reporter on a belief has to preserve the intension, the particular meaning of
the believer's.

There have been various attempts to incorporate the mode of presentation
in the logical form. For example, Schiffer (1992: 503) entertains the possibility
of adding a mode of presentation in the form of 'Φ^*': 'an implicitly referred to
and contextually determined type of mode of presentation'.[2] Sentence (2) is
then represented as in (2a), where *m* stands for a mode of presentation and *a*
for the person called Peter Carey.

(2a) $\exists m$ (Φ^*m & Bel (Jonathan, <a, the best living novelist>, m))[3]

When we adopt this solution of so-called *hidden indexicals*, unarticulated
constituents of the logical form, then the question of compositionality arises.
If the sentence in (2) is not compositional, and in order to preserve compositionality we have added some constituents of meaning which are not overtly
there in the sentence, then what exactly is compositional? It appears that it is
the meaning representation that combines information from the sentence and
from those aspects of thought that are relevant for the meaning. In (2), these
aspects consist of the way in which Jonathan represents Peter Carey to
himself: the mode of presentation he has of the referent *a*.

Propositional attitude reports are discussed at length in Chapter 5, where
Φ^*m is replaced with a more semantically adequate solution. For the current
purpose, however, these nuances of hidden indexicals are irrelevant. All that
matters is that we have to account for more meaning than the sentence gives
us in order to preserve a compositional theory of meaning.

Next, there are sentences that are syntactically complete but semantically
incomplete and hence do not carry meaning in the sense of truth conditions
(see Bach 1994a, 1994b). (3) is only truth-conditionally evaluable when it is
completed as, for example, in (3a).

(3)   *The Blind Assassin* isn't good enough.
(3a)   *The Blind Assassin* isn't good enough to justify the Booker Prize.

Such context-dependent, inferential completions are also elements of the
compositional meaning representation.

Finally, there are sentences that are semantically as well as syntactically
complete but whose utterances carry meaning that is obviously different, that

has been expanded, when compared with that of the sentence. Default interpretations such as social–cultural defaults₁ and cognitive defaults (see *Fig. 2.1) belong here. For example, (4), repeated from (15) in Chapter 2, defaults to (4a).

(4)   Pablo's painting is of a crying woman.
(4a)   The painting by Pablo Picasso is of a crying woman.

Similarly, expansions by means of conscious pragmatic inference₁ (see *Fig. 2.1) belong in this category, as (5), repeated from (7) in Chapter 2, exemplifies.

(5)   Peter's book is about a glass church.
(5a)   The book Peter wrote is about a glass church.

It appears that just as in Fig. *2.1 we identified types of information that contribute to the truth-conditional representation, so did we identify the representation that is best suited to exhibiting compositionality, but we failed to point it out. Rather than try to trace compositionality to the representation of the linguistic input,[4] it seems that we can find it in merger representations. An alternative solution would be to abandon compositionality altogether. But it seems that denying compositionality at *any* level of meaning representation is neither needed nor helpful. Such a move is even unwarranted: there is nothing to undermine the validity of the truth-conditional meaning representation if we allow pragmatic contribution to truth conditions and predicate truth and falsity of such a representation of thought expressed by an utterance.[5] Hence there is nothing to undermine compositionality. It is merely the unit to which composition applies that is at stake. On the strength of the evidence so far, let us take it to be the merger representation.

As a result of accepting this assumption that preserving compositionality on *some* level is justified, the principle of compositionality has to be applied to a level other than that of the sentence. We have to capture the essential, definitional property of merger representations, namely the unbiased merger of constituents of meaning. Instead, let us apply it to *utterances* conceived of as *acts of communication*[6]:

Principle of compositionality for the merger:
The meaning of the act of communication is a function of the meaning of the words, the sentence structure, defaults, and conscious pragmatic inference₁.

*Fig 2.1 can now be revised to represent this level at which compositionality applies. The result is Fig. 3.1.

Stage I : Processing of the truth-conditional content

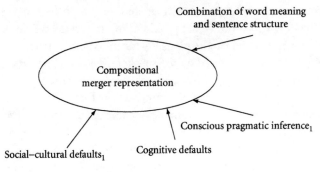

Combination of word meaning
and sentence structure

Compositional
merger representation

Conscious pragmatic inference$_1$

Social–cultural defaults$_1$ Cognitive defaults

Stage II : Processing of implicatures

- Social–cultural defaults$_2$
- Conscious pragmatic inference$_2$

FIGURE 3.1 Utterance interpretation in default semantics

In short, the representation of the speaker's act of communication that the model hearer can be predicted to create in the process of meaning recovery is constituted by a merger of information from the four sources specified in Stage I of Fig. 3.1 and it is this representation that is compositional. Arguments for such a compositional merger representation will occupy us for the remainder of the chapter. To repeat, Stage II identifies the sources of implicated meanings.

It has to be noted that so far I have discussed the 'compositional merger representation' as a representation of utterance meaning. This does not mean that the meaning that arises on the level of larger units of discourse is unaccounted for. Merger representation can also serve as a representation of a discourse that is composed of a series of utterances, just as DRSs of DRT can be representations of multi-sentence discourses. The principles of dynamic semantics are here unchanged.[7] However, will we not need a separate component in Fig. 3.1 called 'rules of discourse structure'? This seems unnecessary because relations between sentences are captured by means of pragmatic inference or by means of default interpretations. For example, anaphoric and presupposing readings of referring terms are accounted for by means of cognitive defaults. This is the topic of Chapter 7.

3.2 Rethinking compositional semantics

Merger representations are semantic representations in that they are representations of meaning of an utterance, or a series of utterances, founded on the principles of dynamic semantics such as DRT. These 'meanings' are, ideally, the speaker's intended meanings and we would like to regard them as such. However, this is only an approximation. In fact, all we can attain is an account of meanings that can be plausibly taken to be constructed by a hearer as meanings that were intended by the speaker. 'Plausibly', because in Default Semantics we want to account for 'normal', predictable processes of meaning (re)construction that yield generalizations such as that in Fig. 3.1. *A fortiori*, 'a hearer' means a model hearer, an imaginary interlocutor whose communicative strategies are fairly predictable and generalizable. Merger representations are theoretical constructs that 'generalize' over the strategies used by a hearer in interpreting the speaker's act of communication.[8] They are not representations of sentences. They are representations of acts of communication that are performed by means of linguistic utterances. They are not representations of thought either. Merger representations are conceived of as, so to speak, abstractions, generalizations over thoughts. They are more coarse-grained than thoughts in that their information content is only what is relevant for their truth conditions. The question of the compositionality of thought is a tangential issue to the compositionality of acts of communication, and perhaps a more difficult one. While in a theory of acts of communication we begin with an assumption that a level of truth-conditional merger representations is discernible, a philosophical theory of thought cannot make an analogous assumption. I shall come back to different understandings of compositionality later on in this chapter. For the moment, we shall accept that the issue of compositionality of thought is tangential to that of the compositionality of acts of communication. We shall also accept that acts of communication are compositional, and semantics is compositional, without discussing the compositionality of thought. They are taken to be compositional in that we start with the assumption that a formal semantic theory can account for meaning construction out of the structure of acts of communication and meanings of their parts. Arguably, Default Semantics will prove to be such an approach.

The justification for this compositional stance is as follows. When a speaker refers to something or someone, he or she does so under some concept or other of this thing or person. This fact has been used in the Fregean and neo-Fregean approaches to language and we are using it here for semantic representations. It will be applied in the following way. A thought about a thing or person contains structured concepts. However, such concepts are not exactly the entities we need in a theory of communication. They contain the guises under which the individual or object are known, which are either Fregean intersubjective senses or some private modes of presentation, ways of thinking. Such concepts are too fine-grained for our purposes. In order to have an explanatorily adequate theory of communication, all we need is those features of concepts and thoughts that make the difference to the truth conditions; the rest is redundant. An alternative to this search for more coarse-grained units of the theory of discourse meaning would be to search for compositionality not in the meaning theory, but rather on some other level. Schiffer (e.g. 1982, 1991, 1994, 2003) draws compositionality from the supervenience of the intentional on the non-intentional and proposes a compositional supervenience theory instead of a compositional meaning theory. Physical states necessitate phenomenal states. For example, the compositional meaning theory would tell us that, to use Schiffer's example, 'Fido is a dog' means <Fido, doghood>. The compositional supervenience theory tells us that 'dog' is correlated with some physical property Φ. The fact that 'dog' means doghood supervenes on the fact that 'dog' has the property Φ. The actual explanation of this correlation is probably best left to intuition, but this does not matter for the purpose of the explanation.[9] It is possible that a compositional approach to meaning may have to be 'reduced', so to speak, to compositional supervenience. But let us first decide whether 'compositional' in a theory of meaning has the same meaning as 'compositional' in 'compositional supervenience'. The question is, what status compositionality has to hold in a theory of meaning.

For formal dynamic semantics, compositionality is a *methodological* principle. In DPL:

it is always possible to satisfy compositionality by simply adjusting the syntactic and/ or semantic tools one uses, unless that is, the latter are constrained on independent grounds. (Groenendijk and Stokhof 1991: 93)

In other words, as long as one can come up with a successful formalization that does not compromise the facts, one is in a position to maintain the compositionality of meaning. Compositionality as a methodological requirement is dictated by the fact that in computational linguistics one aims to produce an interpretation for a logical language that would account for how natural language discourse works. In other words, we need a language of logic, with its syntax and semantics (interpretation) that *models* natural language. DPL provides such a (dynamic) interpretation for an ordinary language of first-order predicate logic. Compositionality becomes a definitional prerequisite for such a language.

Methodological compositionality is a reasonably plausible assumption. It is easy to notice that languages can be conceived of as compositional as long as the meanings of the sentence parts are defined as sufficiently fine-grained and syntax is construed sufficiently freely. In other words, 'meanings' would have to be adjusted as appropriate and 'syntax' would have to be adjusted as a way of composing such meanings. Montague's understanding of compositionality was of this kind, where '*[m]eanings* are functions of two arguments—a possible world and a context of use' (Montague 1970: 228). Compositionality is an assumption, and meanings are construed in such a way that they are compatible with this assumption. Or, in Partee's words, for Montague,

[m]eanings can be anything you like, as long as they form an algebra homomorphic to the syntactic algebra. ('Intermediate levels' must therefore be in principle dispensable.) (Partee 1984: 154)

The next question to ask is what we understand by meaning for the purpose of a semantic theory. Let us assume that meanings are truth conditions in the sense of denotation conditions. If meaning is taken to be truth conditions in the sense of denotation conditions, then compositionality is no longer a methodological principle but instead it becomes a *content* principle. This is the scenario that a semantic theory would like to uncover, but it encounters numerous stumbling blocks. That is why it may seem that one has to go beyond truth conditions in constructing semantic theory. In DRT, truth conditions are predicated of content and semantics goes beyond truth conditions. Compositionality is sought at the level of content. However, as we know from truth-conditional pragmatics and from Default Semantics, truth conditions can also be predicated of utterances or acts of communication. In Default Semantics, truth conditions are predicated of *representations of content* and this allows us to assume that semantics (i.e. the semantics of acts of communication) is compositional—an assumption to be partially supported throughout Part II. Compositionality of content can thus be understood very broadly. But then, compositionality of content need not even necessarily mean compositional semantics, whatever it is a semantics of. In Schiffer's proposal, compositionality seems to be a version of the content principle: it applies to the content matter ('epiphenomenal' on the world). But it does not apply to semantics. Hence, it is a content principle that does not result in compositional semantics. Propositions are *unstructured*, albeit fine-grained entities (Schiffer 2003).

Let us call content compositionality 'compositionality$_c$' and methodological compositionality 'compositionality$_m$'. Next, let us trace the debate in terms of these two senses of compositionality. The problem for post-Montagovian theories is that natural language semantics does not seem to be compositional$_c$ because there are sentences that do not differ in truth conditions (understood as conditions on denotation) and yet differ in meaning, as is demonstrated by numerous types of constructions, for example (2) or (6a) and (6b):

(6a)   I dropped ten marbles and found all of them, except for one. It is probably under the sofa.

[?](6b)   I dropped ten marbles and found only nine of them. It is probably under the sofa. (from Groenendijk and Stokhof 1991: 94, after Partee and Heim).[10]

If this be the case with natural language, then we need representations such as, say, DRSs or merger representations in order to account for the fact that (6a) supports anaphoric reference while (6b) does not. Or, as DPL, we need a dynamic interpretation of the language of predicate logic which, by fiat, makes existential quantifiers of (6a) dynamic, in this way avoiding representations. In more detail, the debate is this. Representationalism and formal semantics are not always close friends. In formal semantic, model-theoretic frameworks, a compositional$_m$ interpretation of sentences has been attempted in which no level of representation was assumed. The most salient example, Montagovian in spirit in this respect, is DPL. DPL eschews representations. It ascribes the difference between (6a) and (6b) to *content*, not to representation. It turns the *content* principle into a *methodological* principle, a set goal to be attained by a semantic theory of natural language. In other words, it turns compositionality$_c$ into compositionality$_m$. The most salient analogous example of representationalism is DRT. In due course, problems with the semantics of anaphoric expressions led to some consensus on the matter and it was agreed that modelling the interpretation of natural language requires some level of representation after all. And in dynamic theories in general, interpretation seems to *be* meaning (see Dekker 2000: 288). Default Semantics, just like DRT, is representational in the strongest sense:

If any two syntactically distinct expressions are associated with the same (independently specified) meaning, and, yet, play a different role in the explanation of certain semantic facts, then the explanation of these facts is (strongly) representational. (Dekker 2000: 295)

This has been exemplified in (6a) and (6b). Or, to use Dekker's examples (ibid.), if semantic theory were non-representational, (7) and (8) should play the same semantic role.

(7)   A man is walking through the park.

(8)   It is not so that no man is walking through the park.

This is so because if semantics were to mirror syntax, (7) and (8) would have to have the same truth conditions and would have to play the same semantic role, and semantic theory would be non-representational. However, the fact that (7) allows for an anaphoric uptake as in (7a) whereas (8) does not strongly suggests that their semantics is different and that we need representations.[11]

(7a)   A man is walking through the park. He is wearing a blue hat.

This representationalism can be achieved through distinguishing content (state of affairs) and character (linguistic meaning, rule of language use; cf. Kaplan 1989)—or linguistic and psychological modes of presentation (Recanati 1993).[12] Alternatively, one can alter the paradigm and instead of supplementing content with linguistic rules of use, specify content by means of a merger representation which approximates content by being a construct of the most likely reconstruction of content by a hearer and does not give epistemic or explanatory priority to sentences over other sources of meaning information. This is what is attempted in Default Semantics. I shall come back to this option later.

So, it seems that the question 'Is natural language semantics compositional?' does not have a 'yes–no' answer. According to compositionality$_m$ (DPL), it has to have one by definition. To take the polar example, according to compositionality$_c$ (Schiffer), it does not, but it does not matter too much: the foundation in the form of the world–meaning relation is compositional. For representational semantics such as DRT and Default Semantics, the formal language aims at compositionality, and at the same time it attempts to present natural language semantics as compositional. But, is it compositionality 'm' or 'c'?

In order to answer this question, let us ask another question: are we dealing with two different meanings of 'compositionality' here? It seems that we are not. The missing link in the above is that meaning representations are not a concession to a non-compositional orientation in semantics. DRT is representational, has mentalistic interpretations (i.e. DRSs as mental representations), but this does not mean that it is less compositional than DPL. It is certainly not less compositional in the content sense, and it may not be in the methodological sense either. As Zeevat demonstrates, mentalistic interpretations are the first step towards a compositional theory:

A compound expression has a certain causal influence on a human interpreter leading him to form a representation. This representation in turn is related to reality in a way that can be captured by a truth definition. (Zeevat 1989: 96)

So, compositionality$_c$ should ultimately result in compositionality$_m$. DRT starts with building compound expressions out of their parts *as if* compositionality *normally* held (that is, as if compositionality$_m$ = compositionality$_c$), and ends up with a programme in which it is likely that compositionality as a requirement for the formal system (compositionality$_m$) will eventually be satisfied.

Zeevat argues for what appears to be the compositionality$_m$ of DRT as follows. To begin with, mentalistic interpretations are the first step towards a compositional theory: a representation of a compound expression has truth conditions. Next, he attempts to turn DRSs into an algebra in the sense of Montague grammar, that is grammar as 'a correlation of the possible functions with the ways in which a compound expression can be built up from its parts' (1989: 96). Next, he shows that it may be possible to 'define an algebra of semantic objects in which the algebra of DRSs can be interpreted by a suitable isomorphism'(1989: 100). To put it simply, he provides a compositional reconstruction of DRT in which the translation of an expression f(A,B) is given in terms of an operation on the meanings of A and B. He provided this reconstruction for DRSs with donkey sentences and discourse anaphora. He points out that this is not the same as providing a rule for reconstructing an arbitrary DRS construction algorithm compositionally. The latter is difficult, or, according to Zeevat, may not be possible (1989: 126) because 'natural language places constraints on the structure of the logical formalisms that can interpret it: natural language is not neutral in this respect' (1989: 129). The conclusion seems to be that representations contain constraints imposed on formalization by natural language, but this need not make these formalizations less compositional. Compositionality turns out to be a flexible notion: natural language has compositional$_c$ semantics *because* we can construe plausible mental representations which are compositional$_m$, they can be translated into algebra, albeit, on the weakest scenario, one type of construction at a time rather than as a universal algorithm.

Now, these constraints imposed by natural language can be conceived of in a variety of ways. In Gricean pragmatics, they are maxims, heuristics, or principles of communication founded on Grice's account of meaning intention and the recognition of this intention. Optimality-theory pragmatics (see e.g. Zeevat 2000; Blutner and Zeevat 2004) adopts neo-Gricean heuristics and reworks them into a formal pragmatic account with formal constraints. Since linguistic meaning underdetermines the proposition expressed, a pragmatic mechanism of completion of this meaning is proposed. It is conceived of as an optimization procedure, founded on the idea of the interaction of violable and ranked constraints. The selected, optimal proposition is the one that best satisfies the constraints. This selection is performed by the pragmatic system whose role is to interpret the semantic representation of a sentence in a given setting. This system is founded on Horn's (1984) and Levinson's (1987, 2000) Q- and I/R-principles.[13] The I/R-principle compares different interpretations of an expression, while the Q-principle assesses the produced structure as compared with other unrealized possibilities: it blocks interpretations that would be more economically connected with alternative forms. Examples of interpretation constraints are STRENGTH (preference for informationally stronger readings), CONSISTENCY (preference for interpretations that do not conflict with the context), FAITH-INT (faithful interpretation, interpreting all that the speaker said). FAITH-INT precedes CONSISTENCY which precedes STRENGTH in the ranking (see Zeevat 2000). In Default Semantics, the equivalent of constraints that natural language imposes on logical formalisms is the interaction of the four sources of information presented in Fig. 3.1. Instead of externally imposed heuristics that give rise to a series of constraints, we have here an interaction of conscious inference, types of defaults, and sentence structure—all derived from natural properties of mental states (intentionality) and the world (linguistic and socio-cultural background). Compositionality still means 'compositionality$_{m=c}$' but this is achieved not by restricting the possible formalisms but by searching for the only plausible formalism that is dictated by the merger. In other words, compositionality is moved 'one level higher', to merger representations, where even the syntactic structure of natural language cannot dictate what the formalization should be like. This will be discussed further in the following section and then such a 'metacompositional' apparatus will be applied to various expressions and phenomena in English in Part II.

All in all, we seem to be back to compositionality$_c$ and, possibly, Schiffer's supervenience version of it: mental representations are compositional$_c$ and this is all that matters. But, as in dynamic semantics, we can go further: once they are compositional$_c$, the semantics can be adjusted. It cannot be adjusted at will but it is justifiable to keep trying, as long as there is a reasonable chance that proposed representations may turn out to be mental representations. This is what merger representations of Default Semantics should be if it transpires that they work. Compositionality is a content principle, but *content* is the content recovered by a hypothetical interpreter (our model hearer) of the act of communication. This is what we called the *meaning* of acts of communication and we sought it on the level of merger representations. As a result, compositionality means compositionality$_{m=c}$. Applications in Part II show that they work for a fragment of English. And although, as Zeevat (1989: 126) says, there may never be a proof that an algorithm for an arbitrary mental representation (there: DRS construction algorithm) can be reconstructed compositionally, we can at least make it worth trying to find one if we discover that compositional merger representations and their formalization can be proposed for a substantial number of semantically problematic expressions. Whether the sample offered in Part II suffices to make it worth trying is for logicians to decide.

The only level in Default Semantics at which we can legitimately talk about compositionality and (pragmatically enhanced) truth conditions in any interesting sense is the level of merger representations. It is, in fact, the only level of representation. This is depicted by Fig. 3.1. The fact that, in some easy instances of utterance processing, the content of the merger representation consists of only one component represented as the top right arrow (*combination of word meaning and sentence structure*), simply means that not all of its constituents are always needed in utterance processing. It does not, however, multiply the levels of representation: there is still the potentiality of a merger and hence it is appropriate to talk about merger representations. Special cases where only the constituent called combination of word meaning and sentence structure is activated are, for example, generics as in (9).

(9)   Pink dolphins live in the Amazon.

It seems that neither pragmatic inference nor default senses need to be activated as sources of information in order to process this sentence.

In Default Semantics, to repeat, truth conditions are predicated of acts of communication. Default Semantics is truth-conditional and compositional *qua* being such a theory of meaning of acts of communication. Compositionality$_c$ is satisfied through compositionality$_m$: it is assumed that there is some level or other of representing meaning that is compositional. This level is called merger representation. We do not know very much about how it works yet, but we can discern the sources of meaning information that contribute to the merger and begin to discuss the interaction of these sources by observing and then formalizing what is taken by a hypothetical model hearer to be intentionally conveyed by the speaker in an act of communication. In a sense, the compositionality of semantics is trivially satisfied: we try to find a level of meaning of acts of communication that is compositional, and then, having constructed a theory of it, we call this theory a 'semantics'. This is how the question 'Is semantics compositional?' turns out not to be a very interesting question. On the other hand, the question 'Is meaning representation compositional?' *is* interesting and will be pursued throughout Part II when we apply Default Semantics to a variety of constructions.

All in all, I have opted here for a rich, strongly representational semantics that equates semantics with utterance interpretation by a model hearer. Semantics is thus a theory of meaning of discourses, has merger representations as truth-conditionally evaluable units, gives no prominence to the linguistic component (*combination of word meaning and sentence structure* in Fig. 3.1), and, at this level of merger representations, is taken to be fully compositional. The foundations of the formal account are presented in Section 3.4. I demonstrate how merger representations work for intensional context when I analyse propositional attitude reports in Chapter 5.

3.3 Metacompositionality

Compositionality at the level of merger representations encounters some difficulties. In general terms, to repeat, compositionality is the idea that the meanings of complex units are constructed out of the meanings of less complex units—be it concepts or expressions. Here I opted for complex units as contents of merger representations. Now, according to Fodor and Lepore (e.g. 2001), compositionality of any kind requires some context-independent concepts as one of its constituents.[14] Accepting this premise would obviously rule out 'meaning as use' theories such as that advocated nowadays in Horwich's semantic deflationism where 'the meaning of a word is engendered by its use' (Horwich 1998: 42). In particular, it would rule out the view that 'the compositionality of meaning can equally well be accom-modated within the use conception of meaning' (Horwich 1990: 70), and, 'if a word's meaning derives from its use, then a complex's meaning consists in its being the result of combining, in a certain way, words with certain uses' (Horwich 1990: 71). Horwich explains the core of this move as follows:

This strategy deserves to be called 'deflationary' for it shows that the compositionality of meaning is much easier to explain than we have often been led to believe. It would not seem to be the case, as contended by Davidson and his many followers, that compositionality dictates an explication of meaning properties in terms of *reference* and *truth conditions*. Indeed, since our explanation did not involve *any* assumptions about how the meaning properties of the primitives are constituted, it would seem that compositionality *per se* provides absolutely *no* constraint upon, or insight into, the underlying nature of meaning.   (Horwich 1998: 158)

Merger representations adopt a mid-way ontology in that context-independent concepts and structures constitute only one of their elements. We need not go as far as Horwich's deflationary strategy.[15] Contextual upgrading of infor-mational content is accounted for by means of pragmatic inference$_i$, cognitive defaults, and social–cultural defaults$_i$. As a result, merger representations preserve context-independent concepts and context-independent grammar, but only insofar as taking this route by the hearer can result in recovering the intended interpretation. In many cases of utterance processing, this context-independent sentence meaning does not suffice. In such cases we do not have compositionality and truth-conditionally evaluable representations on the level of sentence meaning. Instead, we have compositionality and truth-conditionally evaluable representation on the level of the merger with defaults and with the output of pragmatic inference. In other words, as was discussed in more detail in Section 3.1, while simple cases achieve compositionality and truth-conditional representation on the level of the *combination of word meaning and sentence structure* of Fig. 3.1, in the majority of instances of utterance interpretation compositionality and truth-conditionally evaluable representation are achieved at the level of the merger—and hence not at the level of *linguistic* semantics. In fact, merger is the only level of meaning we need to posit. To repeat, compositionality at the level of merger representation does not guarantee compositionality of linguistic units: there need not necessarily be compositionality at the level of the *combination of word meaning and sentence structure*—neither is such a level necessary as an independent construct. Compositionality is then, so to speak, removed from the linguistic 'level' and placed on the level of representing acts of communication. It can be appropriately called metacompositionality.

The spirit of this stance is not new: it has been well acknowledged in Gricean pragmatics that pragmatic inference can contribute to the truth-conditionally evaluable representation. However, it is still disputable to which unit one should assign truth conditions. In relevance theory, thoughts have truth conditions. However, for the reasons discussed in Section 3.1, namely that thoughts are overly fine-grained as units of meaning, thoughts will not do. This does not mean that thoughts definitely cannot have truth conditions. Our search for the unit of meaning is, as was argued in Section 3.1, tangential to the issue of the properties of thoughts. For the purpose of providing a theory of meaning, I have proposed merger representations, theoretical constructs pertaining to the representations constructed by a model hearer, as such truth-conditionally evaluable units. In discourse processing, this unit corresponds to the output of all relevant sources of information about the meaning of the act of communication. In this sense, we can call it a 'thought abstract', or, to employ Slobin's (1996) apt phrase 'thinking for speaking', we can call it 'thinking for discourse processing'. Thoughts are too rich in content to fulfil this role and it seems that the principle of economy of rational communicative behaviour suggests that communicators employ such a 'thought abstract' in conversation. This is what merger representations are meant to capture.[16]

Now, the obvious question to ask is how cognitively real such constructs, called merger representations, are. On what grounds are we assuming them as central units of meaning in the psychological process of meaning production and recovery? Let us look at examples (10), (11), and (12), repeated after (2), (15), and (16) from Chapter 2.

(10)   Tom slipped and broke his leg.

(11)   Pablo's painting is of a crying woman.

(12)   We advertised for a new nanny.

The uptake in subsequent sentences such as in (10a)–(12a) takes as its starting point the 'enriched proposition'—the merger representation. In other words, the causal *and* in (10), the authorship by Picasso in (11), and the female sex of the nanny in (12) all enter into the knowledge base before the following sentence is processed.

(10a)   Tom slipped and broke his leg. The custodian forgot to put out the CAUTION WET FLOOR sign.

(11a)   Pablo's painting is of a crying woman. It must be worth at least a few million dollars.

(12a)   We advertised for a new nanny. She has to start next month.

Similarly, pronominal reference as in (13) and (14) demonstrates that the antecedent of the anaphoric relation is a higher-order entity that is not just the content of the sentence but rather some enriched representation.[17]

(13)   Tom changed the battery and the watch was fine. That was an obvious thing to do.

(14)   A: If you cook the dinner, I will help you sort out your computer.
        B: That is unfair. Sorting out the computer will only take you a few seconds!

It is obvious that in (13) 'that' refers to the situation in which changing the battery caused the watch to work, and in (14) 'that' refers to the situation in which cooking the dinner is the only obvious way to obtain A's help with the computer. So, a semantic representation that stands for such situations seems to be cognitively salient. Now, the move I introduce as compared with post-Gricean approaches is levelling the status of the sources of meaning. In other words, I am not assuming an 'enrichment' of the output of language processing but rather a 'merger' of the output of the linguistic (top right arrow of Fig. 3.1) and the non-linguistic sources of meaning. The difference is not vast, but unnecessary levels of meaning, as well as the unnecessary idea of 'pragmatic intrusion', are avoided. The cognitive status of such representations should not, then, be altered. The difference, however, becomes greater when the output of syntactic processing is overridden by some other source.

Finally, it seems that merger representations, eclectic as they are, are nothing else but postulates of cognitively real equivalents of propositions of possible-worlds semantics. They are modelled on the relation between possible worlds and propositions, but the units that enter into this relation are different. Propositions are (i) functions from possible worlds to truth values, or alternatively (ii) sets of possible worlds. Our 'propositions', that is mental representations, have to be sufficiently fine-grained to capture the difference between, say, '*p* & *q*' and '*p and then q*' as meanings of '*p* and *q*' in, for example, (15). Possible worlds therefore have to be thought of as sufficiently fine-grained to support such a difference.

(15)   I finished Chapter 3 and went skating.

We are preserving here the Frege–Tarski orientation in that merger representations that are semantic equivalents of thoughts or conceptual structures, just more coarse-grained, map onto the real world. As in possible-worlds semantics, sets of alternatives to this real world can give us the meaning.[18] But the unit of this meaning is an act of communication, not a sentence. This act of communication has a merger representation, not a proposition in the classical possible-world semantic sense, as its meaning.[19] Broadly speaking, possible worlds are here irreducible, albeit non-existent entities, just as in Stalnaker's (1976) 'moderate realism' stance.[20] To put it differently: the discussion so far, summed up in Fig. 3.1, has focused on the sources of meaning, their relative status, and the status of the meaning representation they help to produce. What has to be done next is provide a formal semantic account for such a theory of discourse processing. And for this task, possible worlds are necessary, irreducible, theoretical constructs: Default Semantics is a possible-worlds semantics. It is also truth-conditional, model-theoretic, and dynamic in the sense in which DRT is dynamic. These are the foundations for our account, discussed further in Section 3.4.

3.4 Foundations of a formal account

3.4.1 *Truth-conditional semantics and truth-conditional pragmatics*

I have proposed and partially defended the view that compositionality applies on the level of merger representations. I have also proposed that this should mean that the *semantics* is compositional because semantics is to be understood as a theory of meaning of communicative acts that amount to discourse with all its situational context. In other words, I am adopting and further extending and modifying a dynamic semantic view in which context contributes to the truth-evaluable representation. As was discussed above, possible worlds are the best constructs to capture this truth-evaluability. Following Stalnaker (1978), all we need is possible worlds that belong to the context-set. A context-set is the set of possible worlds that the speaker considers to be alternative options for the purpose of a current conversation. In other words, a context-set contains background information, represented as those possible worlds that are not ruled out by what is presupposed.[21]

Any assertive utterance should express a proposition, relative to each possible world in the context set, and that proposition should have a truth-value in each possible world in the context set.... (Stalnaker 1978: 88)

because

[t]he point of an assertion is to reduce the context set in a certain determinate way. But if the proposition is not true or false at some possible world, then it would be unclear whether that possible world is to be included in the reduced set or not. So the intentions of the speaker will be unclear. (Stalnaker 1978: 89–90)

Instead of an 'assertion', in our unified perspective of a merger we are able to talk about the 'act of communication'. Notwithstanding the difference in their realist stances, Stalnaker's idea of a context set is not unlike the accessibility of words in Lewis's (1986: 27) position. Knowledge of the world is, for Lewis, given by the set of epistemically accessible worlds, and a set of an agent's beliefs is given by a set of doxastically accessible worlds. Default Semantics uses possible worlds in this way. In other words, a set of relevant possible worlds is needed in a theory of meaning in order to evaluate merger representations. However, unlike in the dynamic semantic approaches modelled on Stalnaker's idea of assertion affecting the context-set, Default Semantics does not define meaning as having context-change potential.[22] In DRT, meaning is given in mental structures that allow for combining DRSs in a variety of ways. In Default Semantics, *one* such way becomes a merger representation—with the allowance for the relevant differences between these two theories such as, most importantly, a diminished role of syntactic configurations in mergers as compared with DRSs. Only *one* possible DRS becomes a merger representation because representations in Default Semantics are representations of discourse processing, not conversational competence. To repeat, we shall now talk about assertive utterances understood as acts of communication of which linguistic utterance is only a part.[23] It will also be understood that proposition-like structures, as functions from possible worlds to truth values, are here replaced with merger representations. The latter represent the meaning of *utterances* understood as acts of communication and discourses composed of utterances so understood.

3.4.2 *Principles of relational semantics*

In Default Semantics, the language we use for merger representations is modelled on the language of DRT, with its syntax and semantics. But the language is applied to different content in order to incorporate information from non-linguistic sources of meaning. It is also further extended by the introduction of some operators on events, states, and representations, introduced in Chapters 5 and 6. The dynamic contextual update is built on the same general principles for both DRT and Default Semantics.

It cannot be decided at this stage whether, to use Stalnaker's (1975: 191–2) formulation: 'the concepts of pragmatics (the study of linguistic contexts) can be made as mathematically precise as any of the concepts of syntax and formal semantics'. This question can be legitimately posed for theories such as DPL, DRT, or Default Semantics. In Default Semantics, for example, the properties of intentional mental states are important because they can serve as an explanation for some default interpretations.[24] Social–cultural defaults, cognitive defaults, and, to some extent, conscious pragmatic inference,[25] can be modelled in some version of defeasible default logic. But such modelling already assumes the ready output of intentional mental states; it does not account for the process by which these states arise in discourse interpretation in the first place. So, formalization is always epiphenomenal on something that is in itself not formalizable.

The main principles can be taken directly from DRT. DRSs contain discourse referents and conditions. They are structures as in Fig. 3.2 (after van Eijck and Kamp 1997: 191), where v ranges over a set of discourse referents (reference markers), and C is a set of conditions. Most commonly, conditions are predicative: a predicate takes a discourse referent as argument. More formally:

DRS $D := (\{v_1, \ldots, v_n\}, \{C_1, \ldots, C_m\})$.

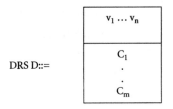

DRS $D ::=$

FIGURE 3.2. The content of a DRS

Fig. 1.1 was an example of such a structure.

Let us now introduce some relevant concepts. Van Eijck and Kamp (1997: 191, 203) define terms and conditions as follows:

i.   terms $t::= v|c$

where c ranges over a set of constants, and v over the set of discourse referents/reference markers. '|' separates the forms which are part of the category to be defined (the category on the left of '$::=$').This shows that, in DRT, proper names also introduce discourse referents that are treated as variables.

ii.   conditions $C::= \top \,|\, Pt_1, \ldots, t_k \,|\, v\dot{=}t \,|\, \neg D \,|\, D;D'$[26]

where P ranges over the set of predicates, '$\top$' stands for atomic conditions in the form of a symbol, and '$\dot{=}$' for identity (in the object language). Symbol is an atomic formula that is satisfied on all assignments. '$;$' is a sequencing operator to be discussed shortly. It stands for the operation of merging DRSs.[27]

The semantics of DRSs begins with a static truth definition. DRSs are interpreted with respect to a model and an assignment function. The assignment function maps discourse referents onto individuals. A model is a domain of individuals and an interpretation function that maps individual constants onto individuals and predicative conditions onto sets of individuals, pairs, triples, or n-tuples of individuals. More precisely, M is an appropriate first-order model for a DRS D iff $M =< M_i, I >$ where I does the following: (i) it maps the predicate names in the atomic conditions of D to n-place relations on M_i; (ii) it maps the individual constants of the link conditions of D to members of M_i; and (iii) M is also appropriate for the DRSs in the complex conditions of D (cf. van Eijck and Kamp 1997: 192). An atomic condition is a condition such as, for example, Jones (x) or owns (x, y); a link condition is for example $v = x$ or $v \neq x$, and a complex condition is a negation or an implication. A DRS is true in M iff there is an assignment that verifies this DRS in M. Let us assume that M is an appropriate model for D, and an assignment s for M is a mapping of the set of reference markers onto M. So, the value of t in M under s ($\nu_{M,s}(t)$) is $I(t)$ if t is a constant, and the value of t in M under s is $s(t)$ if t is a discourse marker (variable, in the sense of DRT). DRS semantics is provided by definitions of verification and satisfaction—and truth, where the latter can be predicated of DRSs:

An assignment s verifies DRS D in M if there is an assignment s' such that $s[\{v_1, \ldots, v_n\}]s'$ which satisfies every member of $\{C_1, \ldots, C_m\}$ in M.

$s[\{v_1, \ldots, v_n\}]s'$ stands for 's' differs from s at most in the values assigned to $v_1, \ldots, v_n$'.

For the purpose of representing a discourse that is composed of more than one sentence, we interpret the subsequent sentences in the context of the previous ones (Kamp and Reyle 1993), or we merge DRSs, standing for separate sentences. I shall summarize the merge approach of van Eijck and Kamp first, and subsequently discuss the utility of both construals, (i) merge and (ii) interpretation in the context of the first DRS, for Default Semantics. The advantage of the language of DRT starts being diaphanous when we try to link sentences of a discourse together: previous sentences become context for what follows. The anaphoric link between 'a man' and 'he' in (7a) repeated below, or 'somebody' and 'he' in (16), can be captured by means of a link condition equating discourse referents.

(7a)   A man is walking through the park. He is wearing a blue hat.

(16)   Somebody was not dancing. He was standing by the window.

This is done by means of a dynamic, relational semantics in which the input and the output assignments are specified for a DRS. The meaning of the sentence becomes a relation between the input context (one DRS) and the output context (another DRS). Before we proceed to the presentation of dynamic semantics, it has to be emphasized that in DRT, this context change potential that belongs to the meaning of a DRS is not part of its truth conditions. In other words, semantic value comprises more than the truth-conditional meaning. This semantic value of a DRS is a relation between input assignments (s) and output assignments (s'). It is called a dynamic value and is represented as $_s[\![D]\!]^M_{s'}$: the dynamic value of the DRS D in model M, where the input assignment is s and the output assignment is s'. Output assignments have to do with the way in which the DRS modifies the context. The dynamic value of a DRS D in model M ($_s[\![D]\!]^M_{s'}$) is defined as follows:

$$D = (V, C) \rightarrow {}_s[\![D]\!]^M_{s'} \text{ iff } s[V]s' \text{ and } s' \text{ verifies } D \text{ in } M \text{ (after van Eijck and}$$
Kamp 1997: 197).

V is a set of discourse referents in a universe of discourse U such that $V \subseteq U$.

In order to capture non-commutative merging in natural discourse, we need an operator that would account for the universes of both D and D'. In order to achieve this, van Eijck and Kamp propose a sequencing operator ';'. DRSs are composed by means of this sequencing operator. The process of merging DRSs (called proto-DRSs) is associative:

$$(D;(D';D'')) \doteq ((D;D');D'') \doteq D;D';D''$$

Since merging DRSs proceeds in the order of producing the sentences ('left-to-right'), then the first DRS D is interpreted in the initial context and brings about context s'' which is an initial context for interpreting D', similar to the case in dynamic conjunction of DPL:

$$_s[\![D;D']\!]^M_{s'} \text{ iff there is } s'' \text{ where } _s[\![D]\!]^M_{s''} \text{ and } _{s''}[\![D']\!]^M_{s'}$$

Relational semantics, RS (DRT), on van Eijck and Kamp's (1997: 200) account, looks as follows:

RS(DRT):
$$_s[\![v]\!]^M_{s'} \text{ iff } s[v]s'$$

$_s[\![v]\!]^M_{s'}$ is the dynamic value of v in M where the input assignment is s and the output assignment is s' iff s differs from s' at most in value v.

Analogously:

$$_s[\![\top]\!]^M_{s'} \text{ iff } s = s'$$
$$_s[\![Pt_1, \ldots, t_n]\!]^M_{s'} \text{ iff } s = s' \text{ and } < \nu_{M,s}(t_1), \ldots, \nu_{M,s}(t_n) > \in I(P)$$
$$_s[\![v \doteq t]\!]^M_{s'} \text{ iff } s = s' \text{ and } s(v) = \nu_{M,s}(t)$$
$$_s[\![\neg D]\!]^M_{s'} \text{ iff } s = s' \text{ and there is no } s'' \text{ where } _s[\![D]\!]^M_{s''}$$
$$_s[\![D;D']\!]^M_{s'} \text{ iff there is an } s'' \text{ where } _s[\![D]\!]^M_{s''} \text{ and } _{s''}[\![D']\!]^M_{s'} \,^{28}$$

In short, DRSs merge in a way that allows one to account for changing context. All in all, D is true in M under s iff there is an s' such that $_s[\![D]\!]^M_{s'}$ (adapted from van Eijck and Kamp 1997: 200).

Default Semantics adopts, revises, and extends the relational semantics of DRT and, in accordance with the assumptions laid out in Chapters 1–3, applies it to merger representations. We can then apply RS (DRT), substituting merger representations for 'D'. For modal and other intensional contexts, Default Semantics extends the language of DRT in a way that differs from current developments there (e.g. Kamp 1990, 1996, 2003) or in SDRT (Asher and Lascarides 2003).²⁹ In modelling speakers' linguistic *competence*, the obvious move is to define the basic alethic possibility and necessity and to apply the obtained formalizations to different types of modal constructions in natural language. But in modelling the process of *interpretation*, we proceed from the opposite end. We start with the mental representation in the form of the merger. The information about the detachment of the speaker from the uttered statement can be conveyed by means of a modal construction, but it can also be conveyed by means of pragmatic inference from a non-modal expression, that relies on any of the sources of meaning information from Fig. 3.1. In other words, we are not starting with grammar and hence we are not defining modality. Our starting point is the merger representation—a mental representation of the output of the processing of an act of communication by means of which modality can be conveyed on a particular occasion. Modality will require an operator on events and states. Such an operator is introduced in Chapter 6. The semantics for propositional attitude constructions is introduced according to yet other principles in Chapter 5: we have operations on *representations* of states and events there. Note that in Default Semantics, default interpretations are resolved prior to the construction of a compositional merger representation in that defaults are parts of information that act on a par with (i) conscious pragmatic inference and (ii) word meaning and sentence structure (see Fig. 3.1). This simplifies the account of modality as compared with other dynamic accounts in that we need no defeasible default in our semantics, no operator for 'normally': defaults are built into the representation of content on a par, so to speak, with the utterance itself. They are sources of meaning information (viz. cognitive defaults and social–cultural defaults), just as word meaning and sentence structure are. To put it simply: in Default Semantics, it is the output of the merger that is formalized, not the outputs of the sources.

There are some variations in the semantics of DRSs in accounting for intrasentential as well as intersentential relations. For example, instead of specifying types of merge for the dynamic value of D;D′ as it was done by van Eijck and Kamp, we can follow Kamp and Reyle (1993) and construct the DRS for the first sentence, followed by the interpretation of the subsequent sentences in that context.[30] At this point, it is necessary to decide whether Default Semantics follows the version of DRT in which sentences are processed first and then their DRSs are merged, as in van Eijck and Kamp's account, or the version in which the initial DRS provides context for further conditions. In other words, are DRSs merged as discourse progresses or is the original DRS expanded? As I argued in Chapter 2, default interpretations do not seem to arise locally, sub-sententially; they are sentence-based. So, the merge operation is a suitable device to render this concept of default interpretations. Merge operates on sentences, it merges DRSs and accounts for the universes of both of the merged representations. On the contrary, Kamp and Reyle's (1993) approach relies on the context of the first DRSs for creating the subsequent conditions. As will be seen in Chapters 5 and 6, the operators that I introduce to DRT in order to handle propositional attitude constructions and modality seem to be well-suited for the merge approach.[31] Finally, it goes without saying that merging DRSs gives us the simplest and most effective way of accounting for context change: DRSs have truth conditions, and sequential merging is introduced as a well-defined operator.

To sum up, Default Semantics adopts and further extends the principles of relational semantics and applies them, so to speak, one level higher, to merger representations. The reason is this. It is precisely *reaching the stage in discourse interpretation at which we can make use of this apparatus which aspires to compositionality* that is at issue in the overall theory of discourse meaning. To make this more clear, let us think in terms of Fig. 3.1. The semantics as presented above will not account for the meaning conveyed through pragmatic inference$_1$, cognitive defaults, or social–cultural defaults$_1$. Therefore, while retaining the relational semantics of DRT, we look for compositionality at a level to which all the components of discourse meaning listed in Fig. 3.1 contribute. This is so because we want to capture the process of discourse interpretation. For example, Default Semantics spells out defeasible inference ('normally', 'by default') on the level of merger representations as *particular types of defaults*, or, in some cases of discourse interpretation, as departures from the defaults. Hence, no formal device is needed to capture default inference.

Relational semantics is applied to the merger of the output of the four sources of meaning information distinguished in Fig. 3.1, and hence to the 'post-default-resolution' output.

Neither shall we need an account of the cases where, for example, imperatives are not used as requests or orders, nor interrogatives as questions, as in (17) and (18) respectively:

(17)   Say it again and you will be fired.

(18)   Can you say it again?

The act of communication with its illocutionary force is established at the level of the merger representation rather than the reanalysis of the grammatical form. So, any account of speech acts that may in the future be developed within Default Semantics will appeal to such merger representations.[32] What we want is a dynamic semantic representation that represents the intuitively correct, intended interpretation of the whole act of communication.

All in all, merger representations are governed by the relational, dynamic semantics. In other words, if we construe merger representations in the manner of DRSs, our DRSs will not be restricted to the sources of DRS conditions that DRT captures at present. Where Default Semantics departs from DRT is in its principles for discourse conditions. While DRT founds the conditions on construction rules that take syntax as input, Default Semantics merges input from various sources as in Fig. 3.1, treating these sources as strictly interrelated.

More specifically, Kamp and Reyle's (1993) construction rules are founded on a triggering configuration, given by syntactic processing of a sentence and formalizable in a generative theory such as, for example, GPSG. Discourse referents and discourse conditions are introduced as output of this syntactic processing. As a result, in DRT, as in any truth-conditional Montagovian theory, the truth conditions of (16), repeated below, and (19) are regarded as being the same:

(16)   Somebody was not dancing. He was standing by the window.

*(19)   Not everybody was dancing. He was standing by the window.

Semantics has to, so to speak, 'go beyond truth conditions'. DRT captures the difference between (16) and (19) by representing the anaphoric link in (16) and its lack in (19) by means of the following move:

DRSs with the same truth conditions, such as [that of 16a] and [that of 19a], may nevertheless be semantically different in an extended sense. The context change potentials of [16a] and [19a] are different, as the former creates a context for subsequent anaphoric links whereas the latter does not.... The comparison of [the DRS of 16a] and [that of 19a] illustrates that meaning in the narrow sense of truth conditions does not exhaust the concept of meaning for DRSs. (van Eijck and Kamp 1997: 194–5)[33]

(16a)   Somebody was not dancing.

(19a)   Not everybody was dancing.

Having adopted the stance that the truth conditions of (16a) and (19a) are the same, DRT has to explain the 'semantics in the extended sense'. It does so by means of employing contextual update: the first sentence of (16) creates a context for the other one, which enables the resolution of the anaphora. In other words, the initial sentence of (16) adds new information to the current context: it changes it.

Let us compare this with the pragmatics-rich stance on truth conditions. In post-Gricean approaches to meaning, including Default Semantics, truth conditions are conceived of in a different way, in that they are applied to a different entity. In relevance theory (Sperber and Wilson 1986; see also Carston 1988, 2002a), pragmatic inference, which is always a context-dependent nonce-inference, can contribute to the propositional representation to form a truth-conditionally evaluable unit (or an explicature, a development of the logical form). As a result, truth conditions are context-dependent and are properties of thoughts rather than sentences. In truth-conditional pragmatics (Recanati 2003, 2004), primary pragmatic processes that operate on the sub-personal, unconscious level contribute to the truth-conditionally evaluable propositional representation. In the theory of GCI (Levinson 2000), implicatures, which can be context-dependent pragmatic inferences or presumed, default meanings, contribute to the truth-conditionally evaluable representation. In Default Semantics, conscious pragmatic inference$_1$, cognitive defaults, as well as social–cultural defaults$_1$ contribute to the truth-conditionally evaluable representation (merger representation). So, post-Gricean pragmatics does not need 'meaning in an extended sense': meaning is not principally syntax-based, it is based on multiple sources of information. Default Semantics is such a post-Gricean approach taken to the extreme in this respect. It goes further than others in that not only do multiple sources of information contribute to the truth conditions, but these sources are treated as temporally interrelated as far as their contribution to the merger representation is concerned. In other words, in processing, there is no level of syntax-based logical form in the process of utterance interpretation that is temporally prior to the output of the other sources.

The fundamental classificatory principle is the following:

Default Semantics (i) is neo-Gricean in accepting a pragmatic contribution to truth conditions and (ii) applies the extended formalism of DRT to merger representations.

To repeat, this programme requires a revised semantics, that is the semantics of merger representations. The formalism of DRT has to be extended, adding new sources of conditions and reference markers. This will also include adding new operators on representations and on states and events.

As a conceptual foundation, putting the formalism of DRT together with the neo-Gricean pragmatic stance on truth conditions seems to be advantageous. The truth definition in terms of M remains the same as in DRT. What differs is the content of the representations in the form of discourse referents and discourse conditions. Merger representations of Default Semantics are no longer principally based on the triggering configurations from the syntactic structure. They can be provided by the social–cultural defaults or by the default, strongly intentional interpretation of an expression. For example, a definite description can, by default, be interpreted as used referentially (see Chapter 4), a belief report as *de re* (see Chapter 5), and a presuppositional link as binding rather than accommodating (see Chapter 7), not because there are rules of context change that 'extend' truth-conditional semantics, but because default interpretations come in these cases from the strong, default intentionality of mental states, and this information is as important for the truth-conditional representation as the output of the syntactic processing of the sentence. [34] In other words, while in DRT context change potential is not part of the truth conditions but belongs to an 'extended semantics' that yields a semantic value, Default Semantics starts with an assumption that truth values apply to dynamic structures captured in merger representations. For example, in Default Semantics, $_s \llbracket v \rrbracket_{s'}^M$ is a dynamic value of a discourse referent v that is given by the merger of the four sources of information distinguished in Fig. 3.1. A more detailed presentation will have to wait until Part II.

3.4.3 *Compositionality in dynamic semantics for (i) DRSs and (ii) merger representations*

We can now return to the compositionality issue. It is likely that the language of DRT is as compositional as predicate calculus.[35] DRSs have a compositional, model-theoretic semantics. But, according to the DR-theoretic (and classical in formal semantics) stance, there is more to meaning than truth conditions. Where problems with compositionality begin is in formalizing the context change potential which DRSs exhibit. They begin when semantics becomes dynamic. The operation of merging DRSs (on van Eijck and Kamp's 1997 account), or processing a new sentence in the context of the previous DRS (on Kamp and Reyle's 1993 account) is responsible for the compositionality problem. In other words, the dynamic semantics for DRSs would be compositional if we had a formal account of the merger operation between DRSs (in terms of sequential merging)—that is an explanatorily adequate formal account of context change potential that would mirror the cognitive process of discourse interpretation. 'New' DRT (van Eijck and Kamp 1997) has a set of strategies for merging DRSs and these have to be taken as part of the language of DRT to make it compositional.[36] The discourse links that are widely investigated in DRT are of the anaphoric kind. The problem of pragmatic enrichment such as, for example, in the case of sentential connectives (and + > and then; if + > if and only if, ...) is largely untouched, save for defeasible rhetorical structure rules of SDRT. And the problem of such enrichment, as well as any context-dependent, pragmatic-inference based enrichment, is precisely the testing ground for discourse semantics.

Default Semantics conceptualizes the merger operation in a different way. Compositionality is the property of merger representations which are 'thought-like objects': they are generalizations over thoughts. Semantics is understood as a theory of meaning that has such merger representations as objects. Since meaning is carried by various vehicles in addition to language, compositional semantics is not the same as compositional semantics of a natural language: the latter is not attempted—and, acknowledging Schiffer's reasons against it, it will not be attempted.

Van Eijck and Kamp write:

It would be unreasonable to demand of a theory of *linguistic* semantics—and it is that which DRT originally aimed at—that it incorporate a detailed account of anaphora resolution, which would have to rely on a host of pragmatic principles as well as on an indefinite amount of world knowledge.

It seems *not* unreasonable, however, to demand of such a theory that it offer a suitable interface to other (pragmatic and/or extra-linguistic) components of a comprehensive theory of meaning which are designed to deal with anaphora resolution ... and to allow these other components to come into action at those points when the information needed for anaphora resolution has become available and the resolution is necessary for interpretation to proceed. (van Eijck and Kamp 1997: 221–2)

What Default Semantics offers is a proposal of such interfaces, viewed as a theory of meaning that is compositional, truth-conditional, and thus a theory that 'semanticizes', so to speak, what was in DRT left to interfaces. It offers a sketch of such a theory of meaning that is partially corroborated by its application to various types of expressions in Chapters 4–9. To repeat, the output of the particular sources of information that add to the merger representation does not interest us: *compositionality does not have to pertain to the output of the particular sources.*

Finally, if Default Semantics is akin to truth-conditional pragmatics and other post-Gricean accounts in its treatment of truth conditions, why is it not 'Default Pragmatics'? The answer lies precisely in the attempted semanticization of the output of the sources of information that produce the merger representation. The *merger* is taken to be truth-conditionally evaluable and compositional. This assumption is dictated indirectly by the supervenience of the mental on the physical discussed in Section 3.2, and directly by envisaging merger representations as more coarse-grained equivalents of thoughts.

3.5 Cognitive principles for merger representations

3.5.1 *PoL, DI, and PI*

Let us now take stock. Merger representations are the result of processing information that constitutes the practice of discourse. This practice relies on linguistic utterances, situational clues, a set of shared knowledge and assumptions about the world, about the participants' mental states, and about the process of discourse interpretation. To repeat, merger representations are not just representations of sentence-based utterances. A representation can pertain to a longer discourse unit. However, we argued that there is no need for separate 'rules of discourse structure' in that the connections between utterances, including the anaphoric links and other cohesive devices, are accounted for by means of pragmatic inference on the one hand, and cognitive defaults on the other (see Section 3.1 and Chapter 7).

This is where the PoL, DI, and PI principles come in. Merger representations conform to the parsimony of levels of representation (PoL) in that there is only one level where all meaning-giving information merges. They also have the output of the processing of intentions as one of the sources of meaning. These intentions are stronger or weaker, depending on the characteristics of the underlying mental state, and in particular its intentionality. This strength of intending contributes to the interpretation of the resulting utterance (by DI and PI principles). Moreover, as was discussed in Chapter 2, intentions are not always processed in conscious pragmatic inference. They can be assumed by default, either (i) due to the fact that intending is normally as strong as the intentionality of the underlying mental act allows (i.e. is 'undispersed'), or (ii) because of the way the culture and society, with their institutions, social behaviour, and interaction are constituted and assumed to be constituted. As Searle put it:

Just as it was bad science to treat systems that lack intentionality as if they had it, so it is equally bad science to treat systems that have intrinsic intentionality as if they lacked it. (Searle 1984: 89)

Differences among various theories of intentionality notwithstanding, this quotation can be taken as a leading assumption for Default Semantics.

It remains to be emphasized that intentions in communication serve here as an explanatory tool in the same way in which they are used in Gricean and post-Gricean pragmatics: they allow one to theorize about meaning with reference to mental states. It is not essential that all intentions be processed by the hearer. As was discussed in Chapter 2, utterances may give rise to unreflective, pre-inferential default interpretations. For such interpretations, there is no need for a separate account: intentions will do perfectly well, with the proviso that their processing may be limited or may not be present. In other words, as was argued in Chapter 2, we have to recognize shortcuts in the processing of the speaker's intentions, but that does not make the account any less intention-based on the level of explanation.

3.5.2 *Semanticization of intentions*

All in all, merger representations are taken to be *semantic* representations because semantics has as its object discourse meaning that is compositional and draws on information that comes not only from linguistic expressions but also from other sources. Such representations can be given using an extended language of DRT. The interpretation of the formalism that would incorporate information from intentional mental states is founded on the relational semantics of DRT and is amended and extended for particular fragments in Part II. This includes introducing new devices into the language of DRT and applying the formalism one level higher, that is to the mergers of the output of the four sources of information distinguished earlier and summarized in

Fig. 3.1. To repeat, although such merger representations are compositional, on the level of the information pertaining to the particular sources no compositionality is expected. In other words, just as linguistic semantics is not compositional, the meaning conveyed through cognitive or social–cultural defaults, or through pragmatic inference, is not compositional either: compositionality can be found at the level of their merger.

I have presented in this chapter some preliminary assumptions for such an interpretation. Most importantly, the semantics has to allow for pragmatic inference and default interpretations to be part of the truth-conditional content, *à la* truth-conditional pragmatics. It also has to make use of possible worlds in its representationalism. In other aspects, the programme of this pragmatics-rich semantics begins with the assumption that the dynamic semantics of DRT can be extended and implemented.

3.5.3 *The inferential end?*

This pragmatics-rich semantics pertaining to merger representations is possibly the most radical move a compositional theory of meaning can make in the direction of pragmatics. Moving beyond that along the Gricean, intention-based path, we would have to equate meaning with inferential role, accepting one or other class of types of inferences.[37] In other words, going any further, one would have to adopt the stance that the content of an expression is given by the role the expression plays in inferences. This would be compatible with seeing discourse in a dynamic way but, at the same time, would prove problematic with respect to pragmatic, inductive, defeasible inference. Conscious pragmatic inferences$_1$ of our merger representations (Fig. 3.1) are not deductive. They cannot be guaranteed to be preserved with the growth of context, they are defeasible. Similarly, cognitive defaults and social–cultural defaults are defeasible. For example, the fact that we interpret 'a nanny' as 'a female nanny' does not necessarily have to persist throughout the whole discourse. Inferential semantics[38] is thus a much less attractive option.

For clarity, I quote the argument presented in Hinzen:

Once we stipulate (. . .) that meaning is determined relative to a specific set of rules (not by virtue of properties of reference, for example), the question of the *stability* of meaning arises. The same expressions may belong to different fragments of a language—when does it [sic] preserve the meaning that it has in one of them, if we turn to another? Take two systems of expressions, S and S′ such that S ⊂ S′ and such that both contain the logical sign '&'. Is an expression containing '&', that plays the inferential role of conjunction in S necessarily also playing the same role in S′? It is, if there are no expressions containing '&', which stand in inferential relations in one of the systems in which they do not stand in the other. If this is the case for all expressions in S, we say S′ is a *conservative extension* of S. This means that when going from S to S′, inferences that you used to draw in S remain valid, and no inferences involving only vocabulary of S which were not valid in S become valid in S′.

(Hinzen 2001: 158)

So, we must not change our inferential commitments with the growth of discourse. In the practice of discourse interpretation, the hearer normally goes through a pragmatic, defeasible inference that can vary from context to context and from person to person. It seems that defining inferential roles is then the same as saying that meaning is all context-dependent and one should quit any attempts at further generalization. Defeasible inference, combined with inferential roles, thus seems a much less attractive option. If this is so, then it seems that going any further in the direction of pragmatics—beyond merger representations couched in a dynamic, cognitively plausible, semantic framework—would be a dead end. The semantics/pragmatics interface ends as a pragmatics-rich dynamic semantics of the representational, possible-worlds based kind.

Notes

1 For an introduction to the semantics and pragmatics of belief and other propositional attitude reports, see e.g. Jaszczolt 2000*b*.

2 For a discussion of this move, called a hidden-indexical theory, see also Schiffer 1977, 1996, 2003; Crimmins 1992; Crimmins and Perry 1989; Ludlow 1995, 1996; Jaszczolt 1998, 1999*b*, 2000*a*, 2000*b*, 2003*a*.

3 See also Section 1.3.

4 Or even to syntax, as in Stanley's approach discussed in Chapter 1.

5 See Section 3.4.2.

6 See Section 1.1.

7 I discuss them in more detail in Section 3.4.

8 I am greatly indebted to Stephen Schiffer for discussing the status of merger representations with me.

9 See Schiffer 2003: ch. 4, and in particular: 'having Φ accounts for the "intuitions" that entitle us to say any particular sentence means the proposition it means, and that is the best "explanation" available to either theorist' [i.e. compositional meaning theorist and compositional supervenience theorist, so we need not have both—KMJ]; Schiffer (2003: 174). See also Fodor 1998, 2001 and Recanati 2002*b* on the compositionality of concepts as opposed to the lack of compositionality of epistemic properties. On a theory of supervenience of cognitive content on the physical see Segal 2000.

10 See also Partee 1984 for numerous examples of constructions that escape this strong version of the principle of compositionality.

11 Dekker (2000: 296) suggests that we have to explain this difference in terms of syntactic structures. In Default Semantics, merger representations perform this task.

12 See also Neale 2001 for the overview of the debate on representations and facts.

13 See Section 1.1.

14 See also other papers collected in Fodor and Lepore 2002.

15 Or any other deflationary strategy, for that matter. See e.g. Brandom 1994, especially pp. 325–6.

16 For the sake of comparison with a well-established account, it can be observed that merger representations take Chomsky's (e.g. 2004) compatibility between language and the conceptual-intentional system one step further. Chomsky says the following:

If language is to be usable at all, its design must satisfy an 'interface condition' IC: the information in the expressions generated by L must be accessible to other systems, including the sensorimotor (SM) and conceptual-intentional (C-I) systems that enter into thought and action. (Chomsky 2004: 106)

In Chomsky's framework, computations result in the last line of derivation <PHON, SEM>, accessed by SM and C-I respectively and in convergence or crashing of the derivation. SEM is what the *derivation by 'narrow syntax'* is mapped onto by the semantic component (for details see Chomsky 2004: 106–107). In Default Semantics, SM and C-I are systems that produce merger representations. Chomsky's theory then covers the application of SM and C-I to one component of my merger representations, namely the *combination of word meaning and sentence structure* (top right arrow of Fig. 3.1).

17 See Gundel et al. (1999) on pronominal reference to higher order entities, and in particular on the use of 'it' and 'that'.

18 One obvious and widely-known alternative is Jackendoff's approach (e.g. 1983, 1991, 2003) that maps conceptual structure onto the world *as humans understand it.*

19 This move, independently supported in Chapters 1 and 2, avoids Stalnaker's (1978) problems with the identity of propositions.

20 Stalnaker is a 'realist' in the sense that possible worlds are for him irreducible entities of the representation of meaning. They are not real in the sense in which the actual world is real, but neither are they merely notational constructs. Cf.:

Is the form of realism about possible worlds that I want to defend really realism? It is in the sense that it claims that the concept of a possible world is a basic concept in a true account of the way we represent the world in our propositional acts and attitudes. (Stalnaker 1976: 75)

This view can be contrasted with the extreme realism of Lewis (1973, 1986) where the actual world is one of many possible worlds and they are all of the same kind.

21 See Stalnaker (1975: 183). See also Hintikka 1962, 1969 on accessibility of possible worlds.

22 See Chapter 1, note 4 and Geurts 1999 on satisfaction.

23 See Section 1.1.

24 In the terminology of Default Semantics, these are cognitive defaults.

25 See Fig. 3.1.

26 This varies between versions. See Kamp and Reyle 1993.

27 For its interpretation see van Eijck and Kamp (1997: 199).

28 For the semantics of different types of sequential merge see van Eijck and Kamp (1997: 204ff).

29 See note 30 on modality in SDRT.

30 Asher and Lascarides's (2003) version of DRT (SDRT) uses an *appending* process. Appending, $D^\frown\gamma$, results in a DRS where γ is appended to D's DRS-conditions:

$$D^\frown\gamma =_{\text{def}} <U_D, \text{append } (C_D, \gamma)>$$

and

$$D^\frown\gamma =_{\text{def}} <U_D, C_D \cup \gamma)>$$

where U_D is the universe of discourse referents of the DRS D, γ is a DRS condition, and C_D is a set of conditions of the DRS D (adapted from Asher and Lascarides 2003: 46). γ is defined as follows:

$$\gamma := P(t_1, \ldots t_n) \,|\, \neg D \,|\, D \Rightarrow D' \,|\, D \vee D' \,|\, D > D' \,|\, \Box D \,|\, \Diamond D$$

where '>' stands for defeasible inference and '$\Box$' and '$\Diamond$' for the modal operators of alethic necessity and possibility respectively. DRSs can be defined recursively as:

$$D := <U_D> \,|\, D^\frown\gamma$$

They define the predicative condition and negation analogously to van Eijck and Kamp. Material inference is defined as follows:

$$_s[\![D \Rightarrow D']\!]^M_{s'} \text{ iff } s = s' \wedge \forall s''_s[\![D]\!]_{s''} \to \exists s'''_{s''}[\![D']\!]_{s'''}$$

Because of difficulties with some other appended DRSs, they propose to consider not only s, but also the world w. Context is seen as a world-assignment pair. Disjunction of DRSs, defeasible implication, necessity, possibility, propositional attitude verbs, imperatives, and all intensional contexts are analysed in terms of possible worlds and hence we need a pair w,s—a world-assignment pair:

$$_{w,s}[\![D \vee D']\!]^M_{w',s'} \text{iff}(w,s) = (w', s') \wedge (\exists s''_{w,s}[\![D]\!]^M_{w',s''} \vee \exists s'''_{w,s}[\![D']\!]^M_{w',s'''})$$

$$_{w,s}[\![D > D']\!]^M_{w',s'} \text{iff } (w,s) = (w's') \wedge \forall w'' \forall s'' \,(_{w,s}[^* (w, [\![D]\!])]^M_{w'',s''} \to$$
$$\exists w''' \exists s'''_{w'',s''}[\![D']\!]^M_{w''',s'''})$$

where '*' stands for 'normally' (defeasible default). On Asher and Lascarides's account, '>' formalizes default interpretations, i.e. the ways in which hearers normally interpret certain contexts. These default inferences are further spelled out in their 'glue logic' that we discussed informally in Sections 1.5 and 2.1.2. Again, as we then observed informally, this solution works very well for modelling language and linguistic competence. Our aim is different: merger representations of Default Semantics are mental representations of particular acts of communication. There is normally *one* merger representation per act of communication. While '>' can be used as an umbrella concept for defaults in a theory of modelling competence, in merger representations of Default Semantics these defaults have to be spelled out in terms of cognitive defaults, social–cultural defaults$_1$ (see Fig. 3.1), or even as interpretations that depart from such defaults, as some mental representations of acts of communications naturally do. In other words, default interpretations do not *always* apply and a theory of the processing of acts of communication has to provide mental representations of the meaning that was recovered from this act on a particular occasion. Next, alethic necessity is defined as follows:

$$_{w,s}[\Box D]_{w',s'}^{M} \text{iff}(w,s) = (w',s') \wedge \forall w''(wR_\Box w'' \rightarrow$$

$$\exists s''' \exists w''' \text{ such that } _{w',s'}[D]_{w''',s'''}^{M})$$

where $wR_\Box w''$ stands for a relation defining all possible worlds relative to a given world (adapted from Asher and Lascarides 2003: 458). Asher and Lascarides also extend DRT to questions and imperatives (see 2003: 50–2) but these will not concern us as they are not discussed among the applications in Part II (see Section 3.4.2).

31 *Nota bene*, in the expression 'merger representation' the term 'merger' applies to combining the output of the sources of information as in Fig. 3.1, which is not to be confused with van Eijck and Kamp's 'merge' as joining DRSs.

32 The semantics of questions and other non-assertive speech acts is currently the focus of research in dynamic semantics. See e.g. Asher and Lascarides 2003; Ginzburg and Sag 2000.

33 My own numbering, examples adapted from van Eijck and Kamp (1997: 194).

34 For the DRS semantics see also van Eijck and Kamp (1997: 196).

35 See the discussion in Section 3.2 and Zeevat 1989.

36 But, '[t]he story of a reasonable definition of merge is a story of memory management'; Van Eijck and Kamp (1997: 212).

37 See Hinzen's (2001) critique of Brandom.

38 For example, Brandom 1994.

Part II
Some Applications

4

Defaults for Definite Descriptions

By definite descriptions I understand expressions of the form '*the* + nominal' that are used about an individual object as in (1).

(1) The man in a blue jumper is my student.

Expressions of this form that are used generically as in (2) will not be subsumed under the category.

(2) The whale is a mammal.

While 'the whale' in (2) belongs to the category of definite noun phrases, it is excluded from the category of definite descriptions.

In this chapter I set out to do the following: (i) analyse different uses of definite descriptions; (ii) represent them in the form of merger representations (henceforth: MRs) of Default Semantics (henceforth: DS), accounting for the degree of salience of interpretations; and (iii) discuss the affinities the category of definite descriptions has with other types of expressions that are used to refer.

4.1 Default referential, non-default referential, and attributive readings

Expressions that are used by speakers to refer are commonly divided into two categories: (i) that of directly referring expressions and (ii) that of expressions whose referring function is provided by the context of utterance. Directly referring (type-referential) expressions are said to contribute an object to the proposition expressed, while contextually-referring (token-referential) expressions contribute descriptive meaning. The category of directly referring expressions is normally said to comprise ordinary proper names, some pronouns including demonstrative pronouns, and demonstrative phrases. Contextually-referring expressions are most commonly instantiated by definite descriptions. But the distinction between type-referentiality and token-referentiality is not as clear-cut as it may seem. As I demonstrated in *Discourse, Beliefs and Intentions* (Jaszczolt 1999*b*), proper names and definite descriptions exhibit many similarities, more than it is customary to admit. Although definite descriptions exhibit an ambiguity of use between the referential reading and the attributive one, these two readings are not on a par in processing: the referential reading is more salient than the attributive one. For example, in (3), 'the best architect' normally refers to a particular, known, identifiable individual. In the context of conversation, such as, for example, when the interlocutors are looking at the Sagrada Família in Barcelona, this salient reading is the one where the description refers to Antoni Gaudí.

(3)   The best architect designed this church.

The referential reading corresponds to the utterance that is accompanied by the mental state with the default, strong, 'undispersed' form of intentionality. I discussed in Chapter 2 the correlation between the properties of mental states and the properties of intentionality and proposed that degrees of intentionality of mental states correspond directly to the degrees of intention (referential, where applicable) of the corresponding act of communication. By this premise, an utterance with a definite description such as (3) comes with a strong referential intention. It is also the unmarked, default reading. If the *hearer* mistakenly thinks, for example, that the Sagrada Família was designed by Christopher Wren, then the reading is also referential but contains a referential mistake on the part of the hearer. Intentionality is then 'dispersed' in the sense discussed in Chapter 2: it 'reaches' the object that was not intended by the speaker and that is not the objective correlate of this description in this situation of discourse. Similarly, when the *speaker* is under the misapprehension that, say, Simon Guggenheim designed the Sagrada Família, then the intentionality is 'dispersed' between the intended person (Guggenheim) and the object recovered by the hearer that is also the objective correlate of this description in this situation of discourse (Gaudí). In what follows, we shall confine the discussion to the process of meaning recovery by the hearer who has the correct and sufficient knowledge base for referential identification of the individual talked about. This is consistent with our earlier decision to consider merger representations as mental constructs of a model hearer. This also means that scenarios such as that when the hearer thinks of Christopher Wren as the best architect in the above situation will not be considered. This is so because the process of discourse interpretation by the hearer does not differ in its mechanism from the one in which the referent is assigned correctly. If the *speaker* makes a referential mistake and this mistake is detected by the hearer and overrides the default, correct ascription of the referent, then the processing differs from the default case. We are interested in the mechanism by which the hearer processes various uses of the description uttered by the speaker. The hearer normally makes assumptions about the speaker's meaning by following defaults and contextual clues and this is the object of our investigation. Similarly, I am going to talk about the attributive reading as ascribed by the hearer to the speaker.

Definite descriptions have often been classified with quantifiers rather than with referring expressions. However, in view of the different uses triggered by different degrees of associated intentionality and intentions, it may be more appropriate to classify them with referring expressions, stipulating at the same time that the default referential interpretation (cf. Gaudí) is type-referential, the non-default referential is token-referential (cf. Guggenheim) and comes with weakened intentionality and *a fortiori* with weakened referential intention, and finally the non-default attributive reading (about whoever the individual who fits the description 'the best architect' in this context might be) is, by definition, not referential. It comes with the weakest intentionality and, again, by definition, with no referential intention. So, as I demonstrated extensively elsewhere (Jaszczolt 1997, 1998, 1999a, 1999b), instead of the binary distinction into type- and token-referentiality for classifying expressions, there are expressions that span both categories and allow for default interpretations, as well as for different degrees of departure from these defaults. In other words, sentence (3) can be represented as (3a) in its default sense, and (3b) and (3c) in the non-default senses progressively departing from (3a) in the degree of referential intention and intentionality (*a* and *a′* stand for individual constants).

(3a) Designed this church (*a*) $a =$ Antoni Gaudí
(3b) Designed this church (*a′*) $a′ =$ Simon Guggenheim
(3c) $\exists x$ (Designed this church (x) $\land$ $\forall y$ (Designed this church (y) $\rightarrow y = x$)
$\land$ Best architect (x))

The demonstrative noun phrase 'this church' is for the moment regarded as an invariably directly referring term and is not analysed here (but see the *Interlude* in Section 4.2).

All in all, I have said here that the salient referential interpretation is also an unmarked, default interpretation. It is so because the default reading corresponds to the default, assumed, undispersed intentionality of the mental state of the speaker's and hence to the assumed, strong, default referential intention of the speaker's. On such readings it is irrelevant under what guise the speaker thinks of the object: all that matters for the semantics is the reference. This fact has important implications for the semantics of *oratio obliqua*, such as the semantics of reports on beliefs, statements, or thoughts whose content can be related by embedding (3) in a context such as (4).

(4) Paula believes that the best architect designed this church.

As I argue in Chapter 5, such propositional attitude reports require variable adicity of the belief operator in order to reflect the degree to which the mode of presentation of the object is relevant for the semantics of merger representations.

4.2 Definite descriptions in merger representations

In DRT, both individual constants and individual variables are terms that are treated as discourse markers: they both, in effect, behave like variables in that they figure in the argument place of discourse conditions such as:

Antoni Gaudí (x)
Best architect (x)

The DRS for (3) in Fig. 4.1 and the DRS for (5) in Fig. 4.2 show how this idea is used in practice.

x y
best architect (x)
church (y)
designed (x,y)

FIGURE 4.1 The DRS for (3)

(5) Antoni Gaudí designed this church.

x y
Antoni Gaudí (x)
church (y)
designed (x,y)

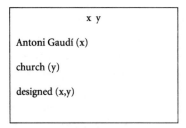

FIGURE 4.2 The DRS for (5)

The DRS in Fig. 4.1 is true iff in our assumed model there are individuals a and a' (animate or inanimate objects) such that they satisfy the conditions 'best architect (x)' and 'church (y)' respectively and they both satisfy the condition 'designed (x, y)'. Analogously, the DRS in Fig. 4.2 is true iff in our assumed model there are individuals a and a' (animate or inanimate objects) such that they satisfy the conditions 'Antoni Gaudí (x)' and 'church (y)' respectively and they both satisfy the condition 'designed (x, y)'.

The distinction between proper names and definite descriptions is captured by altogether different means, namely by anchoring the discourse marker to a particular individual in the world, such as $\{< x, a >\}$ for anchoring x to Antoni Gaudí in the DRS in Fig. 4.2. In other words, x is mapped onto a unique individual in the world. But even here we have a more striking similarity between (i) proper names and referentially used descriptions than between (ii) referentially and attributively used descriptions. Definite descriptions normally have one, unique referent in a particular context and hence can be anchored just like proper names. So, by default, we can use $\{< x, a >\}$ for anchoring x to Antoni Gaudí in the DRS in Fig. 4.1 where x comes with the condition 'best architect (x)'. This just restates our earlier conclusion that token-referential (contextually-referential) expressions in their default reading refer to a unique individual, just as type-referential expressions do.

Kamp and Reyle (1993: 255) observe that '[a] proper account of definite descriptions will have to provide additional processing principles corresponding to the different types of use of definite descriptions'. Their choice is to proceed through a theory of presupposition.[1] Postulating presupposed individuals and anaphoric links results in the DRSs we want. However, it would not yet result in the MRs we want. In our pragmatics-rich DS as laid out in Part I, we capture discourse processing on a particular occasion of use and hence we model a particular act of communication rather than modelling discourse competence. So, in (3), the resulting merger representation has to come with the choice between the default referential, non-default referential, and attributive use of the definite description. Sources of information such as cognitive defaults and conscious pragmatic inference₁ result precisely in such a unique representation for a specific act of communication: an utterance of (3) by a particular speaker, to a particular hearer, at a particular time and place, with the baggage of an assumed shared knowledge base. So, unless the context of this act of communication indicates to the contrary, the merger representation will reflect the default, referential reading of the definite description. We can now attempt to produce MRs, modelled on the compositional merger representation presented diagrammatically in Fig. 3.1. In Chapter 3, we focused our attention on establishing the components that contribute to the merger, justifying their theoretical *raison d'être*, and presenting the output of their interaction which is to be the unique semantic representation (MR) of the particular, contextually situated communicative act. Now we can create the actual MRs for acts of communication. From now on, in MRs, I shall use the following abbreviations for the sources:

WS   for the combination of word meaning and sentence structure
CPI 1   for conscious pragmatic inference$_1$
CD   for cognitive defaults
SCD 1   for social–cultural defaults$_1$

The default reading of the utterance (3) repeated below, in the context specified above, is as in Fig. 4.3. Note also that, until Chapter 6, we are not working out any representation of temporality and we leave verb forms as, for example, 'designed' in Figs 4.1 and 4.2. Similarly, until Chapter 6, the merger representations that we will propose will not contain a representation of temporality. Such representations that contain shortcuts through representing what is still left unresearched or, alternatively, is irrelevant for the purpose at hand, will be marked as *partial representations* with a superscript 'p'.

(3)   The best architect designed this church.

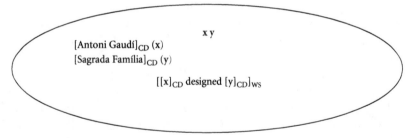

^{P}FIGURE 4.3. MR for the default reading of (3)

The square brackets mark the material for which the particular source specified in the subscript is responsible. So, the referential reading of 'the best architect' is given in the MR as [Antoni Gaudí]$_{CD}$; the referent of the demonstrative noun phrase 'this church' is given as [Sagrada Família]$_{CD}$, and the combination of word meaning and sentence structure operates on the whole sentence, as is shown in the condition [[x]$_{CD}$ designed [y]$_{CD}$]$_{WS}$. Notice that although the noun phrase 'the best architect' is itself a combination of word meaning and phrase structure, we do not have [Sagrada Família]$_{WS,CD}$ in the MR. This is so because the content of the square bracket is the result of the application of the cognitive default analysis to 'the best architect' for this act of communication. So, although WS plays a part in obtaining the constituent [Sagrada Família]$_{CD}$, WS does not apply to the content of the brackets in [Sagrada Família]$_{CD}$. Instead, the content represents the final product of applying CD to [the best architect]$_{WS}$. The latter is an intermediate stage in the processing of the utterance and hence not a constituent of the MR. To recall, MRs are thought-like units, semantic equivalents of utterances and discourses, that are less fine-grained that thoughts: they contain only that information about the content of thought that is relevant for the meaning of the the act of communication—in other words, that is relevant for the (pragmatics-rich) semantic representation called an MR.

Since MRs are thought-like units and they are at the same time the semantic output of utterance (or longer discourse) processing, the order of the constituents in the MR has to reflect the incremental nature of processing. So, instead of the formula 'designed (x, y)' which is standard in predicate logic, we are using 'x designed y'. However, this is not to mean that the subscript 'CD' in Fig. 4.3 is located in the place in processing in which this incremental interpretation is at the time. In other words, this does not mean that [Antoni Gaudí]$_{CD}$ as the meaning of 'the best architect' is resolved as soon as the definite description 'the best architect' is uttered. As argued in Section 2.4.3 above, it is more adequate to adopt the old-fashioned Gricean understanding of default interpretations (his GCIs) as post-propositional, global rather than local. So, CD applies to the description 'the best architect' producing [Antoni Gaudí]$_{CD}$, but [Antoni Gaudí]$_{CD}$ is produced *after* the whole utterance has been processed as 'x designed y'.

Interlude: 'this church' and the Semantics of Complex Demonstratives
I have not said anything about the representation of the output of the processing of the demonstrative noun phrase 'that church'. Demonstratives raise problems of their own for the semantics. Although they are clearly directly referential, they are often complex, like 'that church', as opposed to demonstrative pronouns such as 'that'. The literature on the topic is vast.[2] Traditionally, complex demonstratives such as 'that *x*', 'these *xs*' have been regarded as directly referring expressions, that is as type-referential. So, on this view, 'this church' behaves in a similar way to the demonstrative pronoun 'this': it picks out a referent that is unique for the context. However, let us imagine that the speaker of (3) points at one of the houses in Parc Güell in Barcelona designed by Antoni Gaudí. Does the demonstrative noun phrase 'this church' refer directly to the house by Gaudí in this case? It seems that the noun 'church' should contribute to the truth conditions of the merger representation. On Lepore and Ludwig's (2000) account, it is argued that it

contributes to the truth conditions of the sentence. If so, complex demonstratives belong with quantifiers. But, at the same time, they function as context-sensitive referring expressions. Lepore and Ludwig conclude that:

[t]he key to understanding demonstratives in complex demonstratives is to see the concatenation of a demonstrative with a nominal, as in 'That *F*', as itself a form of restricted quantification, namely, as equivalent to '[The *x*: *x* is that and *x* is *F*]'. (Lepore and Ludwig 2000: 229)

In Fig. 4.3, we took a different route. In the act of communication in which utterance (3) is accompanied by indicating the Sagrada Família, the complex demonstrative 'that church' normally, by default, picks out the referent which is the church called Sagrada Família. This is guaranteed by the default status of the strongest intentionality of the mental state that corresponds to the act of communication in (3), and by the default status of the strongest referential intention with which the utterance is taken by the hearer. So, in the default scenario, complex demonstratives behave like simple demonstratives and function as type-referential, directly referring expressions. The nominal does not contribute to the truth conditions. In the scenario whose location is Parc Güell as described above, the complex demonstrative is problematic. It can behave like a directly referring expression, or it can behave like a quantified noun phrase. Depending on the more fine-grained specification of the situation, 'this church' can be taken by the hearer to refer to some church or other which cannot be identified, or to the indicated, identifiable building in Parc Güell that is not a church. Again, we have an order of priority here: the referential reading with a mistaken use of the noun 'church' takes priority over the use in which the hearer cannot identify the object talked about. This is so because of the cognitive default associated with the strong, 'undispersed' intentionality that applies here. By the DI principle of DS (see Section 2.2.2), the complex demonstrative by default behaves like a directly referring expression in which the demonstration or other contextual indication takes precedence over the semantic content of the nominal. If 'this church' is to be semantically complex, that is quantificational rather than referential, then there have to be contextual reasons for it being so interpreted.[3] In the remainder of this chapter devoted to definite descriptions, these options of interpretation of demonstratives will not be considered. They can be easily worked out by analogy to my account of definite descriptions.

End of interlude

Now, coming back to example (3), the remaining two readings are represented in DS as follows. The non-default referential reading, specified in (3b) repeated below, is as in Fig. 4.4.

(3b)   Designed this church (a') $a' =$ Simon Guggenheim

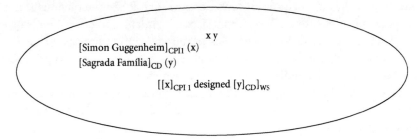

PFIGURE 4.4. MR for (3b)

The attributive reading is as in Fig. 4.5. The description 'the best architect' comes without an accompanying referential intention and the utterance is about whoever fits the description: the referent is not specified. This attributive reading corresponds to the weakest intentionality of the corresponding mental state: intentionality is 'dispersed', so to speak, and it does not 'reach' any object. In less metaphorical terms, the speaker's thought is taken to be about no particular, known, identifiable individual.

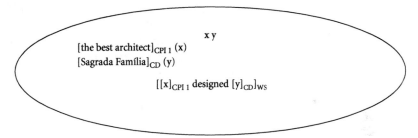

PFIGURE 4.5. MR for the attributive reading of (3)

MRs as exemplified here in their application to constructions with definite descriptions seem to differ significantly from (i) semantic approaches to discourse meaning for which there is more to meaning than truth conditions (such as DRT), as well as (ii) pragmatic approaches such as various types of truth-conditional pragmatics (cf. Recanati 2003) discussed in Chapter 3. The differences between MRs of DS and the representations in (representational) dynamic semantic approaches such as that of standard DRSs of DRT are as follows. First of all, we are capturing here the meaning of *the particular act of communication in a particular context* as recovered by a model hearer. So, if any ambiguity is to be allowed at all in DS, it has to be an ambiguity which is the result of processing. In other words, ambiguity means the unresolved meaning of the act of communication and as such it is quite obvious that it happens not very often: interlocutors normally intend to be communicative and cooperative, as various principles of rational communicative behaviour that stem out of Grice's (1975) Cooperative Principle make clear.[4] By adopting an account of truth conditions according to which all sources of information, namely WS, CPI 1, CD, and SCD 1 contribute to the truth-conditional representation (MR), we obtain an account of meaning of the act of communication which is not restricted to the problems of logical form, 'intrusion' of pragmatics, and related issues that are in the forefront of current debates.[5] Instead of an 'intrusion', we have a merger, a merger representation. This representation is a coarse-grained equivalent of a representation of thought and has truth conditions. To recall, 'coarse-grained' means simply that only those constituents of the content of thought belong to it which are relevant for the meaning of the act of communication. Finally, the advantage over pragmatic theories is that on this construal, the MR is taken to be compositional and as such in the domain of semantics: not the *semantics of sentences* but the *semantics of acts of communication*. In other words, the output, that is the content of MRs, is compositional. The compositional dynamic semantics introduced in Chapter 3 can now be extended to MRs. The semantics applies to MRs on the proviso that discourse conditions of DS draw on the merger of WS, CD, CPI 1, and SCD 1. The relational semantics will now require an amendment in order to capture the readings of referring terms presented in Figs 4.3–4.5. The dynamic value of v, where v ranges over the set of discourse referents, is now as follows:

$$_s[\![v]\!]^M_{s'} \in \{_s[\![v_{CD}]\!]^M_{s'}, _s[\![v_{CPI_1}]\!]^M_{s'}\}$$

The default (CD) and non-default (CPI 1) values are given by the semantics, as components of the compositional MR. From now onwards, in the remaining examples of applications of DS, where the relational semantics of MRs needs to be extended beyond its current form as presented in Section 3.4.2, the required formal devices (or general directions for the solution where the problem is not yet resolved) will be introduced one by one, as is done above. As can be seen from Chapters 5 and 6 respectively, DS for propositional attitude reports and modalities require similar, albeit slightly more substantial extensions in order to account for utterance processing in terms of default and inferred intentions.

4.3 Definite descriptions, proper names, and indexicals: degrees of referring?

In Section 4.1, it was demonstrated how, on the intentionality-based analysis of DS, definite descriptions turn out to exhibit properties that often make them akin to proper names. In example (3), the default, referential reading is at the same time an instance of type-referentiality, as the logical form proposed in (3a) suggests. Referential mistakes can also be accounted for as in (3b).[6] So, it appears that the binary distinction into directly and contextually referring expressions is too strong. As far as proper names are concerned, they are also used differently. They can be subject to referential mistakes or be used by the speaker without giving the addressee any indication as to the identity of the referent. For example, if the speaker utters (6) not knowing who these names refer to, we have a case of purely denotative uses of the proper names that correspond to attributive uses of definite descriptions.

(6)   George Eliot is Mary Anne Evans.

Moreover, a large proportion of proper names are not strictly speaking 'proper': they are semantically associated with the referent they pick out but they are also associated with some descriptive property. Just as complex demonstratives pose problems for the composition of the demonstration and the descriptive content, so some names combine the reference to an individual with a semantically significant description. 'Mrs Susan Brown' conveys information that x is female, married, and that x picks out a certain referent. 'Mount Everest' conveys information that x is a mountain and that x picks out a certain referent. It is easy to illustrate the claim that the descriptive content may matter to the semantic content. In (7), a part of the name ('Street') is discussed with respect to its descriptive content.

(7)   Broad Street is not really a *street*. I would call it an *avenue*.

Examples of this kind can be easily multiplied (see Soames 2002: 117).

   In view of such facts of conversation, it is more and more commonly agreed that the category of referring expressions should comprise expressions capable of being used to refer to an individual or individuals. We can include in this category proper names, demonstrative noun phrases, definite descriptions, and pronouns. The distinction between referential and non-referential occurrences of referring expressions is pragmatic, it is a distinction of use (Bach 1987a), and hence it is a matter of pragmatic input into the meaning (MR). Any other classifications are tangential to the problem of discourse meaning. *A fortiori*, the problems of an adequate semantics of proper names that would decide whether they are akin to complex demonstratives or to descriptions (see Segal 2001) are tangential to the issue of building MRs of DS.

Unlike definite descriptions and proper names, pronouns (including demonstrative pronouns) and demonstrative noun phrases are heavily context-dependent in their interpretation, as sentence (8) exemplifies.

(8)   She said it to those people.

The referring function of such expressions is almost entirely context-dependent[7] and hence the result of this context-dependent reference resolution is properly included in their semantics, as was observed by Grice (1978) when he regarded reference assignment as a pragmatic contribution to what is said. Are proper names and definite descriptions categorially different from such expressions in this respect? In other words, does their referring function not belong to their semantics? As we argued above, all types of expressions that are used to refer can contribute more than a referent to the informational content of the utterance. They can contribute some descriptive content. They do not always do so, but they are capable of doing so. Since the purpose of MRs of DS is to capture the meaning of utterances and discourses as assigned by the hearer who processes them on particular occasions, the fact that expressions *can* in principle be directly referential is of little importance: it is what they can *also* be like apart from being directly referential, and what they *are* like on a particular occasion, that counts for their meaning in the MR. And, as it has been convincingly argued, even pronouns are not uniformly referential. The 'pronouns of laziness' such as 'it' in (9) simply stand proxy for the description but are not anaphoric on it:

(9)   I check *my email* every day but my colleague checks *it* once a week.[8]

Moreover, there have been other classifications of referring expressions available on the market that show the gradation of their referentiality. For example, Gundel, Hedberg, and Zacharski's (1993) Givenness Hierarchy suggests six cognitive statuses with which referring expressions are associated. If a speaker uses, say, a personal pronoun 'he', then it is assumed that the referent is in focus of current attention. If the speaker uses a definite description, then the referent is at least uniquely identifiable. Hierarchies such as that of Gundel et al.'s (1993)[9] clearly demonstrate that referring is a matter of degree and has to be investigated in association with the degree of salience which the referent attained at the particular state in discourse. I have discussed such hierarchies at length in *Discourse, Beliefs and Intentions* (Jaszczolt 1999b) and *Semantics and Pragmatics* (Jaszczolt 2002a) and concluded that such scales are strongly supported by intention-based theories of meaning as well as by empirical evidence (e.g. Brown 1995). So, it seems that whatever type of referring expression the speaker uses, the hearer may have to infer whether the expression was used (i) to refer to a particular individual, and if so, whether it was used correctly, or (ii) to denote whoever or whatever may undergo this term. It is certainly true that definite descriptions give rise to such choices more readily than proper names, and that demonstratives and pronouns normally refer in a sufficiently salient way not to give rise to such alternatives. However, the normal, typical properties of such expressions do not suffice for creating MRs. We need default, intentional meaning, as well as the contribution of contextual clues. Rigid classifications are of little use.

In a not dissimilar way, Peregrin (2000: 273) argues that if meaning is context-change potential, or mapping contexts onto contexts, as in the dynamic-semantics accounts, then we need no strict classification of uses of definite descriptions: definiteness is conceived of 'not as presupposing unique existence, but rather as presupposing unique "referential availability" '. Or, in other words, denotations become 'context-consumers', they are arrived at through inference, and then, by increasing the context themselves, they give rise to further inferences.

Further evidence for the gradation of referentiality with respect to particular contexts of use comes from various attempts to account for the referential use of indefinite descriptions. Ludlow and Neale (1991) describe this use as a situation where the proposition the speaker meant to convey (*proposition meant*) and the speaker's beliefs that lead to the statement (*speaker's grounds*) are both about a specific individual, while what the speaker literally says (*proposition expressed*) is general, in the form of an indefinite noun phrase.[10] In a similar vein, using choice functions (see Section 1.2), indefinite NPs have been given the same semantics as definite NPs, with the proviso that the choice function is free in indefinites and determined by the context in the case of definites:[11]

the F: $[\![\varepsilon_c x\ Fx]\!] = \Phi_c([\![F]\!])$ *with c* contextually determined

where

[e]ach context *c* has its own choice function Φ_c, such that the definite NP *the F* can be represented as the indexed epsilon term $\varepsilon_c x Fx$, which can be paraphrased with *the selected x in the context c such that x is F or the most salient x in c such that x is F.* (von Heusinger 2000*b*: 254)

Analogously, for indefinites:

an F: $[\![\varepsilon_i x\ Fx]\!] = \Phi_i([\![F]\!])$ *with i* free (*adapted from von Heusinger, ibid.*).

The restriction to context is, surely, a matter of degree: we can search for the referent in a more, or less, restricted domain.[12] Choice functions, in effect, select the referent that is most salient (accessible), and accessibility is a matter of degree.[13]

In sum, the strengths of MRs in representing referring by definite descriptions are that they can capture the salience of the particular uses of these expressions and that they account for the particular reference assignment as ascribed to the speaker of the utterance in a particular act of utterance processing. By introducing the level of MR, DS can capture the speaker's intended use of the definite description and the speaker's intended referent, both as recovered from the discourse situation by the hearer.

Notes

1 See also Kamp 2001.
2 See e.g. Kaplan 1989, and for an overview: Larson and Segal 1995 or Jaszczolt 2002*a*. On complex demonstratives see Lepore and Ludwig 2000; King 2001; and Powell 2001.
3 So, my account takes further the following thesis by Powell (2001: 68, my emphasis): 'although they are lexically univocal, complex demonstratives can give rise to genuinely referential or genuinely quantificational truth conditions, *according to speaker intention.*'
4 See Chapter 1 above and Jaszczolt 2002*a*: chs. 10–11 for an overview.
5 See Chapter 1.
6 See e.g. Kripke 1977 and Neale 1990 for a discussion of proper names versus definite descriptions in the case of referential mistakes.
7 'Almost', because the specifications of gender, person, number, and proximity are often inherent in their forms.
8 Van Rooy (2001: 638) discusses the following example of a *descriptive* (non-referential) use of an anaphoric pronoun (originally from Evans): 'Either John does not own *a donkey*, or he keeps *it* very quiet.' Such pronouns are said to go proxy for the descriptions that can be recovered from their antecedents. The speaker need not have had a specific individual in mind while uttering such an indefinite description. The existence of such uses of pronouns is linked by Peregrin (2000) to the role of mapping of contexts onto contexts in dynamic semantics: instead of classifying referring expressions, we access their meaning through inference, as is discussed further in this chapter.
9 The Givenness Hierarchy has been subsequently supplemented with an account of proper names (Mulkern 1996).
10 For a discussion of this account see also Jaszczolt (2002*a*: 137–8).
11 See examples (9) and (10) in Section 1.2 for an introduction to choice functions.

12 The differences in scope-taking between choice functions in the case of definites and indefinites are captured by distinguishing global and local scope functions, for definites and indefinties respectively. See von Heusinger 2002.

13 See von Heusinger 2000*a*: context-change potential affects accessibility.

5

Default Semantics for Propositional Attitude Reports

5.1 Context-dependent substitutivity

When speakers talk about other people's states of mind, they normally use expressions of the form 'A believes that B φs', 'A thinks that B φs', 'A fears that B φs', and so on. Such states of mind have been traditionally, after Russell, called propositional attitudes: they are mental attitudes to a proposition. Expressions of the form stated above are thus propositional attitude reports. The term has remained in common philosophical and linguistic parlance ever since, in spite of the fact that it is rather problematic to accept the *proposition* as the object of such attitudes. The question of the object towards which attitudes are held is still widely disputed in the literature and is variously regarded as a proposition, sentence, thought, or as multiple constituents of a proposition or multiple constituents of thought. We shall consider the latter two options in Section 5.2.

In what follows I concentrate on talking about belief reports as exemplified in (1).

(1)   Tom believes that Peter Carey is a great novelist.

Reporting on people's beliefs is difficult both from the semantic and philosophical point of view. In the philosophy of language, it has been standardly said that *that*-clauses in belief reports pose semantic problems because their content has to be evaluated in an intensional context.[1] In such contexts, substituting a coreferential term in the embedded clause may not preserve the truth value. To put it differently, intensional contexts do not uphold Leibniz's Law. The law states that two things are identical with each other if they are substitutable preserving the truth of the sentence, or, after Frege, *Eadem sunt, quae sibi mutuo substitui possunt, salva veritate.*[2]

So, the main stumbling block is the problem of the identity of meaning between the sentence uttered by the holder of the belief and the sentence embedded in the reporter's description of the believer's state of mind. It has been widely assumed that propositional attitude reports are ambiguous between the *transparent* and the *opaque* reading. For example, sentence (2) has two semantic interpretations that correspond to the wide and narrow scope of the existential quantifier respectively. 'Bel$_T$' stands for 'Tom believes that', 'AoOL' for 'the author of *Oscar and Lucinda*', and 'GN' for 'a great novelist'.[3]

(2)   Tom believes that the author of *Oscar and Lucinda* is a great novelist.

(2a) $\exists x \, (AoOL(x) \, \& \, \forall y \, (AoOL(y) \rightarrow y = x) \, \& \, Bel_T \, GN(x))$

(2b) $Bel_T \, \exists x \, (AoOL(x) \, \& \, \forall y \, (AoOL(y) \rightarrow y = x) \, \& \, GN(x))$

The reading in (2a) is transparent to substitutions of coreferential expressions for the description 'the author of *Oscar and Lucinda*', while (2b) does not allow such substitutions and is therefore opaque.[4,5]

For the purpose of explaining reference assignment, we shall use a related distinction, namely that into *de re* and *de dicto* beliefs and *de re* and *de dicto* belief reports. This distinction is not as clear-cut as the one between transparent and opaque occurrences of expressions but is more adequate for a theory of discourse processing. When the reporter means (2a) by (2), he/she ascribes to Tom a belief about a particular, known individual (*de re*). When (2) is used to mean (2b), the reporter says that Tom believes in the existence of the author of *Oscar and Lucinda* and ascribes to him/her a certain property (*de dicto*). The reading in (2a) is thus transparent and *de re*, and that in (2b) is opaque and *de dicto*. Nevertheless, distinguishing these logical forms does not exhaust the problem with belief ascription as far as a theory of utterance processing is concerned. Let us say that Tom is referentially mistaken and thinks that Frank McCourt, the author of *Angela's Ashes*, also wrote *Oscar and Lucinda*. Let us assume that the reporter is aware of it. Then, the reporter may substititute a correct description or name as in (2c) or (2d), where 'AoAA' stands for 'the author of *Angela's Ashes*' and c is an individual constant associated with the referent Frank McCourt.

(2c) $\exists x \, (AoAA(x) \, \& \, \forall y \, (AoAA(y) \rightarrow y = x) \, \& \, Bel_T GN(x))$

(2d) $Bel_T \, GN(c)$

The belief reported on is *de re* but Tom uses the description 'the author of *Oscar and Lucinda*' erroneously: his belief is about Frank McCourt, the author of *Angela's Ashes*. From the point of view of utterance interpretation that, as in DS, is founded on the merger of different sources of meaning information, it is a case of a referential mistake.

This is a very brief summary of the philosophical and discourse-theoretic problems posed by propositional attitude constructions. Let us now consider belief ascription from the point of view of the process of interpretation of the belief report and how it can be accounted for in DS. In order to do so, we have to point out other difficulties with belief ascription. For example, when the speaker utters (3), the reporter may have doubts whether the speaker under-stands the statement or merely repeats a half-understood astronomical fact. This suspicion may be rendered as in (4).

(3)   Red giants become white dwarfs.

(4)   Tom believes that red giants become white dwarfs but I am not sure if he understands what it means.

Similarly, the reporter may not know what the statement is about. This scenario would normally produce a hedging report like, for example, that in (5).

(5)   Tom believes that something he calls red giants become white dwarfs, whatever it means.

Such situations of discrepancies in knowledge base between the holder of the belief and the reporter, as well as between the reporter and the hearer of the report, have to be accounted for in a theory of discourse *processing* such as DS. In other words, the particular scenarios that affect the meaning of the belief report have to find their reflection in MRs.

Moreover, belief can be ascribed on the basis of non-linguistic evidence. So, the problem of reference assignment is not merely the problem of substitu-tivity in linguistic expressions. Sentence (6) can be uttered of someone getting ready to get off the train.

(6)   He believes that the next station is where he should get off.

Let us now come back to the scenario of referentially mistaken use of definite descriptions taken up in Chapter 4. As we saw earlier, example (3) from Section 4.1, repeated below as (7), can be used referentially in a default, correctly referring way; referentially with a referential mistake; or attribu-tively, with no particular individual in mind.

(7)   The best architect designed this church.

Analogously, on the same scenario, the belief report in (8) can be read as (i) *de re* about Antoni Gaudí, (ii) *de re* about Simon Guggenheim, or (iii) *de dicto*.

(8)   Tom believes that the best architect designed this church.

However, if the referential mistake or the lack of knowledge about the identity of the referent have to be ascribed to the holder of the belief, as they were in

(3), then we can normally expect that the reporter would signal the non-default status of such a report as, for example, in (8a) and (8b) respectively.

(8a)   Tom believes that the best architect designed this church but he mistakenly thinks it was Simon Guggenheim.

(8b)   Tom believes that the best architect designed this church but he doesn't know who it is.

This is an intuitive claim that requires empirical support. But, since it is intuitively plausible and is further strongly supported by the Gricean principles of rational conversational behaviour such as Levinson's I-heuristic,[6] we can proceed with the premises that (a) the different readings have to be distinguished with respect to the reporter's knowledge base; and (b) the default status of the *de re* reading has reasonable support on independent grounds, that is outside the theory of DS. Analogously to the three readings of definite descriptions in extensional contexts discussed in Chapter 4, we can distinguish here (i) the *default de re* reading that comes with the strongest, 'undispersed' intentionality and with the strongest referential intention, and on which the utterance is about Antoni Gaudí; (ii) the non-default reading with intentionality 'dispersed' between the individual intended by Tom (Simon Guggenheim) and the objective correlate of the description in this situation (Antoni Gaudí); and (iii) the *de dicto* reading that corresponds to Tom's *de dicto* belief, about whoever undergoes the description 'the best architect'. Let us come back to reading (ii). This reading corresponds to Tom's belief *de re* with a mistaken reference assignment, namely to a belief about Simon Guggenheim. While the belief is *de re* (about a particular *res*), the report is best called *de dicto* in that, like (iii), it is opaque to substitution of coreferential terms: it does not allow for substituting, for example, 'Antoni Gaudí' for the definite description preserving the truth of the sentence. I have called this occurrence *de dicto about someone else* (or *de dicto₁*), and that in (iii) *de dicto proper*.[7] The MRs of DS will have to account for the fact that propositional attitude reports can be interpreted in either of these three ways and for the fact that one of the readings (*de re*) is the cognitive default, founded on the strength of intentionality of the belief, while the other two are progressive departures from the default (*de dicto₁* and *de dicto proper*) that correspond to the progressive weakening of intentionality. In fact, in the case of the *de dicto proper*, intentionality is so 'dispersed' that it does not reach any object. On the level of properties of acts of communication, this amounts to saying that the utterance comes without a referential intention: it is about whoever undergoes the description. I have developed this theory of *default de re* in various other places and will now resort to summarizing it in the form of a DRS where the options of placement for the discourse referent for 'the best architect' are clearly marked.[8] The informal attempt at a DRS in *Fig. 5.1 represents the fact that the expression 'the best architect' can be used in three different ways. This is rendered by allowing the discourse referent b to belong to the outermost box (our *default de re* reading), the middle box (our *de dicto$_1$*, i.e. *de dicto about someone else*), or the innermost box (our *de dicto proper*). The choices are marked by a box drawn with a broken line.

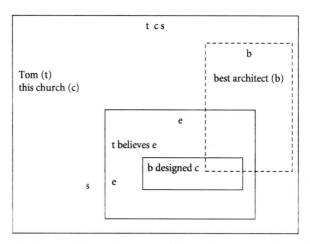

*FIGURE 5.1 Informal representation of the three readings of (8)

This representation of the meaning of (8) does not, for quite obvious reasons, suffice as a representation of the process of interpretation of (8) by the hearer. First, the relation between discourse referents and objects has to be clearly specified in a way that conforms to, or is at least compatible with, the principles of DRT that we are using in DS. Secondly, we need one interpretation for every reading instead of a choice of readings. In DRT, this has been achieved by means of the internal and external anchoring of discourse referents, as is discussed below. Moreover, in DS, we have to be able to render the fact that one reading is the default, presumed, standard one, while the other two are context-dependent departures from it. Just as in Chapter 4 we arrived at various MRs of an utterance with a definite description that can be ordered with respect to strength of intentionality (see Figs 4.3–4.5), so we can arrive at different interpretations of (8) that can be similarly placed on a cline of intentionality and referential intention. I propose such MRs for belief reports in Section 5.3 below. Before that, it is necessary to say more about the degrees of intentionality and intending, as they are directly related to the degrees of importance of the mode of presentation of the object of belief for the MR.

All in all, it seems indisputable that there is more to the meaning of belief reports than just the choice between transparent and opaque readings that can be captured by the relative scope of the existential quantifier and the belief operator when a definite description is involved. First, there is also the mistaken identity reading and hence if we want to account for *utterance* processing as we do in DS, we have, in fact, three types of interpretation available. Secondly, these three types do not mean a three-way ambiguity but rather are ordered on the scale of salience provided by the strength of intentionality of belief and by the strength of the referential intention (from strong, 'undispersed' to non-existent, absent altogether). Finally, in an account in which we model the process of interpretation rather than discourse competence, we have to have a principled way of telling which of the possible readings ensues on a particular scenario.

5.2 Degrees of mode of presentation

It is now evident that, in DS, there is no strict *de re/de dicto* duality of reading of belief reports in utterance interpretation. Neither is there a three-way ambiguity between *de re*, *de dicto₁* (*de dicto about someone else*), and *de dicto proper*. Instead, there are separate interpretations: the default one, and the non-default ones that have to resort to contextual clues. Before venturing into the processing of context, let us focus on the sentence form which is the starting point for the application of such a processes.

Examples (9) and (10) may or may not have the same informational content, depending on the believer's knowledge base:

(9)   The author of *Oscar and Lucinda* is a great novelist.

(10)   Peter Carey is a great novelist.

As was discussed in Chapter 4, the speaker of (9) may not consent to believing (10) because he/she may not know that the description in (9) and the proper name in (10) refer to the same individual. This problem becomes even more apparent when we embed (9) and (10) in belief reports as in (2) and (1) above respectively: the report must not misrepresent the belief. So, the core point in reporting on beliefs and other attitudes is to consider the issue of truth-preserving substitutivity: substitution of coreferential expressions does not always work. Consequently, in a theory of belief reports, we want to be able to say when, in principle, it works and when it does not. The starting point is therefore to define reference in such non-extensional contexts.

The failure of substitutivity of coreferential expressions suggests that we have to either abandon compositional semantics or incorporate contextual information in semantic theory. I suggested a version of the latter approach, redefining the object of study of semantics as a merger representation (see Fig. 3.1). Before proceeding with the compositionality of merger representations in DS, a brief overview of the two major orientations is due.

The current debate originates with Frege (1892) and his distinction between *Sinn* (sense) and *Bedeutung* (reference). According to Frege, the role of reference in intensional contexts is taken by sense, that is by an objective equivalent of a mode of presentation. Subsequently, various solutions have been suggested. Quine (1956) postulated degrees of intensions for quantifying into such contexts. In more recent tradition, it has been suggested that the mode of presentation be incorporated into the logical form, as in the hidden-indexical theory (Schiffer 1977, 1992, 1996), developed also in Crimmins and Perry's (1989) and Crimmins's (1992) concept of a 'notion', an unarticulated constituent of the proposition. Hidden indexicals or notions can be understood as a covert 'so' as in 'A so-believes that...' or 'so-labelled' as in 'A believes that B, so-labelled, Φs' (Forbes 1990, 1997). There is also ample constructive criticism of the Fregean direction in the literature.[9] The *that*-clause can also be taken to refer to a sentence rather than a proposition (see e.g. Bach 1997). Or, one can distinguish linguistic and psychological modes of presentation *à la* Recanati (1993).

Unlike neo-Fregeans, the so-called neo-Russellian approaches deny the contribution of the mode of presentation (henceforth: MoP) to the semantics of attitude reports.[10] The semantic content of a sentence is a *singular proposition*. Within this orientation, Richard (1990, 1995) suggests that the verb 'believe' is indexical, and thereby is contextually sensitive in order to account for various readings of belief reports.[11] Larson and Ludlow (1993) capture the relevance of the actual expression that is used to refer in the sentence by proposing composites of linguistic forms and extra-linguistic objects called by them interpreted logical forms (ILFs; see Section 1.3). Stanley (2000) traces all the contextual factors that affect truth conditions to the elements in the syntactic structure: there are no genuinely 'unarticulated' constituents. In his account of *saying that*, Davidson (1968–9) has a demonstrative 'that' to refer to an utterance. Davidson advocates the so-called *semantic innocence* view according to which an expression in an attitude report contributes exactly what it does in non-intensional contexts. This approach is called a paratactic account.

To sum up, neo-Russellians respect semantic innocence but deny semantic significance of MoPs. In brief, they say that although substitutivity in attitude reports does not *seem* to hold, *in fact* it does. In other words, substitution does not affect the truth value. Neo-Fregeans, on the contrary, have semantically relevant MoPs, as in the hidden-indexical theories. Such theories try to preserve semantic innocence but they have to give up compositional semantics. This is so because hidden indices that stand for MoPs have no counterpart in grammar and as a result the meaning of the sentence cannot be composed out of the meaning of the parts and the sentence structure.

The theory of DS developed in Part I of this book can be classified as neo-Fregean. One of its core premises is that some form of MoP is indispensable in talking about propositional attitudes and attitude reports. In agreement with the outline of the composition of the merger representation proposed in Fig. 3.1, it is clear that the MoP has to come from one of the sources of meaning information there. If it does not come from the combination of word meanings and sentence structure, then it is provided by cognitive defaults, social–cultural defaults$_1$, or by conscious pragmatic inference$_1$. So, the discussion as to whether the MoP belongs to semantics or to pragmatics is circumvented here in that *it does not matter where it comes from.* In other words, in DS, merger representation is the truth-conditional representation and, by definition, it is the output (merger) of the meaning input from the four different sources. As a merger output, it is a representation of meaning that is claimed to be semanticized, truth-conditional, and so should be amenable to a model-theoretic treatment. The exact treatment of belief reports in terms of MRs is the subject of Section 5.3. Before we pursue it, it is necessary to establish what this meaning ingredient called an MoP is, what its epistemological status is, in what way it matters to the meaning of the utterance, and, where applicable, to the meaning of the discourse—and, *a fortiori*, to the merger representation.

The degree to which MoP contributes to the proposition expressed is in the focus of the ongoing discussions on the matter. In Schiffer's hidden-indexical theory referred to above, belief is a three-place relation among the believer, the proposition whose structure can be taken into account, and an MoP under which the person believes this proposition. Let us take Schiffer's example in (11). The logical form is presented in (12), where $\Phi^* m$ is a type of mode of presentation determined by the context, and $<>$ indicate the intensions (cf. (2a) in Section 3.1).

(11)   Ralph believes that Fido is a dog.

(12) $(\exists m) (\Phi^* m \ \& \ Bel(Ralph, < Fido, doghood >, m))$ (after Schiffer 1992: 503)

Introducing a slot for m and a predicate Φ^* for varying m is an ingenious move as it captures the fact that m varies from situation to situation. But in order to use this as a formal solution, we have to be able to answer a few questions such as:

- whether $\Phi^* m$ should be conceived of as a constituent of the logical form of sentences or, perhaps, as a constituent of some other unit (such as the merger representation of DS);
- what information falls under $\Phi^* m$, and how the processor of the belief sentence extracts what is relevant from the total available background information that could in theory fit under $\Phi^* m$;
- whether this information has to be consciously accessible to the processor of the belief report.

Regarding the first question, two answers have been proposed: (i) contextual information that is included in MoP can contribute to the propositional form of an utterance, or (ii) contextual information functions separately from the proposition, as implicatures. Recanati (1994) calls these two standpoints contextualism and anti-contextualism respectively. As was discussed in Chapter 3, the contribution of contextual input to truth conditions remains a matter of debate. While some theories are built on the assumption that semantics has to extend beyond truth conditions, others found the semantics on a propositional form that includes pragmatic (or other extra-sentential) input. In other words, as can be seen from the earlier juxtaposition of neo-Fregeanism with neo-Russellianism, although it is commonly accepted that MoPs are needed in reporting on beliefs, the theoretical question remains as to whether they contribute to the truth-conditional representation. And, it should now be obvious that on the DS account, MoP has to contribute to the merger representation which is construed as truth-conditionally evaluable. As was proposed in Chapter 3, the level of MR is the level to which we apply the extended mechanism of DRT. In other words again, MRs contain discourse referents and discourse conditions just as DRSs do but the sources of these conditions can pertain to any of the sources of the meaning information distinguished in Fig. 3.1: WS, CD, SCD 1, and CPI 1.

Questions two and three above are interrelated. On the assumption that the sources of information about meaning for MRs are as listed above (and in Fig. 3.1), MoP can be either assigned by default by the hearer or it can be consciously inferred. Before we attend to this problem, let us try to confine MoP to the constituent of the MRs that is neither too fine-grained nor insufficient in content for the purpose of *distinguishing between the three categories of readings of belief reports, namely de re, de dicto₁, and de dicto proper*. It seems that although guises under which the person holds the belief may be too detailed, too fine-grained for our purpose, *some* contextual information that pertains to the identification of the belief is what we need. So, we need contextually defined Φ^*m *and* a contextually defined *degree of granularity* of the Φ^*m. In earlier works (e.g. Jaszczolt 1999b, 2000a) I proposed degrees of semantic significance of the MoP that depend on the default or non-default status of the interpretation of the attitude report. In brief, the *default de re* reading is triggered as a cognitive default because it corresponds to the scenario on which intentionality of the mental state (belief) is the strongest. Since this reading is the default reading of belief reports, the contribution of the MoP is null: the degree to which Φ^*m contributes to the MR is 0. If we were to compare the content of the MR of (11) repeated below with Schiffer's logical form in (12), we would have to say that for the *default de re* reading, (12) should be replaced by (13) on this occasion.

(11)   Ralph believes that Fido is a dog.

(12) $(\exists m)(\Phi^*m$ & Bel (Ralph, <Fido, doghood>, m))

(13)   Bel (Ralph, <Fido, doghood>)

We could not make this move within the hidden-indexical theory because Φ^*m does not allow for value 0. In other words, it does not allow for varying the granularity of *m*, neither does it allow for varying the adicity of the *Bel* predicate which results from making *m* redundant for the default *de re*. The general picture in DS is this. MRs of DS are representations of processing and therefore they are separate MRs for separate interpretations of an utterance/ discourse. When the sources of meaning information distinguished in Fig. 3.1 (WS, CD, SCD 1, CPI 1) result in the *default de re* reading of a belief report, it is this reading that the MR represents. If they result in the *de dicto$_1$* or *de dicto proper*, it is this reading that is represented. The representation in (12) has a different theoretical purpose. It is a semantic representation of any belief report that can be made using (11) and as such it captures the fact that belief reports are intensional contexts. It is irrelevant for hidden-indexical theory that in some circumstances of use belief reports behave like extensional contexts. What matters is that they are not always, as a rule, extensional. In other words, we cannot guarantee that substitution of a coreferential expression will not change the truth value. DS takes a different perspective. MRs are situation-dependent. What they give us is a situation-dependent semantics. This situation-dependence can be captured by means of the extended relational semantics of dynamic approaches as introduced in Section 3.4.2. This formal analysis is attempted in Section 5.3.

The reading *de dicto$_1$* corresponds, on our narrowed construal, to a scenario on which the believer has a *de re* belief about an individual who does not in fact undergo the description or bear the name which the believer associates with this individual. So, this is a case of 'weakened' intentionality, intentionality that does not reach the object that is commonly known under the name or description used by the believer. MoP has a role to play here in that it has to distinguish between the allowed and the disallowed substitutions. The guise under which the believer holds the belief is not intersubjectively acceptable. Although the belief is *de re*, there is a referential mistake there that prevents free substitution of coreferential terms. But we do not need the 'whole of $\Phi^* m$', so to speak. For example, if Tom believes (9) repeated below and knows many other facts about the author of *Oscar and Lucinda* such as the titles of all of his other novels, his nationality, his age, what he looks like, who he is married to, but mistakenly thinks the novelist's name is Roddy Doyle, all we need in the MR is the fact that 'Peter Carey' is not substitutable for 'the author of *Oscar and Lucinda*' in the report on the belief expressed by (9), as in (10).

(9)   The author of *Oscar and Lucinda* is a great novelist.

(10)   Peter Carey is a great novelist.

We need only that part of the MoP that distinguishes the correct from the incorrect substitutions of expressions for 'the author of *Oscar and Lucinda*'. So, the MoP does contribute to the MR but, so to speak, not all of its content is relevant. We need only that 'part' of it that distinguishes between the expressions the believer would consent to and the ones he or she would not.

Finally, in the case of a *de dicto proper* report, that is a report that corresponds, on our narrowed field of analysis, to a *de dicto* belief on the part of the original speaker and not the reporter, there is no substitutivity. The belief is held about whoever satisfies the description 'the author of *Oscar and Lucinda*'. The MoP contributes all its conceptual content to the MR. It will normally just be the information that the individual is known as 'the author of *Oscar and Lucinda*', sometimes accompanied by information retrieved from sources other than the expression itself such as the nationality or sex of the author or some other attributes. Example (14) demonstrates that these additional attributes may also enter in to the *de dicto* belief.

(14)   John: Tom believes that the author of *Oscar and Lucinda* won his second Booker prize.
        Tom: I thought the author was a woman.

As can be seen from these three types of reading of belief reports, the situation with the corresponding beliefs is far from clear-cut. The MoP can be very relevant to the representation of meaning of the utterance (MR) as in the latter case where it contributes a fair amount of its content to the semantics

(MR), or it can contribute just that identifying information that resolves the mismatch between the believer's assignment of the name or description to the person and the intersubjectively accepted one as in *de dicto₁*; or, finally, it can be of no semantic significance as in the case of the *de re* reading. The impact this has on the adicity of the *Bel* predicate is discussed in Section 5.3. What matters for the moment is that, in DS, we shall recognize the contribution of the MoP to the MR that varies from null MoP to fine-grained, detailed MoP, depending on the type of reading of the belief report. I shall call *semantically relevant MoP* the content of MoP that contributes to the MR. The scale of the degree of granularity of MoP is also correlated with its status in conscious inference: value 0 corresponds to the *default de re* reading, and the increasing granularity of semantically relevant MoP is directly correlated with the degree of departure from the default and hence the degree of weakening of the intentionality and intentions.[12]

The DS account, as it was set out in Part I, identifies MRs with semantic representations. These representations are the truth-conditionally evaluable representations of content. So, in DS, MRs represent utterance meaning, at the same time being semantic, compositional, and truth-conditional. Such units of meaning allow us to say *not* that belief contexts are intensional and opaque to the truth-preserving substitution of coreferential terms, but rather, that belief reports are transparent by default, becoming increasingly more resistant to substitutions as intentionality of the mental act weakens. So, we end up with variable semantics, justified by the dynamic, context-sensitive perspective.[13] In other words, we end up with different MRs for different readings of the utterance that may be recovered by our model hearer as intended by the speaker on different occasions.

5.3 Merger representations for belief reports

From what has been said so far, we obtain a picture according to which the hearer normally assumes that the subject of a belief report (e.g. Tom in (8)) knows what individual he is talking about. If there are reasons for doubt, the hearer has to assess all the relevant contextual information before interpreting a belief report. This 'normal', default, *de re* interpretation of a belief report, as was argued in Section 5.2, does not require a contribution of the MoP to the MR. This seems to call for a reduction in the adicity of the *Bel* predicate if the semantic (MR) content of the belief report in (11) is represented as in (12), repeated below. Example (12) would then, for this reading, result in (13).

(11)   Ralph believes that Fido is a dog.

(12) $(\exists m) (\Phi^* m$ & Bel (Ralph, <Fido, doghood>, m))

(13)   Bel (Ralph, <Fido, doghood>)

On standard neo-Fregean accounts this is a contentious move. Adicity of *Bel* cannot be freely altered without introducing an ambiguity of the predicate. However, on the DS account, there is no problem with varying the adicity. There is no level of propositional representation that would require stable adicity. Instead, there is a merger of sources of information about meaning and there is no need (and, indeed, no reason) to think of the output of the WS source (combination of word meaning and sentence structure) as a logical form that has an independent status from the merger. So, in the spirit of truth-conditional pragmatics, we can propose a belief relation that has a variable valence. In the case of *de dicto₁* and *de dicto proper* readings of a belief report, there is a semantically relevant MoP m that contributes a *variadic function* (Recanati 2002c) that increases the valence of the *Bel* relation. Variadic function was postulated by Recanati for sentences such as (15) where the rationale for it is the optional locative adverb 'here':

(15)   It rains here.

In 'It rains here', the locative adverb 'here' contributes a variadic function which increases the valence of the expressed relation, and it also contributes a specific location which fills the extra argument-role. (Recanati 2002c: 329–30)

In the analysis of belief reports in terms of MRs, the source of the variadic function is not overt. There is no constituent of the sentence that can be made responsible for the varying adicity of *Bel*. The reason for its introduction is the fact that substitutivity of coreferential terms is not always possible. Where it is not possible, we resort to adding the third argument of the *Bel* predicate. This argument is instantiated as the semantically relevant mode of presentation, that is that part of the guise under which the belief is held that makes a difference to the utterance meaning.

It has been argued that allowing such freedom in construing arguments for a predicate violates constraints on argument structure. There are syntactic constraints on what can function as an argument for a predicate—such as Chomsky's 'theta-role assignment' according to which the argument has to be a sister of the predicate. In the compositional WS theory, that is in a standard way of doing semantics in which the combination of sentence structure and word meaning is taken to be compositional, we can construe a near-equivalent of the variadic function. This equivalent would be the proposal of structured propositions.[14] On Cresswell's (1985) version, the complementizer *that* exhibits different degrees of sensitivity to the structure of the clause that follows it. In my previous accounts of attitude reports, I used structured propositions to demonstrate the default status of the *de re* reading of belief reports, adopting the standard assumption that compositionality should be sought at the level of sentence meaning.[15] In DS, however, the conceptually simpler and cognitively more plausible solution of variable adicity can safely be adopted.

This 'covert' variadic function is not a weakness in the explanation. It is fully compatible with the principles on which the meaning representation is built in DS. MR is a merger of meaning information from various sources and, as was argued in Chapter 3, this level of representation does not prioritize the WS source over the other sources. Since compositionality is a property of MRs not WSs, variadic function applies to the level of MR: an extra argument for the semantically relevant MoP is added when the *default de re* is not the case. In other words, it is added when CPI 1 (conscious pragmatic inference$_1$) or, sometimes, SCD 1 (social–cultural defaults$_1$) signal that the *default de re* that is normally triggered as a CD (cognitive default) is not the case. So, in short, in DS there is no reason why the variadic function should be triggered by WS. By the same token, the arguments brought in against the *Bel* relation with variable adicity will not apply to MR.

Let us now see how the DR-theoretic treatment of belief reports can be transposed, after some amendments, to the level of MR of DS. Attitudinal states such as belief have been represented in DRT as follows. Let us assume that L is a DRS language, MOD a set of mode indicators comprising among others BEL (belief), DES (desire), INT (intention), and [ANCH, x] is an anchor for discourse referents x. An attitude description is then a pair <MOD,K> where K is a DRS. We also have to distinguish internal and external anchors for discourse referents. <[ANCH, x], K> is an internal anchor for the discourse referent x, and external anchor (EA) is a function whose domain is the set of internally anchored discourse referents in K. Its range is a set of referents not occurring in K. External anchors are required because the DRS can only have truth conditions of a singular proposition if it is connected with the entities in the domain to which the conversation pertains (see Kamp 1990, 1996, 2003). Square brackets are employed to signal the special type of condition that is used here: a condition that specifies how a discourse referent relates to the object it represents. Kamp (1990: 55) calls conditions of the type 'ANCH[x]' *formal* conditions, and other conditions such as 'best architect (x)' *predicative* conditions. External anchors play a very important role in DRT. Without them, as in Kamp and Reyle's (1993) basic DRT, we cannot capture the fact that there are singular propositions. In other words, there are scenarios on which all that is needed for representing the meaning is linking the discourse referent with an object it stands for. Descriptive DRS-conditions cannot do it: we have to, by definition, go via descriptions. Formal conditions and external anchors allow the capturing of this direct connection.

Next, a predicate *Att* ('attitude') is added to the vocabulary of L. Attitudes are then states represented as s: Att(x, K, EA) (adapted from Kamp 2003). Sentence (8), repeated below, has the DRS as in Fig. 5.2. For perspicuity, temporal reference is not represented. Also, in agreement with the discussion in the *Interlude* of Chapter 4, the demonstrative noun phrase 'this church' is regarded as directly referential.

(8)   Tom believes that the best architect designed this church.

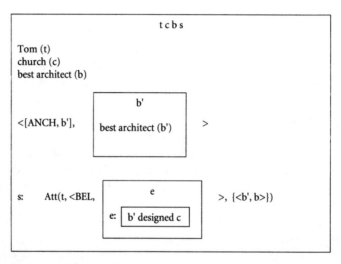

FIGURE 5.2. The DRS for sentence (8)

As can be seen from this DRS, b′ is internally and externally anchored. As a result, it represents a reading on which 'the best architect' is used referentially and in accordance with intersubjectively accepted reference assignment. So, the reading in Fig. 5.2 is the *default de re* one.

Now, from the theoretical stance of DRT, there is no need to specify our cases of *de dicto₁* and *de dicto proper*: if an internally anchored discourse referent is not also externally anchored, then the DRS does not express any proposition (cf. Kamp 2003: 7).[16] But it is not so on the DS approach. In DS, there is an MR that is the output of processing of an utterance that combines ('merges') information from four different sources such as WS, CPI 1, CD, SCD 1.

As was proposed in Chapter 3, truth conditions are predicated of MRs, not of propositions. Also, conditions of DS differ from DRS-conditions in that they are not necessarily triggered by a syntactic configuration of the sentence but are based on the utterance produced in the merger. So, in other words, if the meaning of utterance (16) is (17), it is (17) rather than (18) that enters the MR.

(16)   I haven't eaten.

(17)   I am hungry.

(18)   I haven't eaten [the appropriate meal for the time of the day yet].

Instead of the development of the logical form of the sentence proposed in post-Gricean pragmatics (as in (18)), MR 'leaps' directly to the conveyed sense (as in (17)). By the same token, MR has to be able to account for the fact that the default *de re* reading of belief reports is the cognitive default, and that there are other possibilities for the reading of belief reports that can also be arrived at, albeit by a different combination of WS, CD, SCD 1, and CPI 1.

Let us now see how far we can take the formalism of DRT for representing the three readings of belief reports distinguished earlier. The *de dicto proper* does not have external anchors. In order to represent it, we could borrow from Kamp's earlier (1990, 1996) account of attitudes (NB *not* attitude reports) and allow for internal anchors that do not have external anchoring. Kamp (e.g. 1990: 60) uses formal anchors that have no corresponding external anchors in a more restricted way. He says:

It isn't enough that A takes himself to stand in some suitable relation of acquaintance to b, this relation must actually obtain; otherwise the object of acquaintance for which A's attribution . . . is intended won't exist and the attribution misfires. In such cases A's attitude fails to determine a singular proposition; in fact, it is our view that in such cases it strictly speaking does not determine any proposition at all.   (Kamp 1996: 10)

and

[I]t is quite possible for A to have an internal anchor for some discourse referent although, as a matter of fact, x is not externally anchored for A. These are the cases where A is under the illusion that he is standing in a relation of acquaintance to some object—he thinks that he is acquainted with an object in the given way but in fact there is no such object. (Kamp 1996: 12)

He calls attitudes of this type formally anchored and *formally de re*, while not being *truly de re* because of some deficiency in recognizing the object. So, he classifies formal anchors without external anchors as a case of *formally de re* beliefs. It seems, however, that the category is not clearly distinguishable from what we classify as beliefs *de dicto*: if the person believes that there is someone who designed the Sagrada Família and that this person can be praised as the best architect, then, surely, there is an internal anchor, an imagined person, whoever it might be, about whom this assessment of being the best architect holds. The difference seems to be largely terminological: some of our *de dicto* beliefs are Kamp's *formal de re*. Another case of *formal de re* is a case of a referential mistake: a belief is formally anchored, but, on Kamp's (1996) account, there is no external object that it is anchored to.

All in all, Kamp's *formal de re* belief seems to correspond to our belief *de re about someone else*, as well as to some *de dicto* beliefs. 'Some', because in some cases of the *de dicto* belief there is internal anchoring, that is the believer assumes that there is an individual or other that the belief is about, while in others, as in the case of (19), it may be that one holds a belief without an understanding of the utterance.

(19)   Red giants become white dwarfs.

This distinction, however, is very fuzzy and need not be pursued further. After all, some beliefs are *de dicto* in virtue of the fact that the believer does not know who the individual is, but are 'like' *de re* in that the believer 'imagines' this individual, that is they should, strictly speaking, have an external anchor. Others, like the one in (19), may not have any formal anchors because they are not fully processed: they are not propositional, but semi-propositional (Sperber 1985, 1997), taken as primitive entities, put 'in quotes', so to speak, and stored for future understanding. What we are representing here, however, are belief reports, and these, when pertaining to examples such as (19), are *de dicto* in virtue of being about no one in particular. Since we are interested in belief reports, we shall not venture into this classification of types of beliefs which, *nota bene*, may turn out to be a mater of degree of intersubjective recognition of the object rather than a matter of a two- or three-partite distinction.[17] In fact, typologies of attitudes attempted in the literature testify to this intuition. Asher (1986: 142) summarizes this intuition as follows. The *de re/de dicto* distinction is a generalization over a more detailed taxonomy in which we have to distinguish beliefs without any anchors, beliefs with only external anchors, but also beliefs with only internal anchors, and both internal and external anchors. The situations that correspond to these options need not be discussed here (see Asher 1986), and, indeed, the classification can be adapted depending on the philosophical orientation with respect to direct reference. What matters is the fact that the *de re/de dicto* distinction is not fully compatible with types of anchoring, and, indeed, even combinations of anchoring may not suffice in that formal anchors can be more, or less, well-defined. In other words, there may be a continuum rather than a typology: we can call it a continuum of well-definedness of internal anchors, or, following

Kamp (1990, 1996) and Asher (1986), we could establish a cut-off point by building a condition into the construction algorithm that definite referring terms require some, at least *schematic*, internal anchor.

Let us therefore assume that some, however faint, form of formal anchoring is present in *de dicto* beliefs.[18] Coming back to belief reports, on this construal, Kamp's formal anchoring without external anchoring accounts for the *de dicto* reading. Let us now assess whether it accounts both for *de dicto proper* and *de dicto*$_1$.

The reading *de dicto proper* of (8) would anchor *b* internally as in Fig. 5.3, to

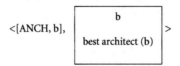

FIGURE 5.3. Anchoring for the *de dicto proper* reading of (8)

represent the sense 'the best architect, whoever he or she is'.

To repeat, the full DRS for a *de dicto* report will not be proposed because there is no need for it in the DRT framework: the truth-conditional content is not well-defined (cf. Kamp 1990: 60; 1996: 10; 2003: 7).

De dicto$_1$ is problematic in DRT. It corresponds to a *de re* belief with a mistaken identity of the referent so it has to be represented in a similar way to Fig. 5.2, but without the intersubjectively accepted external anchor. We have to represent the fact that there *is* an individual, intersubjectively accepted, that Tom's belief is about, but that this individual does not fit the description. This is not possible in DRT as it stands. The problem, in fact, does not arise for DRT: this information does not belong to the proposition expressed. So it is not a weakness of the theory that it does not provide a solution. However, this problem is a genuine problem for accounts that attempt to represent the meaning of a whole act of communication and take the step exemplified in (16) and (17). DS is such an account and as such it has to be able to render that reading of (8) that picks out Simon Guggenheim rather than Antoni Gaudí as the architect of the Sagrada Família ('this church')—analogously to the way it was done for referring terms in extensional contexts in Fig. 4.3.

So, similar to *de dicto proper*, in DRT we cannot provide a full DRS for the *de dicto*$_1$ reading. But the reasons are different. If I am correct, on the DRT account, sentence (8) has the same DRS for the *de dicto*$_1$ reading as for the *de re* reading: the unique individual described as 'the best architect' was an architect of '*this* church' and there is an external anchor. The DRS has well-defined truth conditions. But the intended, referentially mistaken meaning falls outside the theory. It is not so for the DS account. While in the DRT framework we need not be concerned with a complication such as a mistaken identity of the referent ascribed by the believer, in DS we do. It is clear that this reading has a formal anchor, but there is no *intersubjectively recognized* external anchor: the anchoring is, so to speak, mismatched: the intention to refer to Simon Guggenheim by means of this description in this context has misfired. We could say that this case fits the category where there is an internal anchor without an external anchor and therefore no proposition is expressed (see e.g. Kamp 2003). The belief is *de re* (i.e. *formal de re*), similar to Fig. 5.2, while the belief report is *de dicto*, similar to Fig. 5.3. This is as far as we can go in employing the DR-theoretic framework for the task it is not designed to perform. The switch of viewpoint from propositions to compositional MRs now requires different tools to represent the utterance meaning. To repeat, instead of mapping from sentences (or their syntactic structure) into DRSs, that is instead of the DRS construction algorithm, we have mapping from the four sources: WS, CD, SCD 1, and CPI 1 into MRs. MRs are intended to model the content of information obtained through verbal and related non-verbal input. As a result, although we cannot (and need not) provide a DRS for *de dicto*$_p$ in DS we can (and must) provide an MR. To repeat, the MR will have truth conditions because compositionality draws on all the four sources of meaning information there. The fact that 'the best architect' is a description of the architect of the Sagrada Família, as well as the fact that in the speaker's belief this architect is called Simon Guggenheim rather than Antoni Gaudí, are part of the MR. Similarly, in DS, we shall provide a representation for *de dicto proper*.

Now, as Asher (1986: 129) says, from the point of view of semantics, discourse referents are 'pegs' on which the hearer who processes an utterance can 'hang' the ascriptions of properties specified by DRS-conditions. Taking this semantic role of discourse referents all the way conceptually, as we do in DS, we obtain the representations in which we link the object of belief with the discourse referent as we did in Figs 4.3–4.5. The discourse referent x, standing for the person ('the best architect') who designed the demonstrated church ('this church'), was an argument of the following three conditions respectively:

[Antoni Gaudí]$_{CD}$(x)   for the default referential reading
[Simon Guggenheim]$_{CPI_1}$(x)   for the referential reading with a referential mistake

and

[the best architect]$_{CPI_1}$(x)   for the attributive reading.

We shall follow the same procedure for the *de re*, *de dicto₁*, and *de dicto proper* belief reports.

At this point, we can propose the MRs and introduce the semantics of the belief predicate we are going to use. Let us assume that the belief report can be represented as Bel $(x, \quad)$ to mean 'x believes that '. The satisfaction conditions for Bel $(x, \quad)$ are that the individual that corresponds to x on a certain interpretation has the cognitive state that corresponds to   on that interpretation.

In order to explain , let us compare MRs with a well-defined paradigm of SDRT in order to clarify the differences in the objects that they aim to represent. DRT and SDRT aim at compositionality at some level associated with sentence structure. Therefore, the structure of the belief has to be related to the structure of the report. Asher (1986: 171) says: 'in order for a belief report to be true, the DRS that fully describes the structure of the belief must be an *extension* of that constructed from the complement clause of the report.' A DRS D' extends a DRS D iff, when we add conditions and discourse referents to D under a certain assignment, we obtain an alphabetic variant of D. In DS, this requirement need not be posed, although it cannot be disputed either, due to the difference in the assumption as to the level at which compositionality is sought. In DS, belief reports can be construed on the basis of various, also non-linguistic input, and even where the input is mainly linguistic, the extension condition would have to take the structure of the belief to mean the composition of the output of WS, CD, CPI 1, and SCD 1. This, therefore, is a very different understanding of the 'structure' of the belief. To give an example, we are going to allow (21) as a correct report on (20). The report draws on WS and CPI 1.

(20)   Mother speaking to little Johnny who is crying over his injured finger:
       'Oh, you are not going to die.'

(21)   Johnny's mother believes that his injury is not serious.

The MR for (21) contains both the structure and the content of the belief state, but the structure that is of interest there is the structuring of the merger (i.e. the *post-merger structure*) rather than the sentence structure. It is the structure of the belief state, not the structure of the mother's sentence in (20).

From the point of view of post-Gricean semantics and pragmatics, there is every reason to find this admission at least very contentious. After all, the past three decades of interface research have focused on the boundary between what is said and what is implicated and this boundary is regarded as an absolute necessity if we want to preserve truth-conditional semantics: we need a unit of meaning, derived somehow or other from the logical form of the sentence uttered, that can be subject to a truth-conditional analysis. However, preserving this status quo would not be compatible with the assumptions of merger representations that were independently justified in Part I. As was argued in Part I, there seem to be sufficient reasons for seeking compositionality at the level of the merger of WS, CD, CPI 1, and SCD 1. So, in DS, any extension condition would have to mean an extension of the MR rather than of WS alone.

The MRs for the three readings of (8), repeated below, will look as shown in Figs 5.4–5.6.

(8)   Tom believes that the best architect designed this church.

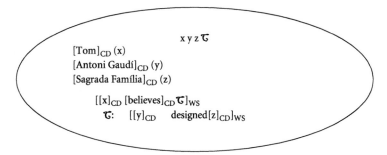

^PFIGURE 5.4. *default de re*

The discourse referent x is associated with the person Antoni Gaudí by means of CD. Similarly, the belief is *de re* by means of CD. As a result, we obtain the *default de re* reading of (8). Bel $(x, \ )$ corresponds here to the condition $[[x]_{CD}[\text{believes}]_{CD} \ ]_{WS}$. The individual who corresponds to x on this interpretation (Tom) has a cognitive state that corresponds to   on this interpretation (Antoni Gaudí designed the Sagrada Família). In other words,   is Tom's *representation of the eventuality* e: [[y] designed [z]]ws.

x y z $\mathfrak{C}$

[Tom]_{CD} (x)

[Simon Guggenheim]_{CPI 1} (y)

[Sagrada Família]_{CD} (z)

$[[x]_{CD} [\text{believes}]_{CD} \mathfrak{C}]_{WS}$

$\mathfrak{C}: \quad [[y]_{CPI 1} \text{ designed } [z]_{CD}]_{WS}$

^PFIGURE 5.5. *de dicto₁*

On this reading, the belief is still *de re* by means of CD, but the discourse referent *x* is associated with the person (Simon Guggenheim) by means of CPI 1.

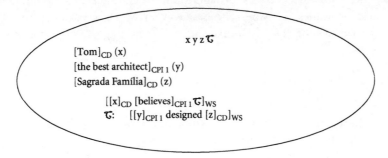

[Tom]$_{CD}$ (x)
[the best architect]$_{CPI\,1}$ (y)
[Sagrada Família]$_{CD}$ (z)

[[x]$_{CD}$ [believes]$_{CPI\,1}$𝒯]$_{WS}$
𝒯: [[y]$_{CPI\,1}$ designed [z]$_{CD}$]$_{WS}$

FIGURE 5.6. *de dicto proper*

On this reading, both the belief (*de dicto*) and the attributive reading of the description are obtained through CPI 1. Two applications of CPI 1 capture the explanation of this reading as the one that is removed the furthest from the default reading of belief reports provided earlier in informal terms in Fig. 5.1. Note that the fact that the belief predicate is interpreted through the CD or CPI 1 source demonstrates how the structure of the belief report is founded on the structure of the belief: *de dicto proper* is the case of [believe]$_{CPI_1}$ and [x]$_{CPI_1}$.

As I argued in Part I, the formalism for the semantics for MRs has to depart somewhat from the relational semantics used for DRSs in DRT. The main difference is that mental representations are created with regard to the four sources of meaning distinguished in DS. In other words, in MRs, the predicative conditions draw on the four sources and compositionality is assumed to obtain at the level of the merger. But this amendment alone will not suffice. We also have to provide the semantics for the belief predicate, as in our MRs 'believe' is a two-place operator on terms and representations of eventualities (   ). To begin with, let us assume that   functions simply as the second argument of a two-place, first-order predicate. The relational semantics in DS for *believe* is now founded on that for *n*-ary predication:[19]

$$_s[\![Pt_1,\ldots,t_n]\!]^M_{s'}\text{iff } s = s' \text{ and } \{[\![t_1]\!]_{M,s},\ldots,[\![t_n]\!]_{M,s}\} \in I(P)$$

For 'x believes   ', in DS, we have:

$$_s[\![Pt_1,t_2]\!]^M_{s'}\text{iff } s = s' \text{ and } \{[\![t]\!]_{M,s}\} \in I(P).$$

However, t_2 will not do. As I argued earlier in this section, *Bel* has a variadic valence. This variability is, in fact, a continuum of degrees of contribution of the MoP to the MR, from no contribution at one end of the scale, to some imaginary fine-grained MoP (whatever it may be) at the other end of the scale. Such variability eschews formalization: the cline has no identifiable and formalizable values for MoP. The best way in which we can capture it is through subsuming the variations under , retaining the appearance of a binary *Bel* (t,):

$$_s[\![Pt, \quad]\!]_{s'}^{M} \text{ iff } s = s' \text{ and } < [\![t]\!]_{M,s'}, \quad > \in I(P) \text{ and}$$

    (i)   is an MR of a mental state of *t* modelled on a DRS for an extensional context and constructed according to the DS-theoretic reanalysis of a DRS for an extensional context;

    (ii) $P \in \{Bel_{CD}, Bel_{CPI\,1}\}$

    (iii) $v \in \{v_{CD}, v_{CPI\,1}\}^{20}$

Conjunct (i) reflects the earlier definition of MRs as a reanalysed DRS in which discourse conditions draw on WS, CD, CPI 1, and SCD 1. As was argued in Part I, we are able to adapt and employ the mechanisms of the semantics of DRT because we added the proviso that MRs have discourse conditions provided by any of the above sources of meaning. Condition (ii) reflects the thesis that the belief operator is *de re* or *de dicto₁* by means of CD or *de dicto proper* by means of CPI 1. Naturally, condition (ii) is not exhaustive. Equating *P* with *Bel* is used here in order to provide the DS for belief reports. We can account in a similar way for other attitude verbs. But this is one of the numerous tasks that will have to be left open for future investigation. Condition (iii) captures the two possibilities of reference assignment to discourse referents: by means of CD or CPI 1. The combination of the resources of (ii) and (iii) allows us to represent the three readings of belief reports that have to be distinguished in DS—the three readings that must be distinguished in a theory of discourse processing.

    The main conceptual difference between DRSs and MRs of belief reports and other intensional contexts is perhaps that, in MRs, instead of eventualities (discourse referents *e* and *s*), we retained the intensional object .[21] This move would not be permissible in DRT and other formal accounts that seek compositionality on the level of sentence structure. They require formal objects such as events with their variable conditions of subjecthood, spatio-temporal location, and so forth. If we were to follow this line and employ discourse referents *e* and *s* for belief constructions in DS, the equivalent of *Bel* (*t,e*), that is $_s[\![Pt,e]\!]_{s'}$, would have to be used instead. However, due to this very variability of *e*s and *s*s, this will not do. In DRT, belief as a relation between a believer and a DRS only works when we sort out the anchoring (see Fig. 5.2). In our DS approach, we have taken a different route. We have 'incorporated', so to speak, the 'anchoring' to the arguments of the belief predicate itself. This was possible because compositionality is not a requirement on WS. Instead, it is a requirement on the whole MR.

Much more needs to be said to resolve finally how an MR for *Bel* (x,) is constructed. All we can do at this stage is suggest this way of looking at attitude contexts through not shunning representations embedded within representations: the semantics of acts of communication, the meaning assigned by a model hearer, needs precisely such a perspective. One may ask at this point: if compositionality is there by fiat by predicating it of the whole MR which is the sum of WS, CD, SCD 1, and CPI 1, then what exactly have we achieved by trying to preserve it? After all,   is an intensional object and hence, by the criteria of, say, DRT, we have not solved the intensionality problem of representing attitude reports. Arguably, the intensionality problem cannot be solved at the level of the expressions themselves. But in DS, our aim is not a formalization of intensional contexts. In the DS account, the aim is to show that intensionality can remain as an in-built property of expressions that serve as belief reports and, at the same time, compositionality is an open and preferred option for a theory of discourse interpretation. In other words, compositionality is not the compositionality of DRSs that is dictated by what we call WS, but a 'post-merger compositionality' of MRs. The liberal attitude to the interaction of the four contributors to the MR allows us to preserve it—retaining the DRT spirit of aiming at a compositional account. To make another comparison: for Schiffer (2003), believing is a relation to unstructured but fine-grained propositions and the compositionality of propositions is to be rejected. DS is not incompatible with this rejection of compositionality on the level of propositions either. Neither is it incompatible with the claim that objects of belief are fine-grained and (linguistically) unstructured. DS has little to say about thoughts and beliefs. It focuses on the representations of utterances which, in their post-merger form, are theoretical constructs and, so to speak, 'abstracts over thoughts'. While beliefs can be relations to finely-grained and (linguistically) unstructured units, belief operators of DS operate on a *structure* made up of the output of WS, CD, SCD 1, and CPI 1. This structure, the MR, has the granularity that is no greater than the requirements of a truth-conditional account make it. Our 'structure' is thus a structure in a different sense from that predicated of propositions. In this sense, in DS, the verb *believe* in an intensional *believe that* context triggers a relation to structured but coarse-grained MRs and, as in DRT, a compositional account is an open, and preferred, option. MRs are coarse-grained generalizations over thoughts and, like thoughts, need not only language but also other, non-linguistic components to have structured, compositional meaning—in the sense in which MRs are structured and compositional.

Notes

1 Belief contexts are also sometimes called *hyperintensional* contexts, in that expressions that can be substituted for one another in other intensional (e.g. modal) contexts cannot always be substituted in attitude contexts. Although such expressions have the same intension, they are not substitutable. Coreferential proper names, for example, are substitutable in modal contexts, but not in attitude context. In DS, instead of the category of hyperintensionality, I distinguish *degrees* to which the guise under which a belief is held contributes to the semantics (see Section 5.2).

2 It has to be remembered that this law also has a more general form, namely the *identity of indiscernibles*: if things have all properties in common, then they are identical, they are one thing. In other words, if all that can be said of one thing can be said of another, then it is said about one thing in two guises. Applied to belief reports, we have substitutivity of terms or expressions rather than 'things'. In addition, Leibniz's Law has been applied to attitude contexts in a version which is in fact due to Quine and which states that if things are identical (i.e. they are one), then they have all properties in common. So, if we take one object described in two different ways, whatever can be said about it under one guise, can also be said about it under the other guise. This law, called the *indiscernibility of identicals*, is in fact what is used in the semantics of belief reports: if A and B are identical, then anything that is true of A is also true of B:

$$\forall x \forall y (x = y \rightarrow (F(x) \rightarrow F(y)))$$

In talking about attitudes, I shall follow the common practice and use Quine's version of the law.

3 See also Russell 1905, 1919; Quine 1956; Neale 1990; Richard 1990; Jaszczolt 2000*b*.

4 The ambiguity of reading of attitude reports is also engendered by proper names, and so it is present in example (1). It is also present even when substitutivity is not the case. In the puzzle presented by Kripke (1979), the problem of reporting on beliefs involves the principle of translation (if a sentence in one language is true, its translation into another language is also true) and the principle of disquotation (if a speaker assents to 'p', then he believes that *p*). Pierre, a speaker of French who lives in France, holds a belief about a certain city unknown to him, called Londres, that it is pretty. His belief, uttered in (i), can be reported on as in (ii):

(i)   Londres est jolie.
(ii) Pierre believes that London is pretty.

Next, Pierre moves to London and acquires a belief expressed by him in (iii), while still holding (i):

(iii) London is not pretty.

It seems that in order to avoid a contradiction, we have to accept that proper names have some semantically significant mode of presentation which comes with the belief. Or, we have to 'anchor' the proper names to real or imagined objects, as in DRT (Asher 1986; Kamp 1990).

5 For the distinction between referentiality, transparency, and substitutivity see also Recanati (2000: 137–50).

6 See Chapter 1 above and Levinson 1995, 2000.

7 See e.g. Jaszczolt (2002*a*: 172).

8 See e.g. Jaszczolt 1997, 1999*b*, 2000*a*.

9 E.g. Clapp 1995, 2000; Salmon 1986; Donnellan 1989; Soames 1987; Recanati 1993.

10 E.g. Salmon 1986; Soames 1987, 1995.

11 However, see the following assessment of Richard's view:

Although Richard's account of ['There is someone Odile believes to be dead'] is . . . structurally similar to the Russellian account, it also features the semantic flexibility of the Fregean account. . . . Richard's treatment quantifies over expressions, for instance, and the Fregean treatment quantifies over senses, which may or may not be construed as linguistic in nature, but which are surely not expressions. But even if senses and expressions have different roles in a psychological story about beliefs and their representations in the mind, they perform the same semantic work in these two treatments of [the above example]. (Spencer 2001: 314)

12 On account of this varying degree of granularity that is required of MoPs in creating MRs, it will not do to equate meaning with conceptual structure. In order to uphold this statement, we would have to introduce matrices over conceptual structures that make the latter more fine-grained, or less fine-grained. It seems that on Jackendoff's (2003: e.g. 305–6) conceptual view of 'pushing "the world" into the mind' this can be achieved, albeit with placing the burden on conceptual structures by making them the criteria for distinguishing between interpretations: 'A speaker S of language L judges phrase P, uttered in context C, to refer to entity E in [the world as conceptualized by S].' (ibid.: 306). In other words, conceptual structures would have to have variable granularity in order to capture the readings *de re*, *de dicto₁*, and *de dicto proper*.

13 So, for example, the following view is incompatible with the DS: 'substitution of linguistically simple coreferential names in attitude ascriptions may result in a change of truth-values in the assertions made using those ascriptions, *without changing the propositions they semantically express* (Soames 2002: 216–17; my emphasis). In DS, what is *semantically* expressed is assertions in the form of utterances and discourses, i.e. the content of MRs. If there is a need to talk about propositions at all, they would have to be identified with MRs, the outputs of processing of all the sources of meaning information that contribute to the MRs.

14 See also Moltmann 2003 for a discussion of structured meanings vs. variable adicity of *Bel.*

15 E.g. Jaszczolt 1999*b*: ch 8.

16 Similarly for no anchoring—albeit that it is assumed in DRT that definites always require at least internal anchoring, as is discussed below.

17 Kamp (1996: 21) allows for a lot of freedom in defining *de re* attitudes, accepting the fact that many proposals are currently on offer. His task in constructing a DRT account of mental states and descriptions of mental states is 'to provide a theoretical "shell" within which the various more specific answers ... can all be coherently expressed'.

18 Note that it would be contentious to represent *de dicto proper* as the case of no formal anchors: no formal anchors intuitively pertain to indefinites used in a non-specific way, e.g. when talking about future eventualities as in (i), 'A computer programme' does not refer to any specific software Tom knows of.

   (i) Tom wants to buy *a computer programme* that would correct his mistakes in reasoning.

   Kamp (1990, 1996) and Asher (1986) stress that definites demand such internal anchors because they are used when the referent is familiar in some way or other. In our account we can remain non-committal: the formal anchor can be more, or less, well-defined and hence we seem to have a gradation of familiarity.

19 See Section 3.4.2 for an introduction to relational semantics.

20 See Section 3.4.2 for the foundations of the formal account.

21 My warmest thanks to Henk Zeevat for his insightful comments on my various attempts to get this right. This, of course, is a non-factive statement: more precise tools than   *must* be possible within DS.

6

Futurity and English *will*

6.1. Futurity and the uses of *will*: two interrelated problems

In this chapter I follow two interrelated aims: (i) to attempt to provide a unitary account of the uses of English *will* in terms of MRs, and (ii) to propose a unitary account of some core expressions used to express future time reference in English. In Section 6.2, I discuss the status of English *will* as a marker of (i) tense, (ii) modality, and (iii) a marker that is ambiguous between the two.[1] I consider clearly modal uses of *will* as in (1) and (2) (epistemic and dispositional necessity respectively), juxtaposed with (3) where *will* has a future time reference.

(1)   Mary will be in the opera now.

(2)   Mary will sometimes go to the opera in her tracksuit.

(3)   Mary will go to the opera tomorrow night.

On the event-semantics approach to temporality adopted here,[2] the classification of *will* as modal turns out to be the most satisfactory solution of the three listed above. I demonstrate that the three readings of *will* differ as to the degree of modality and can be given one overarching semantic representation. Since future *will* is best accounted for with reference to possible worlds (see e.g. Parsons 2002, 2003), it is not qualitatively different from modal *will*. Similar to the procedure followed in the previous two chapters, I first try to apply the solution proposed in DRT, extending and reanalysing it subsequently to match the theoretical assumptions that underlie MRs. To repeat, MRs draw their content on four different sources of meaning information, namely WS, CD, SCD 1, and CPI 1. As in the previous applications, CD will turn out to be of great importance for representing the essential similarity among the uses of *will*. As before, I use the properties of (i) the intentionality of mental states, and their pragmatic equivalent of (ii) communicative, informative, and referential intentions in communication in order to show that the degrees of intentions involved result in different interpretations of *will*. The strongest referential intention directed at the eventuality results in the strongest commitment to the communicated eventuality and by the same token in the 'weakest degree of modality'.

This discussion of the properties of *will* is supplemented with a discussion of the semantic category of futurity in Section 6.3. Sentence (3) is juxtaposed with expressions of futurity that use futurative progressive and so-called 'tenseless future' (Dowty 1979) as in (4) and (5) respectively.

(4)   Mary is going to the opera tomorrow night.

(5)   Mary goes to the opera tomorrow night.

Similar to (1)–(3), from the analysis of (3)–(5) the purely future *will* in (3) also turns out to be modal. However, more has to be said about the meaning of (4) and (5). Contrasted with the regular future in (3), the forms in (4) and (5) seem to involve a sense of planning. This is evident when we look at (6). Let us assume that Mary is at the stage of preparing to put pencil to paper. Then 'drawing a rabbit' is true, although no part of the rabbit has as yet been drawn.

(6)   Mary is drawing a rabbit.

So, perhaps the stage of planning, or some other predetermination, is included in the activity, at least with some classes of verbs.[3] Moreover, when no planning is involved, futurative progressive and tenseless future are not applicable or their application is heavily restricted as in (7) and (8):

[?](7)   Mary is feeling unwell tomorrow night.

[?](8)   Mary feels unwell tomorrow night.[4]

The argument for modality comes from Dowty (1979): there is a hierarchy of predetermination involved in these three ways of expressing futurity. Tenseless future comes out as the strongest assertion, then futurative progressive, and finally the neutral regular future:

I'm doing such and such tonight should amount on my account to saying that I will do it only if I don't change my mind, but saying *I do such and such tonight* is saying in effect that something else besides my intention leads me to do it. *I will do such and such* makes a more neutral prediction about the future. (Dowty 1979: 162, emphasis in original)

This scale of predictability, involving external force, intentions, and a mere statement of future eventuality, seems to provide strong evidence for the modal character of futurity. Even if regular future comes out as neutral, it is so because it is the weakest step in expressing essentially evidential futurity. And, as a member of the class, it has to be classified as an expression of the semantic category of futurity. Futurity and its linguistic realizations cannot be kept apart.

The affinities (3) exhibits with (1) and (2) on the one hand, and (4) and (5) on the other, are best explained by a scale of epistemic modality. The gradation of intentions strongly suggests that *will* is modal. Instead of the ambiguity/temporality/modality trilemma, there is a gradation of the strength of intending the eventuality that results in various degrees of modal meaning communicated by *will*, as well as in various degrees of modality communicated by various future-oriented forms such as futurative progressive and tenseless future.

In Section 6.4, I corroborate this argument by providing a DS analysis of examples (1)–(5). The scales of modality for (1)–(3) and (3)–(5) are founded on Grice's (2001) unitary theory of modality. According to Grice's Equivocality Thesis, alethic and deontic modalities are univocal, derived from one conceptual core of *acceptability*. In the formal analysis, I entertain the possibility that Grice's acceptability can be introduced as a modal operator (ACC) to DRT. However, since the treatment of *will* in DRT relies on representing tenses, ACC is not compatible with it. But it is compatible with an account where the representation of meaning draws on all the sources of meaning information that are active in the process of discourse interpretation. So, it is compatible with DS and can be introduced to the MR. I suggest such MRs for examples (1)–(5). These MRs also capture the gradation of modality in the two interrelated scales (1)–(3) and (3)–(5).

6.2 The modality of *will*

One way of accounting for the various senses of *will* as exemplified in sentences (1)–(3) would be to admit its ambiguity. This descriptive solution is offered, for example, by Hornstein:

the various readings of *will*... indicate that it is an ambiguous morpheme in English. In one of its guises, it is a future-tense marker. In addition, it is a modal that underlies the imperative. In this latter role, it is roughly translatable as *must*. (Hornstein 1990: 38)

The main question is to assess the status of this alleged 'ambiguity'. If it is to mean that *will* acquires different readings in different contexts, there is no harm in adopting this term. However, the term 'ambiguity' is so theoretically loaded in semantics and pragmatics that assigning this property to *will* would be at least confusing. First, as Grice (1978) proposed and post-Griceans have endorsed, senses are not to be postulated beyond necessity. Where no ambiguity appears as a real, verifiable stage of utterance processing, it should not be postulated. This is captured by the principle of MOR.[5] The generally accepted alternative to an ambiguity account is to invoke the generality of sense and the underspecification of the semantic representation. In other words, at some early stage of utterance processing, *will* can go either way: to stand for futurity, or epistemic or dispositional necessity. This solution is more plausible than a postulate of ambiguity based on different syntactic constructions into which *will* can enter.

Hornstein rejects the attempts to assimilate the future tense to a modal and provides a range of examples showing their different behaviour. However, this rejection seems to rest on a conceptual mistake. In a unified treatment of *will*, the future tense need not be *identified* with a modal. One merely points out that *will* allows for a unified semantic representation that makes use of the degrees of modality. In other words, it is perfectly natural to say that *will* marks primarily the future temporal reference and at the same time that this temporal reference is a subcategory of modality, notwithstanding the different syntactic patterns and collocations into which the various senses of *will* can enter. Nevertheless, as I shall argue shortly, this is not necessarily the optimal solution.

Now, as I have argued in Part I and extensively elsewhere,[6] underspecification does not stand up to the fact that some interpretations of such multiple-reading sentences are more salient than others and arise without the help of the context. In other words, since there are default interpretations, under-specification need not always ensue. Instead, there is a default reading and the departures from the default which correspond to the lower degrees of the relevant intention. These departures are ordered on a scale that is driven by these degrees of intentions and intentionality. 'Unreal' ambiguities, that is ambiguities that do not arise in utterance processing, need not be postulated, but neither do underspecified representations. It is important not to equate this thesis with the claim that there is no semantic ambiguity and no under-specification. Both may be the case in utterance processing but neither needs to be invoked for the semantics of, say, definite descriptions, propositional attitude reports, various senses of *will*, and, we can say tentatively, various senses of sentential connectives and number terms (see Chapters 8 and 9). In DS, *will* obtains an analysis along these lines: there is no ambiguity, no underspecification, and there is a gradation of modality exhibited in the various uses of *will*. Before moving on to the analysis, let us briefly assess some of the relevant extant arguments pertaining to the modality stance.

Tense, aspect (including aspectual class of a verb), mood, and adverbials are the most obvious means of conveying time reference. But temporality is the property of events and states and it is not an exaggeration to say that all sentence components can contribute, in one way or another, to conveying the temporality of the described situation. The sentential connective *and* frequently triggers a temporal reading such as *and then*. Tense interacts with these other vehicles, for example with aktionsart properties, and produces the message of temporality. Seen in this way, this 'conspiracy' can be given an universalist formal account, without resorting to unnecessary ambiguities or language-specific mechanisms for embedded tense. For example, the overlapping reading of (9) is associated with the stativity of 'be at home', as evidenced by the contrast with (10) where an overlapping reading is not possible.

(9)   The president will/may/must be at home (now).

(10)   The president will/may/must leave (now). (from Gennari 2003: 45).[7]

Now, for our purposes of elucidating the semantics of futurity, we have to establish whether the assumption that *will* 'conspires' with other elements of the sentence to render the future or present time reference is sufficient to assume that future temporal information is the default for *will*—a default that is overridden by stativity. Contra Gennari (2003: 49, fn 8),[8] the fact that *will* patterns with modals in the test in (9) and (10) suggests that this assumption is unwarranted. Similarly, Gennari's (2003: 50) example, quoted here as (11), obtains a future or overlapping reading, depending on the contextually specified reference time.

(11)   John will be at home.

The situational context, the lexical and syntactic knowledge of what 'being at home' means, combined with the information about John's customs and habits, give us one or the other meaning. Dowty (1986: 41) mentions specifically (i) principles for interpreting the ordering of sentences in discourse, (ii) Grice's conversational implicature, and (iii) common-sense reasoning of the hearer as factors that influence the interpretation. Translating (i) and (ii) into current theoretical discourse, we obtain accounts such as (i') the rhetorical structure theory of Asher and Lascarides (e.g. 1998a, 2003) with its rules of the interpretation of consecutive events as the order of *Narration*, state plus event as *Background*, etc., and (ii') post-Gricean principles such as Levinson's (1995, 2000) Q, I, and M heuristics.

Aspectual oppositions of verbs are often subjective. They are such by force of referring to situation-internal time. We have just discussed their interaction with the semantics of *will*. This interaction has been thoroughly researched in the long tradition from Reichenbach (1948) and Vendler (1967), through Dowty (1979, 1986), to new formal proposals (e.g. Leith and Cunningham 2001; Gennari 2003). It has been acknowledged that information from the aspectual category the verb can express in a particular context of use is part and parcel of the semantics of temporality. So, does it follow that the semantics of temporality must be a subjectivist semantics? Insofar as the relation between the eventuality and the sentence is concerned, it does, because we want to get the truth conditions right. In other words, if *will* produces an overlapping reading in sentences about states, then we have to make it relevant for the truth conditions that the sentence concerns a state. If we do not, we have to search further for an explanation of the differences between (5) and (3). However, it is only the speaker's decision concerning the way of presenting a situation (as a state or process for example) that is subjective. The semantic theory, pertaining to uttered sentences rather than mental processes preceding them, is not subjectivist. All that we need seems to be the agreement that there is a one-to-many relation between situations and the aspectual classes used in their descriptions.

All in all, the semantic status of *will* is as yet unresolved. Some linguists take *will* to be modal (e.g. Enç 1996), others to be ambiguous between tense and modal (Hornstein 1990), and yet others as predominantly a marker of tense (Dahl 1985). Enç (1996: 350) observes that *will* does not pattern with the Simple Past as far as the sequence of tense is concerned. While (12) can have a simultaneous reading, in (13) the second occurrence of *will* is shifted into the future with respect to the first:

(12)   Mary said that she was tired.

(13)   Mary will say that she will be tired.

Further, when the present tense is embedded under past, the present retains its reference to the time of speaking as in (14). On the other hand, when the present is embedded under *will*, it may have a shifted reading as in (15). In this respect *will* patterns with modal expressions rather than with tenses, as is evidenced by comparing these examples with (16). *Will* behaves like future-shifting modals in that the present tense of the embedded sentence may refer to the future rather than to the time of speaking.

(14)   John said that Mary is upset.

(15)   John will say that Mary is upset.

(16)   John must claim that he is sick. (from Enç 1996: 352–3).

By force of this argument, *will* seems to be modal. It involves a prediction which is a type of modality. It often refers to the future, but so do other modalities as in (17):

(17)   You must visit us next weekend.

Now, reference to alternative possible worlds is often taken to be characteristic of modality. But (18) is undoubtedly modal although it refers to one world:

(18)   It is certain that Copernicus discovered heliocentrism. (see Enç 1996: 348).

So, the fact that sentences with *will* refer to one possible world is not an argument against its modal status.

Note that Enç (1987) also demonstrates that while *will* and its temporal sense patterns with modals, past and present are 'true tenses'. On this account, past and present are tenses and are to be regarded as referential expressions standing for intervals. They are not operators but temporal arguments of the verb. Let us now gloss over a couple of sample views that accept some version of the argument analysis of *will*. Ogihara (1996) adopts the standpoint that verbs have argument places for temporal terms. *Will* is a modal with a future reference. Following Abusch (1988: 9), he analyses *will* as *Pres+woll*, and in particular Pres[woll[V]], where *woll* is the English future auxiliary, neutral as to tense, that is realized as *will* or *would*.[9] *Pres+woll* accounts for the futurity of the embedded *is* in (19) and for the 'double access' of (20):

(19)   Next year, John will claim that Mary is his wife.

(20)   Bill sought a man who will be leaving. (from Ogihara 1996: 123, 178).

While in (19) *is* is interpreted as future because it matches in tense with *will*, in (20) two readings are available, on one of which *will* refers to a time prior to the time of utterance. Ogihara's relative tense theory, where tense morphemes are embedded in structurally higher tenses, allows for this explanation. So, while it is possible to hold that tenses are not operators and are not a species of modality (see e.g. Higginbotham 2001; Hornstein 1990), the term 'tense' has to acquire an intra-theoretical specificity there.

It has to be observed that the analyses that begin with the composition of the English *will* are conspicuously anglocentric. Arguably, they are also committed to the relativity of conceptualization in that even if there is a future auxiliary in English that is neutral with respect to tense, it would be very difficult to postulate its existence on a conceptual level in languages without the sequence of tense (henceforth: SOT). Alternatively, we would have to say that the future tenseless modal is a theoretical manoeuvre and has nothing to do with the level of concepts. If, on the other hand, the conceptualization of time and modality can be brought down to some common, universal level, perhaps even a non-linguistic level,[10] then the decomposition of *will* has to be compatible with this universal conceptual system and we would have to have a well supported mapping from concepts to their linguistic generalizations. This can only be done on the level above the 'submodal', that is the semantic level of futurity. In addition, there is substantial evidence that modality has semantic scope over time, not the other way round (see Nuyts 2001: 335). So, all that remains is to pursue the semantic line of argument for the modality of the future.

In what follows, I shall adopt the operator analysis, for the reasons discussed above and because it best captures the interrelations between (1)–(3) and (3)–(5).[11] The problems with the SOT phenomena, standardly brought in as an argument against the operator analysis, will obtain a solution by employing eventualities and relations between eventualities in DS. MRs allow for expressing such interrelations by incorporating the earlier-than/later-than devices.[12] To repeat, since my MRs are no longer derived principally from syntax (DR-theoretic 'triggering configuration') but instead rely on a variety of contextual clues for temporal information, they capture the shifts of the temporal deictic centre. The working of such MRs is demonstrated in Section 6.4.

Let us now see how DS, with its intentionality-based argumentation, applies to English *will*. To repeat, the ambiguity position seems to be a dispreferred option by force of Grice's MOR. It seems that if we can provide an explanatorily adequate unitary analysis, this analysis is to be preferred. Moreover, by PoL of DS, we avoid unwarranted levels of meaning representation. Communicating temporality by means of *will* can be intended very strongly, less strongly, or to various other degrees culminating with very weak 'temporality' intention. If we accept this gradation of intentions, then various degrees of intentions correspond to various interpretations and neither ambiguity nor underspecification ensue. In sum, the intentionality-based explanation proceeds as follows. Intentionality is a property of mental states that makes them have objects as correlates. Derivatively, intentionality is instantiated in the property of linguistic expressions that makes them refer to individuals or states of affairs. This association can be stronger or weaker, it can be captured in an analysis in terms of possible-worlds semantics. In modal expressions, the degree of the speaker's commitment to the described eventuality is involved. This gradation entitles us to conclude that the future *will* is not qualitatively different from modal *will*. In sum, the gradation of intentionality strongly suggests that *will* is modal. However, the association of the degree of intentionality with the default reading of a modal expression will have to change. The 'most modal' reading is the one that corresponds to the *weakest* intentionality and at the same time is the default. Modal operators express detachment from the propositions they operate on and this reversal of the default connection comes as a natural concomitant of this fact. This proposal is taken up in Section 6.4 in the context of Grice's unified account of modality translated into DS.

All in all, this intentionality-based argument supports Enç's (1996) view that futurity and dispositional modality are not disjoint. The future *will* can be regarded as a type of a modal *will* in that it involves a prediction that is itself a type of modality.

6.3 Future as modality

In *De Interpretatione*, Aristotle classifies future with modals. While propositions about the present and the past must be true or false, with regard to
future events he talks about 'potentiality in contrary directions' which gives
rise to corresponding affirmation and denial (Aristotle, in 1928: 16a–23b).
Similarly, Prior puts forward a conjecture that we might try to treat past and
future differently, 'with one type of solution for future-existers and a different
one for past-existers' (1967: 174).

The modality of the semantic category of futurity is intuitively plausible
when we consider that the future is not the mirror-image of the past: while the
past can be represented as a time line, the future is a bunch of possible time
lines stemming out of the present moment, as in Fig. 6.1.

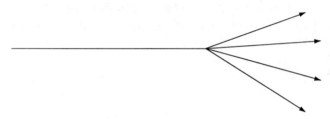

FIGURE 6.1. Past, present and future

The overlapping reading of (21) (epistemic *will*, 'what can reasonably be
expected') and the reading of obligation of (22) (deontic *will*) testify to the
modal status of *will*.

(21)   Mary will be eating her breakfast now.

(22)   You will/shall get it back tomorrow.[13]

The volitional and habitual *will* are further evidence that the expression of
futurity is interwoven with the expression of the degree to which the proposition can be accepted. In most Indo-European languages, the forms for
future tenses can be traced back to the expressions of intention, desire, the
subjunctive, and general expressions of non-factivity (see Palmer 1979: 5–6;
Lyons 1977: 809–23). Fleischman (1982: 23)[14] proposes a more detailed account. Future tenses arise historically out of the following forms: (i) inceptive
or inchoative aspectuals; (ii) modals, mostly of obligation, volition, uncertainty, and unreality; and (iii) goal-oriented categories, such as verbs of
motion meaning 'go'. Now, Fleischman observes that verbs with modal
functions also function as futures. But instead of collapsing tense and mood
into one category or subsuming future tense under modality, she proposes a

'bidirectional semantic shift': modals evolve into tense forms, which in turn acquire modal meanings. Uncertainty and modality seem to be part of futurity in many languages in that future tenses are neutralized in subjunctive and negative contexts (see Ultan (1972: 94–5) for an extensive list of relevant languages). In sum:

Futures are universally temporal/aspectual or temporal/modal or all three; and the ratio of these elements to one another in a given form is subject to diachronic fluctuation as a function of the shifting 'division of labour' within the verbal system at various periods in the development of a language. (Fleischman 1982: 84–5)

For example, Fleischman claims that in Romance and English the Simple Future becomes more and more modal in character, whereas the future tense function is taken over by periphrastic constructions such as the *go*-construction in 'to be going to' (cf. Fleischman 1982: 135). Next, quite independently of this diachronic hypothesis, it is the fact that 'willan' meant 'to want' in Old English and some of this meaning still permeates the uses of *will*. Werth (1997: 112) derives the senses of *will* from differences in intentionality: the volitional *will* conveys the subject's intention, and this intention in turn conveys the high probability that the eventuality will take place.[15] Woods (1997), reaching similar conclusions, proposes that *will* reports a 'tendency' or a 'disposition'.[16]

The modal tint of *will* is reflected in Steedman's (1997) proposal to regard the form in (23) as 'true future tense', symmetric to the past tense, as presented in the diagrams in (23a) and (23b). Steedman uses here Reichenbach's (1948) distinction between reference time (R), speech time (S), and event time (E).

(23)   I go to London next Tuesday. (after Steedman 1997: 907).

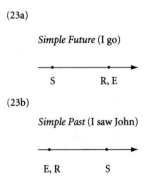

(23a)

Simple Future (I go)

S   R, E

(23b)

Simple Past (I saw John)

E, R   S

'I shall go' is regarded as the modal future, with the modal overlay that is orthogonal to the information given in the Reichenbachian diagrams in (23a) and (23b). To compare and contrast, we shall retain the concept of the 'degree of modality' in expressing the future. However, instead of 'true future tense', we shall use the concept of the 'strength of intending' in order to explain how the form in (23) becomes the 'pure' expression of future time reference.

All in all, evidence and theoretical arguments in support of the view that *futurity*, not just *will*, is modality are as yet very fragmented. Some of these views are embedded in a more radical view that time in general is just modality; others distinguish qualitatively between the past and present on one hand, and the future on the other. Just as for Parsons '[t]ensed properties are dispositional properties' (2002: 18) and for Ludlow (1999: 157) future is probability and possibility, I will now argue that in DS the future comes with degrees of probability, commitment, or acceptability of a proposition. These characteristics are definitional of futurity and hence also apply to the analysis of the English *will*. So, DS will provide a uniform theory to unite extant evidence.

6.4 The analysis

6.4.1 *Tense-free futurity?*

In Part I it was argued that a psychologically plausible theory of discourse processing has to postulate one level of meaning representation to which information is contributed by WS, CD, SCD 1, and CPI 1. Merger representations of DS, that is reanalysed DRSs, were proposed to serve this purpose. They allow for representing multisentential discourses as units, for accounting for anaphoric (including presuppositional) links even in long discourses, and most importantly for contextual update, including both semantically encoded and pragmatically conveyed information on one level of representation. Accounting for changing context is the definitional property of dynamic semantic theories. Just as discourse interpretation is incremental, so MRs are constructed, so to speak, bit by bit, where earlier chunks of the representation constitute the background for interpreting the following chunks.

Kamp and Reyle's (1993) account of *will* is couched in terms of the 'earlier–later' relation, where times are regarded as intervals, and the reference point is fixed and is normally the utterance time (n). Sentence (3), repeated below, acquires a representation as in Fig. 6.2 according to this account:

(3)   Mary will go to the opera tomorrow night.

In terms of construction rules for temporal reference, for future tense we introduce into the DRS condition set the conditions $n < t$ and (i) $e \subseteq t$ for events, and (ii) $s \circ t$ for states, where t stands for the time of the eventuality,

FIGURE 6.2. The DRS for sentence (3)

e for an event, *s* for a state, < for temporal precedence, ⊆ for temporal inclusion, and o for temporal overlap. The sentence structure is rendered as normal by the predicate-argument(s) structure. In Kamp and Reyle's version of DRT, this is a way of representing grammatical tenses. The general principle is this:

The algorithm must represent the temporal information that is contained in the tense of a sentence and in its temporal adverb (if there is one). (Kamp and Reyle 1993: 512)

and

[The feature] TENSE has three possible values, *past*, *present* and *future*, signifying that the described eventuality lies before, at, or after the utterance time, respectively. The value of TENSE for a given sentence S is determined by the tense of the verb of S. When the main verb is in the simple past, TENSE = *past*; when it is in the simple present, TENSE = *pres*; and when the verb complex contains the auxiliary *will*, TENSE = *fut*. (Kamp and Reyle 1993: 512–13)

Just as 'goes' by default expresses simple present and 'is going' continuous present, so 'will go' by default expresses simple future. Kamp and Reyle's analysis works well for these default meanings. Where it becomes problematic is the departures from these defaults such as tenseless future of (5), futurative progressive in (4), and also *will* of epistemic and dispositional necessity as in (1) and (2) respectively.

In the DS-theoretic analysis of the future time reference, this reliance on tense is abandoned. MRs contain information from the context of interpretation of the utterance of the sentence and the output of all the four sources of meaning information merges before we obtain a compositional representation. To make a further comparison with DRT, just as in DRSs we can anchor the feature TENSE to the grammatical tenses, so (and even more so) in MRs we can anchor *time* to the situation of discourse. And the situation may call, for example, for the interpretation of *will* as a marker of epistemic or dispositional necessity. Similarly, the context, and even the linguistic context in the form of a temporal adverb as in (5) and (4) repeated below, may dictate the assignment of future time reference where there is no future tense. If the prediction of (3) were expressed by means of tenseless future or futurative progressive as in (5) and (4) respectively, the representation would have to remain the same as far as representing temporality is concerned because (5) and (4) are interpreted as referring to a future time.

(5)   Mary goes to the opera tomorrow night.

(4)   Mary is going to the opera tomorrow night.

The differences between (3), (4), and (5) concern the strength of the assertion, the strength of evidence or claim. In other words, they pertain to modality. In Section 6.4.3, this difference will be captured in DS as a unitary modal operator with varying 'strength'.

All in all, in addition to the properties of *will* exemplified in (1)–(3), the DS approach has to account for the concept of futurity. As was exemplified in (3)–(5), futurity can be expressed not only by the feature TENSE using the auxiliary *will/shall*, but also by tenseless future and futurative progressive. It can also be expressed by periphrastic forms such as *to be going to + verb, to be about to + verb*, etc. We have observed that there is a significant difference in semantic behaviour between the present and the past on the one hand, and the future on the other, and have gathered a collection of partial arguments in support of the future as modality. Whether this is a qualitative difference, that is whether the present and the past are definitely not modal, is a question taken up in Section 6.6. We can now strengthen this tentative proposal by testing how a modal future can be accounted for by using a general modality operator in MRs. This operator will have to account for the affinities among (3), (4), and (5) that are not (and need not be) captured in DRT. More importantly, it will have to render the degrees of modality of *will*, as was proposed in Section 6.2 in line with the principles of DS.

6.4.2 *The* Acc *operator*

Modality is not a clearly demonstrable category. Deontic and epistemic modalities are clearly distinct concepts. Furthermore, epistemic modality includes both judgements of necessity and possibility and the degrees of commitment based on evidence (see Palmer 1986: 224). However, the concept of the degree of commitment permeates all the modal terms. I shall use this intuition in proposing MRs which capture various degrees of such commitment.

The first task is to demonstrate how (1)–(3) on the one hand, and (3)–(5) on the other, are interrelated. The next task is to provide a formal account of (1)–(5) that would make these interconnections explicit. Sentence (3) obviously has future time reference. One may argue that this is so because of the temporal adverb 'tomorrow' and hence there is no context-free default involved. However, (3a) evokes the same sense of futurity:[17]

(3a)   Mary will go to the opera.

In DR-theoretic terms, we simply have an event *e* of Mary's going to the opera at a time interval *t* which follows the utterance time *n* (see Fig. 6.2). Now, (2) should have present time reference with the habitual aspectual marker. On the other hand, (5) should have future time reference. So, taking tense as a starting point will not do. Intuitively, what differs between (3), (4), and (5) is the *degree* of certainty, speaker's commitment, or speaker's evidence that the event of Mary's going to the opera will take place. On the other hand, what the tokens of *will* in (1)–(3) have in common is constituting a scale of degree of modality with which *will* is used. It seems that a common framework for all these cases is needed and the best place to start would be to identify the category which can allow for such degrees of commitment. Having provided reasons against ambiguity of any kind, we will settle on a modal operator. We shall use for this purpose Grice's argument for deriving modals from the common source of *acceptability*.

Grice (2001: 90) proposed that modals are 'univocal across the practical/ alethic divide'. He called this an Equivocality Thesis. In the formal argument he introduced a rationality operator '*Acc*' meaning 'it is (rationally) acceptable that'. This operator accounts for both the modality of (24) and that of (25):

(24)   John should be in London by now.

(25)   John should take more care of his business affairs.

He introduced modal operators for modalities in (24) and (25), alethic ($\vdash$) and practical (!) respectively, and demonstrated that practical and alethic 'must' and 'ought/should' fall under the general concept of acceptability. We obtain the following senses:

Acc $\vdash$ p   'it is acceptable that it is the case that *p*'
Acc ! p   'it is acceptable that let it be that *p*'

For our purpose, it is convenient to think of practical and alethic as deontic and epistemic; nothing will hinge on this adjustment of conceptualization. So, in other words, there are reasons for belief (alethic, epistemic, dynamic) and reasons for action (practical, deontic) and they are traceable to the same concept.[18] Grice also attempted to derive practical modality from alethic in that if something 'must [deontically] be the case', it is so because it 'must [epistemically] be the case, (see Grice 2001: 90–1). This philosophical discussion will not be further pursued here. Suffice it to say that this seems a strong and intuitively plausible argument for the underlying identity of various types of modality as 'it is reasonable to think that'.

In the light of Grice's arguments for the uniform operator of *Acc*, it is at least plausible to suggest that *will*, being a species of modality for the reasons to do with avoiding unnecessary ambiguity or underspecification provided earlier in this chapter, can be subsumed under the same category of acceptability. Namely, there is epistemic *will*, derived from the concept 'it is acceptable that', followed by the specification of time. If this move proves successful, it will account for the modal status of *will* and allow for its differing time reference. Acceptability, meaning 'it is reasonable to think that', 'it is rationally plausible that', allows for degrees. An event can be more, or less, acceptable due to being more, or less, certain, allowing for more, or less, commitment on the part of the speaker. For example, dispositional necessity in (2) comes with stronger acceptability than epistemic necessity in (1), which in turn comes with stronger acceptability than the regular future *will* in (3). In (3), the reading is 'it is to be expected that she will go', 'she will probably go'.

Now, just as the modal and temporal *will* can be subsumed under *Acc*, so can the futurative progressive and tenseless future in (4) and (5) respectively. If I am correct, then in terms of DRT, they should ideally both result in DRSs as in Fig. 6.2. This is so because DRSs have to capture the mental representation of the discourse and hence although there is no future tense expression involved in (4) or (5), the DRS will have to reflect the true semantic temporality of the event. This is, however, problematic. The indications in the grammar and lexicon are contradictory: tense and the temporal adverbial cannot be straightforwardly reconciled.

On DS, tense is no constraint because compositionality applies after information from the four sources has merged. Just as we can account for different strengths of *Acc* in (1)–(3), so, and even more so, can we account for them in (5), (4), and (3). 'Even more so' because describing the properties of a lexical item *will* in its different uses in terms of degree of certainty as in (1)–(3) comes at a price of making comparisons across different eventualities. On the contrary, making comparisons between different ways of expressing the future is inherently graded in terms of certainty and commitment: (3), (4), and (5) refer to the same eventuality, signalling different degrees of commitment on the part of the speaker.[19] Following Dowty (1979), we take it that tenseless future corresponds to the strongest assertion, futurative progressive comes next, and regular future comes out as the weakest, neutral. In DS, this strength of assertion can be accounted for by means of the degree of the informative intention, paralleled on the level of mental states by the degree of intentionality. The MRs for (1)–(3) and (4)–(5) will now have to obey these findings concerning their interrelations and gradation of the strength of intentionality and intentions. For convenience, I repeat this set of examples below. In representing the set A, we are implementing the earlier findings concerning the properties of *will*. In the set B, we are implementing the earlier findings concerning expressions of temporality. The sentences in each set are presented in the order of decreasing intentionality.[20]

Set A

(2) Mary will sometimes go to the opera in her tracksuit. (dispositional necessity)

(1) Mary will be in the opera now. (epistemic necessity)

(3) Mary will go to the opera tomorrow night. (regular future)

Set B

(5) Mary goes to the opera tomorrow night. (tenseless future)

(4) Mary is going to the opera tomorrow night. (futurative progressive)

(3) Mary will go to the opera tomorrow night. (regular future)

The first principle to be followed in representing them is Grice's MOR, that is avoiding unnecessary ambiguity. So, if five distinct representations can be avoided because there is a more 'unified' and otherwise equally adequate analysis, the latter should be preferred. Just as the senses of *will* in Set A are related, so are the expressions of futurity in Set B. However, neither should we relegate Set B to one representation, say, as in Fig. 6.2. The difference of the degree of intentionality and intentions is meaningful and it has to be captured in an MR. When we make use of the *Acc* operator, we can capture all these dependencies.

6.4.3 *The application of* Acc

In DS, I introduce into merger representations the operator 'ACC' that is essentially modelled on Grice's *Acc*. The main difference is that ACC in MRs operates on eventualities. Following the well-tested practice of DRT, we distinguish two types of eventuality, namely states and events.

Bringing sets A and B together conforms to our earlier proposal that (i) *will* is modal, and, as a related issue, that (ii) the semantic category of futurity is modality. I will now attempt to account for these examples by using this overarching modal category of acceptability in the form of the ACC operator. As before, I shall be frequently comparing and contrasting MRs with the DRSs of DRT in order to make the differences in aims and assumptions clear.

In (3), it is not only the future time reference that we have to represent but also the degree of acceptability. In DRT, we could try to add the ACC operator to the language and represent (3) as in *Fig. 6.3. *ACC e* stands for 'event *e* is acceptable to the speaker'. Note that we replaced Grice's 'Acc ⊢ p' with 'ACC e', omitting the specification of the alethic/epistemic 'it is the case that'. This omission is justified by the fact that 'it is the case that *p*' does not mean a departure from the interpretation of non-modal assertions, as well as by the gradation of modality. I shall return to this issue in more detail a little later in this section, once the required machinery for representing modality is in place.

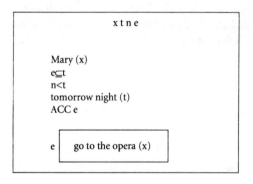

*FIGURE 6.3. A DRS with ACC e

It has to be remembered that DRS-construction rules operate on relevant parts of syntactic configurations. Therefore, in order for *Fig. 6.3 to work, it is essential that the syntactic theory adopted reflect, or at least be compatible with, our account of futurity as modality on the one hand, and our account of *will* on the other.

However, *Fig. 6.3 is problematic for various other reasons. The most important one is that the ACC operator does not yet give us the required distinction between different ways of expressing futurity. Next, operators on eventualities are not, at present, part of the DRT language and would have to be formally introduced. Let us focus on the first difficulty before we move on to the condition *ACC e*. What we need in order to represent how (3) fits in the scales for (1)–(3) and for (3)–(5) is distinguishing degrees of commitment to the proposition expressing *e*, or degrees of probability. In other words, we need degrees of modality. The simplest thing to do would be to index ACC for these three sentences. But this will not yet capture the concept of *acceptability to a degree*. We can use here a device well-known from hidden-indexical theory where the type of mode of presentation accounts for the differences between different readings of, say, propositional attitude reports. In Chapter 5, I used for this purpose Schiffer's (1992) $\Phi^* m$. To repeat briefly, sentence (11) from Chapter 5 (here (26)) has the logical form as in (12) from Chapter 5 (here (27)):

(26)   Ralph believes that Fido is a dog.

(27) $\exists\, m(\Phi^* m\ \&\ \mathrm{Bel}(\mathrm{Ralph}, <\mathrm{Fido}, \mathrm{doghood}>, m))$

where Φ^* is 'an implicitly referred to and contextually determined type of mode of presentation' (Schiffer 1992: 503). In Chapter 5, I proposed instead the degrees to which *m* has to be specified. In other words, *m* can be coarse-grained or fine-grained. In default interpretations, it does not contribute to the representation at all. Sometimes it is relevant to the meaning of the utterance under what guise we think of the referent (say, Fido as a gold medallist of a dog show but not as your neighbour's noisy poodle), at other times it is irrelevant, yet on other occasions all that may matter is the referential mistake made by the speaker. It seems that we can use an analogous principle for futurity. Sentence (3) will now be represented by a DRS in *Fig. 6.4.

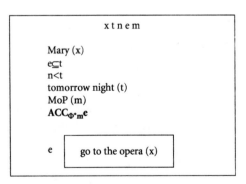

*FIGURE 6.4. A DRS with $\mathrm{ACC}_{\Phi^* m}e$

Using some elements of neo-Davidsonian analysis of events (Parsons 1990), adapted to match our earlier theoretical orientation, the simplified logical form for the sentences in Set B will now be as in*(28):

*(28) $\exists m \exists e (\Phi^* m \ \& \ ACC_m (\text{Going-to-the-opera } (e) \ \& \ \text{Subject (Mary, } e)$
&Tomorrow-night $(e)))$

Note that in *Fig. 6.4 m is treated as a discourse referent. The following argument will show why this is an unnecessary complication. Instead, information about modality will be introduced directly into the semantics.

The representation in *(28) will not suffice. As was argued in Chapter 5 when we attempted MRs for attitude reports, Schiffer's $\Phi^* m$, as an element of MR, would suffer from overdetermination. It would provide more information than is necessary for getting the compositional meaning right. Hence, for attitude reports, I have introduced the degree of m instead, where $\Phi^* m$ takes values from 0 to 1. The logical form for Set B will now incorporate information that m matters to a certain degree of granularity. In place of m, I introduce Δ that stands for that ingredient of ACC that makes it into a particular type of modality. Δ^n stands for the degree n of granularity of Δ and is substituted for $\Phi^* m$ as in ?(29):

?(29) $\exists \Delta \exists e \exists n (\Delta^n \ \& \ ACC_\Delta^n \ (\text{Going-to-the-opera } (e) \ \& \ \text{Subject (Mary, } e) \ \&$
Tomorrow-night $(e)))$[21]

Note that Δ is left unspecified. As was remarked earlier in more general terms, Δ can take on Grice's '⊢' or '!' for 'it is the case that...' and 'let it be that...'. However, our ACC is not exactly Grice's *Acc* operator. For one thing, it takes states and events, rather than propositions, as arguments. Next, we do not want to commit ourselves to Grice's 'alethic/practical' divide; ACC may require more types of Δ. The latter issue cannot be resolved quickly; it is a topic for an in-depth, data-based investigation. So, at present, we will not discuss the typologies of modalities.[22] But what we can do is leave Δ unspecified for the task at hand, namely for the analysis of examples (1)–(5). The modal senses they exemplify all rely on '⊢', 'it is the case that', and 'it is the case that' is not specific to modals: it can be left out as a default ingredient of the interpretation of assertions.

I am aware of the fact that 'it is the case that' introduces the problem of the time of evaluation of propositions, and, in DS, the time of evaluation of MRs. This is the philosophical issue of presentism vs. the tenseless theory of time that we will have to put aside until Section 6.6, and even there we will be able to afford only a limited insight into this big philosophical problem. So, for the time being, let us go along with Grice's theoretical assumptions and accept his '⊢', as well as with the DS-theoretic assumptions and accept its default status. In short, we will have ACC_Δ^n that reads as 'it is acceptable, to the degree n, that it is the case that $[e$ or $s]$'.

The next point of departure from *Fig. 6.4 is obvious: we cannot proceed to construct DRSs if our aim is to represent post-merger meanings. For this purpose, we need MRs. To repeat, MRs combine the output of various sources of meaning information and as such are not so reliant on the triggering configuration. The various uses of *will* in (1)–(3), as well as the various ways of representing futurity in (3)–(5) are not problematic. The move from the grammar or lexicon to the use of the word or construction is by no means mysterious: the WS is not compositional, it is the merger that is.

We can now come back to the second problem with *Fig. 6.3 (and also *Fig. 6.4): operators on eventualities are not at present part of the DRT language and would have to be formally introduced. We should thus attempt to introduce them, not into DRT, but rather directly into DS. Let us look at the logical form in $^?$(29). It seems that we need not make any significant adjustments in order to do so. Unlike τ of Chapter 5, e is a Davidsonian construct, not a representation of a particular event with its spatiotemporal and other specifications. Whatever we say about es and ss by adding ACC_Δ^n, we can also say by means of adding another argument to $^?$(29). Unlike *Bel* of belief contexts that operates on τ, ACC operates on extensional objects. The correct representation is arrived at by means of MR conditions other than ACC_Δ^n e or ACC_Δ^n s and e/s: [...]$_{WS}$. The operator analysis is innocuous.[23] As we shall see later on in this section, the formalization will also be innocuous.

The MRs for (3), (4), and (5) are constructed as in Fig. 6.5, with the Δ^n varying from, let us say, Δ^{tf} for the tenseless future form in (5), through Δ^{fp} for the futurative progressive in (4), to Δ^{rf} for the regular future in (3). The referential reading of the proper name 'Mary' is given by the CD. 'ACC_Δ^n e' is to be read as 'event e is acceptable to the speaker to the degree n of the type of modality Δ'.[24]

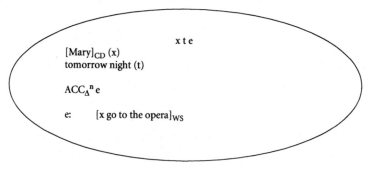

FIGURE 6.5. Generalized MR for (3)–(5)

Fig. 6.5 is just a generalization over the representations of the particular utterances made by means of (3), (4), and (5). It is not yet a full MR of a particular act of communication performed by means of (3), (4), or (5). To recall, in DS we represent acts of communication rather than linguistic competence and Fig. 6.5 is not such a representation. We can call it a *generalized MR*. We can now move on to representing the particular utterances. Note that the representations of temporality of the event such as

$e \subseteq t$ (event e is temporally included in time t)

$n < t$ (the present moment n precedes time t)

are not needed in the MR because the value n of Δ takes care of the specification of time. It does so by drawing on the combination of WS and CD or WS and CPI 1, as is represented in Figs 6.6–6.8.

The three indices of Δ, namely *rf*, *fp*, and *tf*, correspond to three degrees of modality, derived from the three degrees of informative intention[25] and at the same time three degrees of intentionality of the corresponding mental state, as was summarized in the DI principle of DS in Section 2.2.2. In Δ^{tf}, reference is made to the future event without expressing any degree of detachment from the proposition expressed. Hence, this is the case of the strongest intentionality. In Δ^{fp}, the degree of commitment of the speaker to the proposition expressed is lower and hence a higher degree of modality is present: modality is in an inversely proportional relation to the degree of commitment or assertability, possibility, evidence, etc. It is also in an inversely proportional relation to the degree of intentionality of the corresponding mental state as well as to the degree of the communicative intention with which the proposition was uttered. In Δ^{rf}, we have the highest degree of modality and the lowest degree of commitment.

In other words, the degrees of detachment are assessed when we juxtapose the *grammatical forms* used in a language to express a future eventuality. I am not suggesting that the form with tenseless future (and hence with no, or very little, detachment) as in example (5) is the default way of expressing the future just because it corresponds to the strongest intentionality. It would be the default if future were merely time rather than modality. However, we have argued that it is modal and have brought in a variety of arguments in support, that led to including (5) as a sub-case of Fig. 6.5. Hence, the default is the 'most modal' of the three forms, that is the standard, regular future in (3). Its MR reflects this default status by indexing ACC for the CD source of meaning information as in Fig. 6.6.

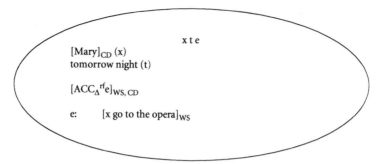

FIGURE 6.6. Regular future

Examples (4) and (5) can now be represented as progressive departures from the cognitive default of expressing futurity by means of the regular future. Both futurative progressive and tenseless future are output of the sources WS and CPI 1 as in the MRs in Figs 6.7 and 6.8. WS accounts for the futurity of 'is going' by combining it with the meaning of the temporal adverbial present in the sentence structure, and CPI 1 produces the final inference to, so to speak, *futurity with a stronger commitment than the default,* namely, judging by all the evidence available, futurative progressive.

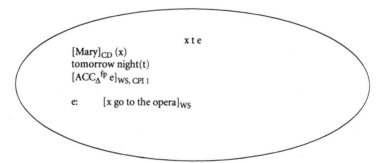

FIGURE 6.7. Futurative progressive

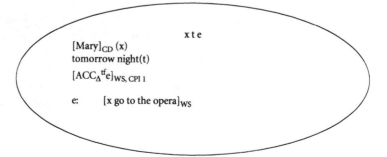

FIGURE 6.8. Tenseless future

Note that just as the temporal specification is excluded from *e*, so is the identification of the subject *x*, and, even, the identification of the route to the intended subject as recovered by the model hearer, namely $[x]_{CD}$, $[x]_{SCD\,1}$, or $[x]_{CPI\,1}$. In other words, *e* cannot be represented as in *Fig. 6.8a.

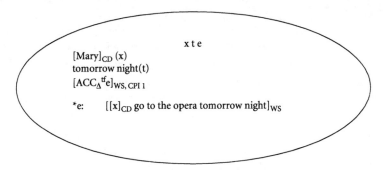

$$x\ t\ e$$

$$[Mary]_{CD}\ (x)$$
$$\text{tomorrow night}(t)$$
$$[ACC_\Delta^{tf}e]_{WS,\,CPI\,1}$$

$$*e:\qquad [[x]_{CD}\ \text{go to the opera tomorrow night}]_{WS}$$

*FIGURE 6.8a. Tenseless future

Since the operator ACC acquires its specification of the type and degree of modality elsewhere in the MR, and there is no need to resort to the content of the unit on which it operates in order for it to acquire these specifications, *e* will suffice. By contrast, in the case of the belief operator discussed in Chapter 5, we could not make do with extensional objects such as *e* and *s*. The type of belief context was dictated, so to speak, 'from within τ'.

Examples (3), (4), and (5) do not exhaust the possibilities of referring to future eventualities. Neither has it been empirically confirmed that (3) differs from (4) to the same degree, so to speak, as (4) from (5) as far as the degree of modality and the degree of intentionality are concerned. Hence, the super-scripts *rf*, *fp*, and *tf* cannot be replaced by numerical values for intentionality of, say, 0, 0.5, and 1 respectively. A thorough data-based study of the usage of various ways of expressing the future may reveal some quantitative depend-encies but this is a separate large project that will have to wait until the theoretical preliminaries prove adequate.[26] For the present, we can render the gradation of modality within the semantic category of futurity by means of a somewhat impressionistic scale of intentionality as in Fig. 6.9, with *n* of Δ^n varying between *tf*, *fp*, and *rf*. These values represent some, as yet unspecified, points on the scale of *n* with values for intentionality from 1 to 0.

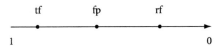

FIGURE 6.9. The gradation of intentionality and modality for the future

To repeat, the placement of the values on the scale reflects only the relative values as the absolute ones have not been determined. While we know the relative positions of *tf*, *fp*, and *rf* from the properties of use of these forms, their absolute placement on the scale will require a detailed empirical study.

We can now move to the different uses of *will* in examples (1)–(3). Example (3) is well accounted for by $[ACC_\Delta{}^{rf}]_{CD}$ based on Fig. 6.5. As far as (1) and (2) are concerned, we can now account for them by comparing the relative degree Δ of ACC in (1) and (2) with that of the regular future in example (3). First, it has to be noted that we have adopted the position that temporal markers have their unmarked, default interpretations. This standpoint is founded on the principles PoL, DI, and PI of DS. As was presented above, the default sense of *will* can be intuitively and correctly accounted for by ACC and Δ^{rf}. Now, just as tenseless future is not the default use of the form 'goes' nor is the futurative progressive a default use of 'is going', so the epistemic necessity *will* and dispositional necessity *will* are not the default uses of *will*. Each of these expressions can be used with its default sense or with a sense that departs from the default. This departure corresponds to a different strength of ACC, explained by different degrees of intentionality and relevant intentions as in the DI principle. In the present investigation of futurity and markers of the future, pursuing the topic of scales for modalities would not be relevant. Suffice it to say that the respective degrees of strength would have to be constructed by analogy to the degrees of *will* discussed below. [27]

In short, scales of intentionality are useful in two ways. First, we can represent the observation that future time reference is scalar, as in Fig. 6.9, adding other forms such as epistemic *may*, epistemic *can, might, could* with future-time reference towards the zero end of the scale. Secondly, and more importantly, we can present the interrelations between different uses of a particular linguistic form such as *will, goes,* or *is going*. Just as future time reference has its default expression in (3) rather than (4) or (5), so every such expression belongs to its own scale of defaults and departures from defaults. In this way, the sense of *will* in (3) is the default among (1)–(3).

Regular future *will* has an MR with the ACC operator and the modality Δ of the degree *rf*. *Will* of epistemic necessity in (1) can now be presented as overriding ACC Δ^{rf} by the condition 'now (t)'. Even if the temporal adverb 'now' were not overtly present in the sentence, 'now' would have to be recovered from the context by the hearer. MRs, which are, so to speak, 'post-merger' representations, have means of accounting for this type of conversational inference. If 'now (t)' were not communicated, *will* would remain of the default, ACC_Δ^{rf} type. To repeat, this is so because it is an MR, not a sentence-based object, that has compositional semantics.

In order to distinguish epistemic *will* from epistemic *must*, etc., we specify the index *rf*. We represent it as $[ACC_\Delta^{rf}s]_{WS,\ CPI\ 1}$. CPI 1 signals that rf *will* is not the case, but instead *will* is processed by WS in the context of the structure that contains the temporal adverb 'now', as well as by CPI 1 that renders the final result as epistemic necessity *will*. The MR for sentence (1), repeated below, is now as in Fig. 6.10.

(1)   Mary will be in the opera now.

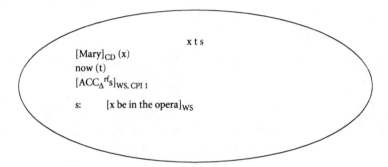

FIGURE 6.10. Epistemic necessity *will*

$[ACC_\Delta^{rf}s]_{WS,\ CPI_1}$ in Fig. 6.10 uniquely identifies the form used in (1), that is epistemic necessity *will*. Naturally, epistemic *will* enters into scales of strength with other expressions of epistemic modality, just as the future *will* entered into the strength-of-modality scale with tenseless future and futurative progressive forms. But, as I indicated above, this is an issue separate from the current investigation of the future.

Finally, the dispositional necessity *will* of (2) acquires an analogous representation. It is slightly more straightforward to represent sentence (2) than (1), in that the adverbs 'sometimes', 'normally', etc. are almost always present, either in the sentence under analysis or in the preceding sentences of the discourse, and hence can be easily included in the MR—and also in the DRS. The analysis of ACC is as before: $[ACC_\Delta^{rf}s]_{WS,\ CPI_1}$ and the difference between epistemic and dispositional necessity is guaranteed by the information contained in the adverb—either overtly expressed or recovered from the context. The partial MR for (2) repeated below is as in Fig.6.11:

(2)   Mary will sometimes go to the opera in her tracksuit.

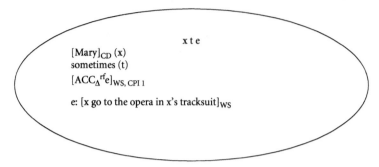

FIGURE 6.11. Dispositional necessity *will*

The difference between *will* and, say, *would* is maintained by retaining the *rf* index on Δ.

The next step is to add the formalism for the semantics for MRs so as to include the ACC operator. Unlike in the case with the belief operator in Chapter 4, here we need not depart far from the relational semantics used in DRT. But we have to remember that the object on which this semantics operates is different in DS. In DS, compositionality is predicated of MRs. To repeat, predicative conditions draw on WS, CD, SCD 1, and CPI 1. Now, ACC is a one-place operator on eventualities, where eventualities are conceived of as states or events. The relational semantics in DS for $ACC_\Delta^n\ e$ is not straightforward because events are still ill-defined constructs. However, it can be safely accepted that events are arguments of predications. The semantics can be built by analogy to that for predication:[28]

$$_s[\![Pt_1, \ldots, t_n]\!]_{s'}^M \text{ iff } s = s' \text{ and } \{\ [\![t_1]\!]_{M,s}, \ldots, [\![t_n]\!]_{M,s}\} \in I(P)$$

So,

$$_s[\![ACC_\Delta^n e]\!]_{s'}^M \text{ iff } s = s' \text{ and}$$

   (i) $[\![e]\!]_{M,s} \in I(ACC_\Delta^n)$
   (ii) $ACC_\Delta^n \in \{[ACC_\Delta^n]_{CD}, [ACC_\Delta^n]_{CPI}\}$
   (iii) $\Delta = \vdash$

Unlike the belief operator, ACC is an operator on events. In the above preliminary attempt at a formalization, conjunct (i) stands for the claim that event *e* obtains a semantic value (becomes an MR) on a particular assignment *s* in a particular model *M* within the limits provided by the interpretation of acceptability of a particular type Δ and degree *n*. The type and the degree are accounted for in (ii) and (iii). Conjunct (ii) reflects the thesis that the n value of Δ is its default value, obtained through CD, or some other value obtained by means of CPI 1. Conjunct (iii) states that the type of modality is 'it is the case that'.

It has to be observed that ACC obtains the value for Δ and n from the MR. Hence, this is as far as we can go with the application of relational semantics at present: WS, CD, or CPI 1 have to be brought in to render the values such as dispositional necessity, regular future, and so forth.

Naturally, condition (iii) is not exhaustive. '$\Delta = \vdash$' is used here in order to provide the DS for the three readings of *will* in (1)–(3) and for the three ways of expressing futurity in (3)–(5). Modal expressions other than those used in these five examples may require a different value for Δ. I return to this question below, but the DS for other modals will have to be left open for future investigation. The combination of the resources of (ii) and (iii) allows us to represent the possible readings of *will* in (1)–(3), as well as the future-time reference of (3)–(5).

Note that we can eschew here the talk in terms of the 'world-assignment pair' (w, s) discussed in Section 3.4.2 as necessary for representing modalities. In other words, we have $_s[\![MR]\!]_{s'}$, not $_{w,s}[\![MR]\!]_{w',s'}$. If I am correct, this can be attained because Δ^n of ACC performs the same function as relations between possible worlds. In other words, instead of:

$$_{w,s}[\![\Box D]\!]^M_{w',s'} \text{ iff } (w,s) = (w',s') \wedge \forall w''(wR_\Box w'' \rightarrow \exists s'''\exists w''' \text{ such that }$$

$$_{w',s'}[\![D]\!]^M_{w''',s'''})$$

where $wR_\Box w''$ stands for a relation defining all possible worlds relative to a given world, as discussed in Section 3.4.2, note 30, after Asher and Lascarides (2003), in DS we have ACC_Δ^n for the degree of acceptability of an eventuality under a default value of Δ ('it is the case that').[29] This move is not possible when compositionality is sought on the level of sentence structure as in DRT. However, it is perfectly compatible with the DS account where composition-ality is post-merger compositionality of MRs. To repeat, this is not an advantage of DS over DRT: it merely reflects the difference of objectives.

Note also that other modals, such as *may, might, can, could, would,* can be accounted for by extending the current analysis so as to include further specifications of Δ. In the analysis of (1)–(5), we had no need to specify the type of modality, that is the value of Δ, because all of the discussed expres-sions could be subsumed, very generally, under Grice's 'Acc $\vdash$ p', 'it is acceptable that it is the case that p'. Combined with the index on Δ, this gave us the expressions that were actually uttered by the speaker. But Δ may also assume the value '!', 'let it be that', as in Grice's 'Acc ! p', 'it is acceptable that let it be that p'. It remains to be seen whether varying Δ in this way, that is its value and its indexing, accounts for all the modal senses in natural language. Their analysis, as well as the analysis of conditionals related to it, are separate, albeit very relevant, projects for future research.

Similarly, a formal semantic analysis of temporal adverbials will not be pursued here. The main purpose was to give some theoretical support to the idea that temporality is an aspect of commitment to the communicated eventuality, and hence a constituent of modality. This has been attempted through an analysis of the relevant expressions with respect to the degrees of relevant intentions of the utterance and the degrees of intentionality of the corresponding mental state. The development of this idea and the possible empirical precisification of the values on the relevant scales will be the next step.

6.5 Conclusions

I have attempted to address two interrelated questions, namely (i) whether the English *will* is a marker of modality or tense, and (ii) whether futurity is temporality. I answered question (i) in the DS framework by suggesting the default temporal status of *will*, and the degrees of departure from the default explained by the degrees of intentionality associated with the mental state, and, by the same token, by the degrees of intentions associated with utterances with which these states are expressed. The highest degree of modality, and hence the weakest intentionality, corresponds to *will* as the marker of future time reference. This gradation suggests that future time reference can be modal in itself. In other words, if the gradation of intentionality is simple because there is no category-boundary crossing from modal to temporal sense, then it is modal. So, the answer to question (ii) is needed to complete the answer to (i). Question (ii) was approached through comparing three ways of expressing futurity.

The final conclusion is that there is a general notion of modality that subsumes all the senses of *will* on the one hand, and various expressions of futurity on the other. This has been found in Grice's notion of acceptability that I translated into the DS-theoretic operator ACC, following the intuitively plausible hypothesis that modality can be subsumed under 'it is reasonable to think that'. By introducing ACC to DS, we can account for the scalarity of (1)–(3) on the one hand, and (3)–(5) on the other, with respect to the *degree of acceptability* (n) and the default or non-default use of an expression (CD or CPI 1). To be more precise, we established interrelations between different uses of *will* by accounting for the degrees of intentionality (including default intentionality) as in (1)–(3). This was done by specifying the value n as *rf* by means of CD, and accounting for other uses by means of WS and CPI 1. For (3)–(5), which contain various expressions of futurity, we varied the value for n, as well as the source of reading (CD and CPI 1). The values for n of Δ^n were tentatively placed on the scale of intentionality.

Since MRs are 'post-merger' representations of utterance/discourse meaning, I departed from the DR-theoretic practice of representing *tenses*. Tense belongs to WS. However, DS does not have a separate sub-theory of every source of meaning information: as it is presented here, it focuses on what happens after the merger. This is so because the compositional, truth-evaluable representation is the 'post-merger representation' (MR). As a result of this perspective, I could attempt to account for the dependencies between different uses of English *will* on the one hand, and different ways of expressing futurity on the other in relegating the differences to Δ^n. This move was dictated by our earlier conclusion that temporality, at least with respect to the future, if not generally, is more adequately described as modality, degree of commitment, or $ACC_\Delta{}^n$. The issue of *temporality in general* is taken up as an open question in Section 6.6.

6.6 Temporality as modality: some open questions and further extensions

Future as a modality can be argued for in two ways. We can argue for the asymmetrical status of the future and the past where only the future is modal, or for the modality of time itself. In other words, the question is whether future is modality because it has not yet taken place or because *time* is modality.

A brief disclaimer is required at this point. The objective of Sections 6.1–6.5 was to establish the semantic and epistemological status of futurity. Any light this proposal might shed on the status of the past is a topic for a separate investigation. Nevertheless, I shall point out some aspects of the philosophical background to futurity in order to suggest some future directions in which a DS analysis of temporal expressions can be taken.

The modality of the expressions of futurity that I am defending here can be traced back to ample philosophical debates on the nature of time, and in particular the question as to whether time is an attribute of the objective world or of our experiencing the world. Kant, Hegel, Husserl, and Heidegger are among the representatives of the latter view, to give some seminal examples. According to Kant, time is subjective; it cannot be classified with real, empirically given objects, but rather is a way in which our mind orders sensations that constitute experience. For Hegel, time is an illusion, but an illusion that is closely tied to the logically organized reality. Husserl's time consists of subjective phenomena, categorically different from the objects that happen in time. Acts of consciousness have their immanent temporality. The climax of the unreality of time advocated by the phenomenological tradition is Heidegger's (1953) *Being and Time* (*Sein und Zeit*). Being is characterized by temporality, experienced as the awareness of the end (death). Time is not linear. Instead, it amounts to reaching the past and the future. Future, past, and present are derivative concepts, grounded in the 'potentiality of being', 'having been', and 'being that is': '[t]ime must be brought to light and genuinely grasped as the horizon of every understanding and interpretation of being' (Heidegger 1953: 15). The idea of most importance to my discussion of the status of futurity is that the reference point, so to speak, for temporality is the future rather than the past. Future is not a series of 'nows' that have not yet arrived. Neither is the past a series of 'nows' that have already passed. Instead, 'the present arises from the future' (1953: 391) just as time itself arises out of the possibility of the end of being (death). In other words, time is a *possible horizon for the understanding of being*.

It is not my aim to contribute to the philosophical debate on the reality or unreality of time. However, some aspects of this debate provide an important starting point for the assessment of the semantics of time. First, even if time is not subjective, it still has to be true that objects exist in space and time in the most 'folk' sense: for most sentences, we know their meaning if we can interpret them with respect to situations which are themselves world-time structures. In most versions of truth-conditional semantics they amount to models. Secondly, Heidegger's claim that existence can only be grasped in its totality when we can entertain the possibility of its end provides a possible explanation for the 'folk' concept of time. If the 'folk' concept of time is an arrow going from the past, through the present to the future, then this infiniteness of time has to rest on some conception of what it would be for the time to end. It is at least conceivable that we 'start', so to speak, thinking about time by assuming an end in the future, which is a reference point for calling something present or past. This gives a privileged status to the future. Hence, it is at least worth investigating whether futurity is categorially differ-ent from the past and the present. If so, then the schema for the concept of the future would perhaps be a series of lines standing for possibilities, stemming out of the present as in Fig. 6.1. This would amount to saying that possibility, which is itself a type of modality, is the defining characteristic of the future, and the temporality of it is just derivative. In the case of the present and the past, other possibilities are counterfactuals and hence are a separate phenomenon.

Let us now see if the extant arguments for the modality of the past are equally strong. We will begin with two theories of time distinguished a century ago by McTaggart. The current debates on the semantics of temporal expressions stem out of McTaggart's distinction between the A series and the B series:

I shall speak of the series of positions running from the far past through the near past to the present, and then from the present to the near future and the far future, as the A series. The series of positions which runs from earlier to later I shall call the B series. The contents of a position in time are called events.... A position in time is called a moment. (McTaggart 1908: 111)

Both series are equally essential as characteristics of time, but the A series is more fundamental and cannot be defined. We know, however, that present, past, and future are incompatible: no event can be more than one. Nevertheless, every event can be at some point described as future, present, and past. In order to explain this, we have to assume the succession of time. So, in order to account for time, we must presuppose time and this is circular. Time series is thus a property of our perception; events may not be temporal.

The A series gives rise to a so-called A-theory of time, known as tensed, or *presentism*, and the B series to a B-theory, known as untensed. For B-theorists, events are ordered as earlier-than/later-than. They are not intrinsically past, present, or future: we speak of them as past, present, or future from the perspective of the utterance that provides a point of reference. For B-theory, time is psychological, it belongs to the observer. Events do not change. For A-theorists, there is no sequence of events: there are no future or past events, just 'present' events, so to speak, that are, will be, or were.

Now, we know that time is not conceptualized for all cultures as an axis pointing from the past to the future. For the Ancient Greeks and the Maori, time travels from the future to the past. The past for the Maori is *ngara o mua*, 'the days in front', and the future is *kei muri*, 'behind'. Observers move into the future, facing the past (see Thornton 1987: 70). For the Hopi, past events come back (see Allan 2001: 353). These conceptualizations seem to be compatible with both of McTaggart's series. For the Ancient Greeks and the Maori, events move before the observer's eyes but the experiencer faces the past, not the unknown future. So, the days in front are the days that passed, and the days behind are in the future: this is a conceptualization of time relative to the speaker. This is compatible with two schemas: the observer 'slides', so to speak, along the timeless events, or events 'slide' from being future, then present, to being past. We are in the present and know, face, the past, while 'the future, being unknown, is of little importance', it cannot be seen, it is behind us (Thornton 1987: 70). So, such cross-cultural differences in the conceptualization of time cannot help us in choosing between the two theories. Such differences in the direction of the time axis or the shape of the time line are tangential to the principle on which the A series and the B series are distinguished. This principle consists in ascribing change to the events or to the observer and hence making time real (A series) or psychological (B series).

It is sometimes claimed that B-theory cannot account for the problem of indexicality. It is so on the assumption that (30) and (31) have the same semantics if the time of uttering them is 5 o'clock. That is to say, the time matters for the truth conditions but the linguistic expression by which it is stated does not.

(30)   The meeting is at 5 o'clock.

(31)   The meeting is now.

On such a semantics, Kaplan's (1989) *content* is truth-conditionally relevant, while the *character* (linguistic expression) is not. On the other hand, there is an intuitive difference in the amount of knowledge one has when one utters (30) and (31) at 5 o'clock: uttering (30) does not have to come with knowing that the meeting is *now*. This objection to B-theory can be easily handled in DRT and DS. In DRT, the semantics is extended beyond truth conditions and allows for the Kaplanian character (the linguistic expression) to contribute to the meaning of the sentence. Similarly, in DS, we are not constrained by saying that (30) and (31) should have the same semantic properties; in DS, semantic representation is a post-merger representation (an MR) and need not be restricted by the lexical items and structures used in the WS source of meaning information. To repeat, meaning is created as a merger of the output of all the four sources: WS, CD, CPI 1, and SCD 1. So, this argument against the B-theory collapses. B-theory can thus be upheld both by DRT and by DS. In DRT, the indexicality of temporal expressions is captured 'separately', so to speak, by adding the time of utterance. The discourse referent n standing for the time of the utterance ('now') is added. This introduction of an indexical component allows us to anchor the shift of the truth conditions to some stable reference point (Kamp and Reyle 1993). This addition[30] also allows for shifts of the 'now' into the future or the past as in (32) and for accounting for the anaphoric dimension of tenses by using Reichenbach's (1948) distinction between reference time, speech time, and event time required in (33). In (33), the reference point for the second sentence is the time of Tom's arrival, which differs from the speech time.

(32) You know the whole truth now. I knew it a few days ago when I was writing this letter.

(33) Tom arrived in Cambridge at 11 a.m. He had left London at 10 a.m.

Reichenbach's distinction between the point of event (E), point of reference (R), and point of speech (S) gives rise to the conceptualization of Simple Future as in (34) (cf. Reichenbach 1948: 290).

(34)

Simple Future (I will go)

S, R   E

If we were to place this conceptualization within the A-theory or the B-theory, it certainly fits better with the B-theory in that it relies on the earlier-than/later-than relations on the time line. However, the speech point 'contaminates' it, so to speak, with the speaker-centred perspective, or, in Reichenbach's explanation, with token-reflexivity: 'The tenses determine time with reference to the time point of the act of speech, i.e. of the token uttered' (1948: 287–8). And this is precisely the perspective that is used in post-Montagovian dynamic semantics. So, if this reasoning is correct, contemporary dynamic formal semantics combines the resources of B-theory with some aspects of A-theory. In order to maintain a tenseless B-theory, one has to find a way of anchoring the B series, at least in the form of entities that make tensed propositions true. Mellor (e.g. 1993, 1998) proposes that instead of a 'now', 'temporal presence', we appeal to the presentness of our experience and beliefs. Some events that we experience now are not present: an explosion of a star perceived now happened in a remote past.[31]

As far as the intuitive appeal is concerned, if we were to choose between A-theory and B-theory, at first glance A-theory seems more attractive:

Unfettered by the burden of delivering tenseless truth conditions, the A-theory can use indexical predicates in the metalanguage to deliver tensed truth conditions that preserve the indexical character of temporal phenomena. (Ludlow 1999: 97)

What Ludlow proposes is that

x is the semantic value of PAST iff x was true,

where x stands for a 'proposition-like object', differing from a proposition in that it is devoid of temporality.[32] Predicates PRES and FUT for the present and the future are treated analogously. The logical form of future sentences is as in (35), where [...] stands for some conventional dating system.

(35)   FUT[S] when FUT […] (Ludlow 1999: 133).

This rescues the A-theory by not committing us to the existence of the past and future events. The price, however, is a need to introduce implicit constituents of sentences. It seems that this proposal gives A-theory no real advantage over B-theory as conceived of in DRT and DS. On DRT, semantics is extended so as to account for indexicality in the way proposed by Kaplan. In DS, truth conditions are post-merger and, therefore, indexicality is a legitimate ingredient of the MR.

I shall not venture into detailed arguments for and against real time.[33] Suffice it to say that, it seems, the debate is far from resolved and both options—that is (i) time belongs to events and (ii) time is psychological and all events are real—are open. Ludlow follows the A-theory all the way and suggests, albeit tentatively, that perhaps there is no future and no past in language but merely modality and evidentiality. If we subsume evidentiality under the category of modality,[34] we can rephrase Ludlow's conclusion as follows: there is no future, no past, but merely epistemic modality—possibility, necessity, and evidentiality. Instead of saying that we use modals to express future tense, and aspect to express the past, we should say that we use modals to express modality and aspectual markers to express aspect. Expressions of past tense can then be regarded as evidential markers (see Ludlow 1999: 161–2).

Now, Prior's tense logic is a modal system, as Prior's definition of the possibility and necessity operators (M and L in his notation) shows:

if we define M (or 'Possibly') as 'It either is or will be the case that', and L (or 'Necessarily') as 'It is and always will be the case that', these operators will meet [… the] conditions for being modal operators … (Prior 1957: 12)[35]

Similarly, Montague (1973) treats tense and modals alike, as operators that have a sentence as their scope.[36] So, the operators 'it was the case that' and 'it will be the case that' look strikingly similar to the possibility and necessity operators of modal logic. In order to find how far this similarity can go, Parsons (2003), like Ludlow (1999), entertains the possibility that time is modality, or '[m]ore precisely, let the tense logician replace all talk of truth-at-a-time with talk of truth-at-a-world' (Parsons 2003: 5). In order to do so, Parsons suggests we take it to be a fact that it is possible to say for each world what time is present in it. Model theory will now have to work on those possible worlds that differ in what time it is at these worlds. Being true at time *t* now becomes reanalysed as being true in a world *w* in which the time is *t*. For example, we may have in the domain a world like ours, except that the present time in it is 50BC. That is, that world is *now* as ours *was* in 50BC. All in all, temporality as modality is an attractive option and it may be worth pursuing it within DS.

To further the argument from evidentiality, it is worth rethinking Whorf's discussion of time in Hopi. The differences in the conceptualization of time in Hopi and English, used by Whorf (1956) as one of the core arguments in favour of linguistic relativity, can in fact be used as an argument in favour of universalism. For both languages, at some level of conceptualization, we have the strength of evidence and hence evidentiality. Tenseless languages are a very useful window on conceptualization. Burmese, for example, has sentence-final particles that signify realis and irrealis. Realis corresponds to the present and past time reference, while irrealis is used for future time reference or for modality (after Comrie 1985: 50–1). While this evidence does not help with the philosophical problem of the reality of time, it certainly provides evidence that in Burmese futurity groups with modality. Combined with some evidence that the conceptualization of modality is universal, perhaps even non-linguistic, provided in Nuyts's (2001) data-based study, we have a strong argument for the modality of the future. What we have not considered in great detail is the argument from the existence of binary grammatical distinctions of past–non-past as in English, or 'future–non-future' as in one of the languages spoken in New Guinea (Hua). By this criterion, there is future tense. However, this may simply be a modal distinction in which present and past go together as non-modal and future as modal.

The next move to make is to draw conclusions from linguistic relativity research to the A series–B series dilemma. As we saw in Section 6.2, various linguistic vehicles conspire to produce a message of temporality of a conveyed event or state. The interaction of tense, aktionsart, and lexical and situational information can explain the behaviour of *will* in various contexts and various grammatical environments. There is no argument from the discussion of the semantics of futurity for postulating language specific reasoning about the future. The rejection of linguistic relativity in the domain of temporal distinctions is supported by the apparent lack of analogy with the conceptualization of space. The research on the conceptualization of space in various cultures strongly suggests the influence of the spatial lexicon on thinking about space. This is so because humans can conceptualize spatial locations either in absolute terms, or relative to the speaker, or as intrinsic where one object is located with reference to another.[37] When we try to map these ways of thinking onto time, future in the A series by necessity assumes the relative conceptualization[38], while the B series seems to assume an intrinsic (earlier-than and later-than) conceptualization. But people normally have access to conventional calendar systems that are the equivalent of an absolute categorization. This seems to suggest that the A series–B series controversy is not a genuine alternative. Instead, by adding a point of reference, we obtain a satisfactory system: A series plus anchoring the 'intrinsic' conceptualization, or B series plus anchoring the relative one to the temporal position of the speaker. So, we can tentatively suggest that a mix of the B-series and the A-series resources is conceptually correct and if post-Montagovian formal semantic approaches to time do indeed mix A- and B-series resources, they are conceptually correct in doing so.

The evidence discussed above strongly suggests that time and modality are closely connected and perhaps even that there is no semantic category of temporality but instead that there are degrees of certainty, evidence, or acceptability. Evidential markers that dominate the Amerindian language Hopi are not qualitatively different from temporal markers found in English. They can all be brought to the common denominator. Thai, a 'tenseless' and 'aspectless' language, also seems to corroborate the evidentiality/modality solution (see Srioutai, in progress). In Steedman's view (1997: 932), this common underlying conceptualization relies on goals, actions, and their consequences. Temporality constitutes only part of this conceptual frame-work. So, perhaps, instead of investigating language dependence, we have to focus on the speaker's process of conceptualization, that is on speaker-dependence.

To sum up this already rather lengthy discussion of open issues, it would seem justified to adopt the assumption that temporality is not a real semantic category but an amalgam of various conceptual distinctions. The next task would be to see if this assumption works for expressions of the present and the past, just as in Sections 6.1–6.5 we saw how such a conceptual amalgam can work for the future. In order to do so, we utilized modality, strength of evidence, and acceptability. DS proved to be an ideal methodological frame-work to explore this hypothesis.

Notes

1 See e.g. Fleischman 1982; Enç 1996; Werth 1997; Ludlow 1999.
2 E.g. Parsons 1990; Kamp and Reyle 1993; Pratt and Francez 2001.
3 Here: Vendler's (1967) *accomplishment*. See Dowty (1979: 154).
4 For detailed references and a literature review on this topic, see Dowty 1979.
5 See Section 1.2.
6 See e.g. Jaszczolt 1999a, 1999b, 2002a, 2004.
7 Dowty (1986) contrasts (i) states and activities with (ii) accomplishments and achievements in this respect.

8 Gennari (2003: 45) talks about an 'influence of stativity on the temporal reading'.

9 This is a development of Ladusaw's (1977: 97) analysis of auxiliary as Aux → Tense (Modal) with the semantics λp [Tense′[^ Modal′(p)]].

10 Nuyts (2001) provides a thorough, empirically supported argument for the universality of epistemic modality.

11 After Prior. Prior's (1957, 1967, 1968; also 2003) tense logic is an extension of propositional or predicate logic that makes use of tense operators: *P*, a one-place sentence connective as in *Pp* ('it was the case that *p*'), and *F*, as in *Fp* analogously ('it will be the case that *p*'). In other words, 'the future-tense statement is true if and only if the present-tense statement will be true'; Prior (1957: 9).

12 See McTaggart 1908; Reichenbach 1948.

13 I am not concerned with the *will/shall* distinction at present.

14 Following Ultan (1972).

15 In Dahl's (1985) empirical study of sixty-four languages from a wide range of genetic groups, the most typical uses of the future involve an element of planning (intention) rather than pure prediction. While he argues that intention is not a necessary condition for the use of a future form, the quantitative finding suggests a strong correlation.

16 Cf. also Allan's (2001: 358) to 'act on one's will, desire, want, hence insist on doing something'. So, '[a]lthough often spoken of as a tense marker, English *will* and its past tense form *would* are primarily modals'.

17 The default sense of futurity for descriptions of states is weaker than that of events but does not contradict the current argument.

18 There have also been other attempts in the literature to provide a unitary semantics of modals. See e.g. Papafragou 2000, where unitary underspecified semantics for modals is supplemented with pragmatic inference that contributes to the truth-conditional content. Note that Papafragou also assigns special status to epistemic modality as an exemplification of human ability to metarepresent. This is compatible with my claim in this chapter that epistemic modality is the basic type of modality.

19 Different degrees of commitment can be caused by a variety of reasons: the speaker's assessment of the situation, reporting the commitment on Mary's part, an attempt to provoke a denial by expressing an insincere strong commitment, etc.

20 It can be argued that tenseless future expresses a lower degree of commitment than regular future in that it can be hedged as in (5a):

(5a) Mary goes to the opera tomorrow night, it seems.

However, hedging is caused here by the fact that the statement communicates a high degree of commitment that results, for example, from checking the daily schedule in Mary's own diary. In other words, 'it seems' signals the illocutionary force rather than hedging the propositional content.

21 This is not the only way of representing the type of ACC. If we were to depart from the Montagovian tradition of the operator-based analysis and adopt the stance that

temporality is to be expressed as an argument, the logical form would change accordingly. However, as was argued earlier on in this chapter, I adopt the operator analysis as it best captures the degrees of intentionality and intentions that differentiate between the uses of *will* in (1)–(3) and the uses of different expressions of futurity in (3)–(5).

22 But see e.g. Palmer 1986; Papafragou 2000; Condoravdi 2002; van der Auwera et al. 2001; van der Auwera and Plungian 1998; Traugott 1989; Traugott and Dasher 2002: ch. 3.

23 It is also justified on independent grounds. See the discussion and further references in Section 6.2.

24 For the sake of simplicity, we ignore the detailed representation of the state *s*/event *e*.

25 I have ascribed the degrees of strength to the informative intention but it is perhaps more plausible to ascribe them to the referential intention with the proviso that whole eventualities are referred to. Nothing important depends on choosing this option.

26 Nuyts's (2001) 'scale of likelihood of a state of affairs' could prove of use here, with the proviso that futurity *is* modality. See also Jaszczolt 2003*b*.

27 It has been attempted in the literature to explain the uses of *will* in (1)–(3) as 'colouring' of the future reference by some modal overtones such as volition (e.g. Wekker 1976: 67). There are various disadvantages to this move. First, one has to assume that futurity counts as a basic function and modality as an overtone. Secondly, one has to classify such modal overtones and specify descriptively when they are likely to occur. Next, one has to postulate an ambiguity between, e.g., volitional and non-volitional future *will* as in (i):

(i) Ludwig won't eat his food.

Finally, one has no means of accounting for the epistemic *will* as in (1), or for the dispositional *will* in (2), where under the latter we can include Wekker's (1976: 2) 'characteristic' (habitual) and 'inference' readings as in (ii) and (iii) respectively:

(ii)   Mary will often listen to loud music just to annoy me.
(iii) Water will conduct electricity.

On our current account, these problems do not arise as futurity is incorporated in the overarching category of modality, accounted for by various values and various conditions associated with the uniform operator ACC. Instead of colouring of the future, 'degrees of modality' can be taken as the working hypothesis for the explanation of the diversified uses.

28 See Section 3.4.2 for an introduction to relational semantics.

29 See also van der Auwera (1985) on the limitations of possible-worlds semantics for the study of modalities.

30 See also Bennett and Partee 1972; Ladusaw 1977; Saurer 1984. In contrast to Montague, Bennett and Partee use no translation language. Instead, they give a

direct semantic interpretation of natural language expressions. Their system is non-compositional in that, among others, it interprets an expression containing an adverbial as a whole. For example, 'Tom met Mary yesterday' cannot be compositionally accounted for as either P[Y[Tom met Mary]] or Y[P[Tom met Mary]] because of the scope paradox. 'P' stands for past tense operator and 'Y' for 'yesterday'. See also Binnick (1991: 254).

31 To take another pro-B-theory philosophical stance, Mellor (1998: 45) resorts to postulating the timelessness of *experiences* as well as events. Merely our beliefs, intentions, memories about these experiences are tensed. It seems that this shifts the problem of temporality from propositions to beliefs but does not get rid of it. Since linguistic expressions are means of externalizing beliefs (or, are *vehicles of thought*), such a qualitative difference between beliefs and propositions (meanings of these expressions) will not do. Beliefs are propositional, and propositions are tensed. An account of tensed beliefs ends up as being not very different from an account of tensed propositions about events in time.

32 Cf. Ludlow (1999: 97).

33 See also Dummett 1969; Mellor 1998; Parsons 2002, 2003; Mozersky 2001; and mainly the articles in Jokić and Smith 2003.

34 '[T]he term "epistemic" should apply not simply to modal systems that basically involve the notions of possibility and necessity, but to any modal system that indicates the degree of commitment by the speaker to what he says. In particular, it should include evidentials'; Palmer (1986: 51). In many languages, including English, the epistemic system is mixed and involves both judgements and evidentials.

35 Note that any semantics of time must commit itself to some units of time. For Prior, time is analysed as instants and this is a weakness of his tense logic. Even the time needed for uttering a sentence is an interval rather than an instant. As Kamp (1979: 394) argues, thinking in terms of intervals is conceptually prior to thinking in terms of instants. For example, being in the process of writing an article contains instants during which the author is not actually writing but instead is eating or is asleep. Now, in order to be able to tell that such instants belong to the process of writing an article, we must think of the latter as an interval. Otherwise the instant of eating would not be distinguishable from another instant of eating which occurs before the article was begun or after it was finished.

What is essential is the introduction of some kind of extended units into semantics. This has been successfully performed in Bennett and Partee's (1972) amendment of Montague tensed intensional logic in the form of intervals, followed by Dowty (1979), and subsequently by DRT in the form of states and events (Kamp and Reyle 1993), based on Davidson's (1967, 1969) semantics of events. In DS, we follow DRT in distinguishing states and events.

We have to remember, however, that reality is not given to us in the form of eventualities. Moreover, the notion of an event is not sufficiently precise. For example, arguably, negation can convert events into processes or states as in (i) and (ii):

(i)   John arrived.   (event)

(ii) John didn't arrive.   ($^?$process) (from Crouch and Pulman 1993: 272).

While events facilitate the treatment of adverbials, they complicate, for example, sentential negation. See also Parsons 1990; Pratt and Francez 2001; Jaszczolt 2002a: 257–8.

36 See Montague 1973; Ladusaw 1977; Dowty et al. 1981: ch 5.

37 See e.g. Pederson et al. 1998; Levinson et al. 2002, 2003; Levinson 2003; Li and Gleitman 2002; Papafragou et al. 2002.

38 These types of conceptualization must not be confused with so-called absolute tenses (e.g. Simple Past) and relative tenses (e.g. Past Perfect). Both absolute and relative tenses assume a speech point. See Comrie 1985 and Reichenbach 1948.

7

Default Semantics for Presupposition as Anaphora

7.1 Binding and accommodation

Van der Sandt (1992) convincingly argues that presuppositional expressions should be accounted for neither in terms of some non-standard logic, nor relegated to pragmatics. He proposes that presuppositional expressions be regarded as *anaphoric expressions*. In other words, their properties are comparable to those of pronouns and other anaphors. First, I shall summarize van der Sandt's proposal and next move on to an amendment that is dictated by DS. This amendment consists of replacing van der Sandt's admittance of some degree of ambiguity of presuppositional anaphors with a scale of salience of possible anaphors from the default anaphor to the most unlikely one. The relevant readings are represented by means of MRs.

Van der Sandt points out some problems with the view of presuppositions as referring expressions. He says that sentences (1)–(3) should be devoid of a truth value because the second component of the complex sentence suffers from presupposition failure. For various reasons evident from the first clause, the presupposition that John has children does not carry over to the whole compound. Nevertheless, (1)–(3) are not truth-valueless.

(1)   John has children and *his children* are bald.

(2)   If John has children, *his children* are bald.

(3)   Either John does not have any children or *his children* are bald.

He also points out the problems with (4) in that the pronoun is bound by an external quantifier and the phrase 'his child' is not a referring expression.

(4)   Someone had a child and his child was bald. (from van der Sandt 1992: 334).

Moreover, defining presupposition in terms of entailment does not work, essentially because presupposition is a non-monotonic relation and may disappear as a result of the growth of information, as in (5b) compared with (5a):

(5a)   It is possible that *Harry's child* is on holiday.

(5b)   It is possible that Harry does not have a child, but it is also possible that {*he/Harry's child*} is on holiday. (from van der Sandt 1992: 335).[1]

If presuppositions appear to be non-monotonic, then they are cancellable and defeasible and should best conform to a pragmatic treatment. However, a pragmatic approach is equally rejected by van der Sandt. He argues that semantic content should not be regarded as computed prior to presuppositions. According to him, all *pragmatic information may exhibit binding* with the original expression. For instance, let us take van der Sandt's example in (6) and its presupposition in (7). In order to specify the presuppositional link, we have to ensure that we are specifying the same child–cat pairs. In other words, the truth-conditional content has to include the information that (6) and (7) concern the same child–cat pairs.

(6)   A child beats his cat.

(7)   A child has a cat. (from van der Sandt 1992: 340).

Essentially, all he claims is that, as far as presuppositions are concerned, the semantics/pragmatics distinction need not be drawn—or at least need not be observed. This claim is perfectly compatible with the current views on semantics and pragmatics as interrelated 'processors' of information, in the sense of feeding information from one to the other.[2] Here we shall take it further. Van der Sandt's proposal of *binding to context* seems best realized in a theory in which sources of meaning information all conspire to render a compositional merger representation. DS is such a theory. In Section 7.3 I demonstrate that in DS we can take van der Sandt's proposal further and shed light on its most murky aspect which is, I think, his claim of a 'genuine ambiguity' of partial matches that is introduced in Section 7.2 below.

On the pragmatic account, adding presuppositions to context is treated uniformly. It is a result of inference and accommodation—adjusting the context to make them fit the discourse. On the contrary, on van der Sandt's picture, presuppositions, when accounted for in terms of a dynamic semantic theory such as DRT, exhibit the capacity either (i) to bind to an antecedent or (ii) to accommodate in the relevant context. To repeat, DRT mirrors the incremental process of utterance interpretation by providing discourse referents that collect whatever semantically relevant information concerning the given referent is available as discourse progresses. Options (i) and (ii) can be spelled out as follows. Presuppositions are anaphors and can be analysed in the same way in which pronominal and other anaphors are handled. In other words, they are subject to *binding*. But, in addition, since they contain some descriptive content, they can also be informative when the antecedent cannot be found. In this case, they are subject to contextual repair, that is they are contextually *accommodated*. Accommodation is performed with respect to the previous discourse, so, in terms of DRT, the antecedent is normally found in the main DRS (the outer box). In (8) the presupposition 'John has children' is accommodated in the main DRS.

(8) If John has grandchildren, his children will be happy. They wanted to have offspring long ago. (from van der Sandt 1992: 351).

Sometimes, however, the presupposition is bound in a subordinate box instead. In (9), the presupposition 'John has children' cannot be added to the main DRS because its content is in fact uttered, and it is uttered in the scope of a conditional:

(9) If John has children, he will regret that all of his children are bald. (from ibid.: 353).

Van der Sandt's account of DRS construction differs somewhat from that of Kamp and Reyle's (1993) 'standard' account, in that he allows a structure of unresolved anaphoric elements (a so-called 'A-structure', a set of DRSs) for further processing when an appropriate amount of information in discourse interpretation is reached. The DRS for a sentence is merged with the main DRS, after which the anaphoric structures are processed, subject to the constraints of accessibility. Both anaphoric binding and accommodation are accounted for in this way, by postulating the so-called projection line along which looking for the antecedent proceeds (see also Kamp 2001; van Eijck 2001). I discuss some benefits of this move when I introduce MRs for presuppositional anaphora in Section 7.5. There is a conceptual problem with this change of perspective though. Proposing a collection of DRSs well represents the multiple choice for anaphora resolution that is superficially present, but it needlessly suggests the presence of a semantic or pragmatic ambiguity. As I argue in Section 7.2, ambiguity in processing anaphora is rare, even when the match of the antecedent with the potential anaphor leaves room for bridging information.

7.2 Genuine ambiguity of partial matches?

Van der Sandt's account is partly a response to the widespread view that presuppositions must be entailed by the context.[3] He points out that the relation of entailment between a potential antecedent and an anaphoric expression is not a sufficient condition for selecting this potential antecedent. For example, there can be several potential antecedents to a masculine pronoun available. It is not the case that as soon as a suitable antecedent is encountered, it is selected. Rather:

presuppositional anaphors may be *genuinely ambiguous*, that is, there should be cases where we can either select among different antecedents or have the choice between either binding or accommodating. (van der Sandt 1992: 349)[4]

For example, in (10), 'his girlfriend' may or may not be coreferential with 'an oriental girlfriend' (from van der Sandt, 1992: 350). In other words, the presuppositional anaphor 'his girlfriend' can be bound to 'an oriental girl-friend' or otherwise has to be accommodated.[5]

(10)   If John has an oriental girlfriend, his girlfriend won't be happy.

He calls such examples *partial matches*: the match with the antecedent is not precise and two readings are possible. Let us now discuss what he means by 'genuine ambiguity' and whether this genuine ambiguity really ensues. First, intuitively, (10) is not obviously ambiguous. The sentence is rather unnatural but let us accept it for the sake of this argument and, moreover, let us assume that it has been uttered with a 'normal' intonation pattern, that is without, for example, stressing the second occurrence of 'girlfriend' as in (10a):

(10a)   If John has an oriental girlfriend, his GIRLFRIEND won't be happy.[6]

It is not at all clear that we have an ambiguity in processing (10). 'His girlfriend' seems to be more saliently matched with 'an oriental girlfriend' than with some made-up antecedent. In other words, it seems to be bound, rather than accommodated, and we have a salient bound, non-presupposing reading.

This intuition, however murky, helps in two ways. It sheds some doubt on the genuine ambiguity view and, ironically, it seems to be supported by van der Sandt's own theory of preferences for binding and accommodation sites. Van der Sandt proposes that accommodation normally takes place at the end of the projection line, that is at the 'highest accessible level such that the resulting structure does not violate general constraints on (un)binding and acceptability' (1992: 357). Generally, accommodation ensues when binding cannot work. Accommodation proceeds in the opposite direction to binding: binding takes place at the *nearest* accessible site, going from the anaphor upwards along the projection line. Intuitively, the process works as follows. In the search for binding, we may go all the way up and not find a suitable antecedent, at which place, that is on the top of the projection line, accommodation takes place. For example, sentence (11) obtains the preferred interpretation in (12) rather than, for example, (13), because of the preference for binding over accommodation:

(11)   Every man gossips about his ex-wife.

(12)   Every man who had a wife gossips about her.

(13)   Every man gossips about Richard Gere's ex-wife. [when the previous discourse was about Richard Gere]

The search for the sites for accommodation in discourse processing is thus governed by the default: only when all potential antecedents for binding fail, do we repair and accommodate. We are not told why accommodation proceeds in this way but the proposal is a common-sense one: we try to find an antecedent for an anaphor in the discourse and failing that, we 'make it up', so to speak, within constraints laid out by the principles summarized in Gricean or post-Gricean rules of rational conversational behaviour.

So far we have no explanation of 'genuine ambiguity', unless we are prepared to treat the notion of a 'suitable' antecedent in a very rich, context-dependent way. According to the rules for binding and accommodation, there is normally one preferred reading. This conclusion seems to be compatible with van der Sandt's construal, especially that he himself admits pragmatic interference in the process of anaphora/presupposition resolution, and this pragmatic inference aims at providing a unique interpretation. On the other hand, by the same argument, if pragmatic inference is at work, then ordering of binding and accommodation, including the ordering of sites within them, seems unnecessary. Since van der Sandt follows this route and orders the readings, he is obliged to provide conditions on the suitability of various possible binding/accommodation sites. He suggests an order of preference that is determined by full vs. partial matching, the relative distance along the projection line, as well as two somewhat general factors of the principles of discourse and non-linguistic knowledge. Prior to all this, there are also general conditions on binding and accessibility. It seems that the only way to reconcile pragmatic inference with the need for the ordering of sites is this. The process of anaphora resolution is governed by rules that provide sites for binding and accommodation, ordered along the projection line. At the same time, pragmatic processes interact with this ordering and contribute to the final result of binding and accommodation. Notice that this interpretation fits well in the DS-way of accounting for discourse processing: WS, CPI 1, as well as defaults of various kinds (CD and SCD 1) contribute to the final reading of an utterance.

In view of the postulate of all these helping hands in finding an antecedent, the genuine ambiguity view seems to have a dubious theoretical plausibility. Combining it with the murky intuitions on the ambiguity in the processing of (10) allows us to conclude that there are not sufficient arguments to regard (10) as 'genuinely ambiguous' in processing. This preliminary rejection of the genuine ambiguity is further supported by the DS-analysis in Section 7.5.

7.3 Presupposition and focus

Van der Sandt (1992: fn 23) admits that contrastive stress may partly disambiguate presuppositional anaphors.[7] However, he does not provide detailed conditions for contextual acceptability. The latter task is attempted by Krahmer and van Deemter (1998). They say that in partial matches such as (10), the non-identity reading tends to have an accented anaphor. This conforms to the rule that strong quantifiers (i.e. quantifiers that come with an appropriate domain of quantification) and accented weak quantifiers induce an existence presupposition.[8] Accenting, as in (10a) repeated below, can, in effect, disambiguate sentences where there is no identity anaphor.

(10a)   If John has an oriental girlfriend, his GIRLFRIEND won't be happy.

Similarly, in example (14), when there is no accent on 'children', then all the partygoers are understood to be children. With the accent, as in (14a), 'the children' are a real subset of the set of partygoers or some other set of children.

(14)   If John talks to some partygoers, the children will laugh at him.
(14a)   If John talks to some partygoers, the CHILDREN will laugh at him.
         (from Krahmer and van Deemter 1998: 364).[9]

Information structure has, in fact, been successfully incorporated in dynamic semantics.[10] The focused element has been given a precise semantics by means of comparing it with the set of alternatives in Rooth's alternative semantics.[11] The overall principle behind this approach is that quantificational domains can be restricted through (i) binding, (ii) accommodation of presuppositions, or (iii) focusing. The idea is that focusing induces presuppositions. The interrelation between focus and presupposition seems to be more intricate though. Geurts and van der Sandt (1999) view focusing and presuppositions as separate phenomena. Nevertheless, focus is part of contextually given information and one of its 'normal' roles, so to speak, is to induce presuppositions. As a result, it seems that to regard focus as a constraint for domains of quantification on a par with binding and accommodation amounts to dividing, so to speak, the explanandum into an explanandum and an explanans: presupposition realized as focusing is explained by focusing. Or, even, this approach reverses the true roles of the explanandum and the explanans: it is *presupposition* that gives us alternatives for the semantics of *focus*, rather than the other way round. This is so because focus induces presuppositions.[12] Last but not least, in addition to the methodological problems pointed out above, the fact is that special accenting is not present very often.

Moreover, the topic-hood can help with the hierarchy of preference of interpretations. For example, in (15) where 'the mother' is clearly in the topic position, 'she' selects it as its antecedent:

(15)   The mother picked up the baby. She had been ironing all afternoon.
       (from de Swart 1998: 149).

Topics are good antecedents for pronouns: their referents are more salient than those of other referring expressions of the sentence (cf. Lambrecht 1994). Further, as Krahmer and van Deemter (1998) say, the information properties of the phrases that qualify as antecedents have to be considered. For example, if 'the man' has two suitable antecedents, 'a man' and 'an uncle of mine', it is more likely that 'a man' will be selected, independently (within some range) of the distance from the anaphor.[13]

In spite of the disambiguating role of focus, the authors still uphold the 'genuine ambiguity' between binding and accommodation in partial matches: in many situations of discourse, there are no helpful disambiguating factors for utterances such as (10) or (14). In DS, however, this genuine ambiguity seems unwarranted. I present the argument in Section 7.5, but let us first gloss over some alternative DR-theoretic treatments of anaphors, including presuppositional anaphors, in order to test the intuition about ambiguities in the processing of anaphoric expressions.

7.4 Other principles for selecting anaphors

Kamp (2001) argues for the need to recognize intermediate stages, so to speak, between binding and accommodation. When binding fails, it is not the case that global accommodation takes over. Instead, some missing contextual information can be added so as to make binding possible. As he rather briefly remarks, we may need a theory of presupposition types. This, however, takes us only part of the way. Whatever presupposition types are, it seems that they would amount to a useful typology, but a typology that cannot be but an intermediate stage in the search for a cognitively plausible explanation of what the interlocutors actually do while resolving anaphoric links.

Asher and Lascarides (1998*a*, 2003) do not distinguish binding from accommodation. They have a discourse update through *binding presuppositions to the context* by 'rhetorical links'.[14] They provide a list of factors on which presupposition projection depends, including the semantic and pragmatic properties of the relevant utterances, the type and strength of the rhetorical relations, as well as the preference for global attachment, that is, in our terminology, global accommodation (1998*a*: 282). For example, in (16), the interaction between the rule 'Prefer Global Attachment' and 'Maximize Discourse Coherence' results in the local accommodation of the presupposition that the problem has been solved.

(16)   Either John didn't solve the problem or else Mary realized that the problem has been solved. (from Asher and Lascarides 1998*a*: 265).

Presupposition projection is explained there by the type and strength of rhetorical relations. In Asher and Lascarides (2003: 23–4), they explain the oddity of sentence (16) by employing a relation of Alternation that contrasts the two disjuncts. All that matters for our current purpose is that, in their SDR-theoretic account, there are general rules that explain the behaviour of anaphors, without giving rise to unwarranted ambiguities.

Following Asher's (1986) and Kamp's (1990) work on the anchoring of discourse referents, Zeevat (2000), discussing the semantic behaviour of demonstratives, suggests intensional anchoring of referents in DRSs.[15] Such anchors contain information from the speaker's concept and are therefore richer than the referring expression itself and can aid the reference resolution process. Instead of postulating a discourse referent that is linked directly to an object in the world (externally anchored; see Kamp 1990: 51–5; 1996), he proposes adding new conditions to the DRS which define this individual for the particular universe of discourse. In this way he captures the observation that anchors must include the ways in which the objects figure in discourse. Presuppositions are resolved on the basis of considering such relevant guises under which the referent is known or perceived. The role of the presuppositions concerning the descriptive meaning of referring expressions is rendered with much more fine-tuning in this theory: '[t]he objects that are found by presupposition resolution in the common ground are anchored by an intensional anchor' (Zeevat 2000: 307). In other words, the speaker's concept has more content than the referring expression itself. How exactly these anchors can be created in the process of interpretation is a separate problem for research on the cognitive aspects of discourse processing. But again, all that matters for our present argument is that anaphora resolution seems to be by default regarded as unambiguous, resulting in a unique antecedent.

Geurts (2000) attempts to explain the properties of presupposition by an informativeness principle. Example (17) induces a presupposition in (18) in spite of the initial modal expression.

(17) Perhaps Fred does not know that the dean is a woman.

(18) The dean is a woman. (from ibid.: 316).

He observes that if it is the case that presuppositions are accommodated as closely as possible to the main DRS, it must be so for a reason. This reason could be informativeness, as specified in the Informativeness Principle (IP): stronger, more informative readings are preferred. Geurts dismisses it though. He claims that in examples (19)–(22), the more informative reading (reading (i)) is not the preferred reading.

(19) Fred picked a fight with a Yankee.
  (i) Fred picked a fight with an inhabitant of the Northern States of the US.
  (ii) Fred picked a fight with an inhabitant of the US.

(20) Barney's social circle consists of inarticulate philosophers and literary critics.
  (i) inarticulate [philosophers and literary critics]
  (ii) [inarticulate philosophers] and [literary critics]

(21) The cover of Betty's latest novel is decorated with pink fruits and vegetables.
  (i) pink [fruits and vegetables]
  (ii) [pink fruits] and vegetables

(22) Everybody in this room speaks two Romance languages.
  (i) Two Romance languages are spoken by everybody in this room.
  (ii) Everybody in this room speaks two Romance languages. [some or other, KJ] (from Geurts 2000: 327).

Let us briefly consider these examples in the light of DS and the four sources of compositional MR. Sentence (19) is accounted for because it is a case of social–cultural conventions and reading (ii) is produced by SCD 1. Examples (20) and (21) are instances of syntactic ambiguity and hence a 'genuine ambiguity' which no one would question. If there is a preferred interpretation, it would have to be context-driven, or possibly driven by some weak social–cultural defaults assumed by the interlocutors, such as, for instance, that literary critics are not *normally* inarticulate or that vegetables are not *normally* pink. Finally, (22) is a case of a cognitive default where 'two Romance languages' defaults to 'exactly two Romance languages' rather than, for instance, to 'French and Italian'.

The DS solution does not stand in a vacuum. Levinson (2000: 270–1) also points out that anaphoric linking lies largely outside the domain of grammar and has to be resolved pragmatically, with the help of default interpretations in that semantically general expressions such as pronouns I-implicate local coreference, whereas semantically specific expressions such as definite descriptions M-implicate disjointness from the local potential antecedent. DS goes one level up from these heuristics-based defaults to types of defaults that are motivated by (i) the properties of the processor (CD) or, in other words, the cognitive apparatus of a model hearer; (ii) the environment (SCD 1); or (iii) both (CPI 1). It is also akin in spirit to constraints of Optimality-Theory pragmatics: Blutner's (2000) constraint 'Avoid Accommodation' accounts for the preference for binding, even binding with partial matches and binding with bridging, over introducing new objects, and his 'Be Strong' accounts for the preference for the strongest interpretation consistent with what the speaker says.[16] OT constraints, it seems, are directly translatable onto our cognitive-default based preferences. But a detailed comparison will have to wait for another occasion.

7.5 Scales and defaults for presuppositional anaphors

In view of the above discussion, it seems that we can accept default interpretations for presuppositional-anaphoric expressions as a plausible assumption. In DS, we shall attempt to explain such default interpretations with reference to one overarching principle of the strength of intentionality and the strength of intending. The feasible alternatives will be placed on a scale of the 'degree to which the referent is salient', in a manner resembling Gundel, Hedberg, and Zacharski's (1993) proposal of the hierarchy of givenness of the referent that groups referring expressions on a scale of salience.[17] Furthermore, this scale is compatible with the degree of *being in focus* which, as was discussed in Section 7.4, contributes to the disambiguation of quantificational domains.

In DS, preferences in reference resolution are accounted for by appealing to the properties of the mental states. Just as in the case of referring by definite descriptions in extensional and intensional contexts, in partial matches we can appeal to the degree of intentionality, translated into the degrees of the informative intention (the DI principle of DS), and, where applicable, into the strength of the referential intention embedded in it (the PI principle of

DS). Binding and accommodation allow for degrees of salience of the sites for the antecedent, and hence they allow for the degrees of salience of various potential antecedents. This salience corresponds to the degree of intentionality with which the utterance was produced: or, strictly speaking, the degree of intentionality of the underlying thought. In the stressed version of (14), the referential intention is weaker than in the unstressed version: the set of children is not clearly specified, it can be either a subset of the partygoers or some other group of children. When there is no stress on 'children', this presupposing reading is not the default: the stress helps bring it about. The intentionality of the underlying mental state and hence the referential intention of the utterance are weaker as compared with the unstressed, non-presupposing reading. The strength of intentionality yields intuitively correct results: binding with a partial match is preferred to accommodation and the presupposing, accommodating reading is marked, it is not the default.

So far I have looked at presuppositions of existence. Similarly, in the case of presuppositions other than existential ones, it seems to be the case that non-presupposing readings come with stronger intentionality and are the default. In (23), the presupposition of the consequent, that someone solved the problem, cannot percolate up to the top of the sentence because it is prevented from doing so by the content of the antecedent:

(23)   If someone at the conference solved the problem, it was Julius who solved it.

In (23a), stressing 'at the conference' results in a reading in which the antecedent shares the presupposition (that someone solved the problem) with the consequent. Stressing 'at the conference' results in a presupposing reading.

(23a)   If someone AT THE CONFERENCE solved the problem, it was Julius who solved it.

Analogously, in (24a), stressing 'murdered' gives rise to a presupposing reading.

(24)   If John murdered his wife, he will be glad that she is dead.
(24a)   If John MURDERED his wife, he will be glad that she is dead. (from van der Sandt 1988: 158).

These examples are partial matches in that 'John's wife being dead' is entailed by 'John's wife being murdered' and 'solving the problem' is entailed by

'solving the problem at the conference'. The presuppositions of the consequent, that someone solved the problem and that John's wife is dead in (23a)
and (24a) respectively, can be either anaphoric on the antecedent or have to be
accommodated. In the case of binding to the partially matching proposition,
the non-presupposing reading ensues. In sum, we can have the (i) binding,
anaphoric on the antecedent, non-presupposing reading, or the (ii) accommodating, presupposing reading.

Let us now compare the intentionality of the mental states associated with
(23) and (24) on the one hand, and (23a) and (24a) on the other. In (23) and
(24), the eventuality stated in the consequent relies on the eventuality condi-
tionally stated in the antecedent. In other words, what is intended in the
antecedent is merely developed in the consequent, preserving the condition-
ality of the whole statement.[18] On the other hand, in (23a) and (24a), what is
intended in the consequent has to be resolved as to its strength with respect to
the presuppositions of the antecedent. To use the DS-theoretic explanation,
the intentionality of the mental states that correspond to (23a) and (24a) is
'dispersed' between the presupposing and the non-presupposing reading.
This is so because although the presuppositions that someone solved the
problem and that John's wife is dead are strong there because of the accenting,
they need not necessarily be there. It is also possible to read (23a) as part
of (23b).

(23b)   If someone AT THE CONFERENCE solved the problem, it was Julius
        who solved it. But, of course, the problem may not have been solved
        at all.

Similarly, (24a) can be part of (24b).

(24b)   If John MURDERED his wife, he will be glad that she is dead. But she
        may not be dead for all I know.

In the unstressed (23) and (24), intentionality is stronger. The way to think
about it is that there are no interfering factors between the antecedent and the
consequent: the consequent comes with the intentionality that is clearly
associated with the conditional status of the antecedent clause. Intending
the eventuality represented in the antecedent is, by this reasoning, the case of
stronger intentionality. Hence, the non-presupposing readings again turn out
to be the default.

As always, I have switched seamlessly between 'stronger intentionality' and
'stronger intending'. This is dictated by the DS-theoretic assumption
defended in Chapter 2 that the degree of intentionality of the mental state is
reflected in the degree of the speaker's referential intention. To repeat, if we

define referential intention as intending eventualities as well as individuals, referential intention is the only type of intention we need for the purpose of explanation. If, however, we confine it to referring to individuals, then we have to add to the theory the degrees of the informative intention as well. All in all, in (23) and (24), the intention is stronger: the eventuality is, so to speak, communicated more strongly. If we allow the referential intention to apply to states, events, and processes, not merely to individuals, then the referential intention is present and is also stronger.

We have established that binding and accommodation allow for scales of preferred sites for antecedents. The scales reflect the degrees to which the potential antecedent is salient in the discourse. In DS, salience of referents translates directly into the degree of intentionality of the mental state and the degree of referential or informative intention that accompanies the use of the expression that introduces this discourse referent. The 'degree of being in focus' is equally translatable, albeit focus has a different status as a constraint on quantification domains from that of binding and accommodation (*pace* Geurts and van der Sandt 1999), as I have argued in Section 7.4. Focus is a 'helping hand', or a repair device that has to be signalled by accent or sentence structure and triggers the search for what is, by default, the strongest referent. Focus induces a presupposing reading, and hence indicates some degree of accommodation. Let us take example (14a) again:

(14a)   If John talks to some partygoers, the CHILDREN will laugh at him.

Here 'the children' is a subset of the set of partygoers or some other set of children. Generally, backgrounded material in the nuclear scope tends to be interpreted as belonging to the quantifier's restrictor and focused information is in the nuclear scope. The referential intention is weaker than that of the unstressed version: the subset is not further specified, neither is the other set of children. Hence, from the strength of this intention, as well as from the strength of the intentionality of the underlying mental state, we can conclude that the presupposing reading is not the default. We can also predict that binding with a partial match is preferred to accommodation as the referential intention is stronger in the first. The presupposing reading is the result of accommodation and so it is not as strongly communicated as the non-presupposing reading.

We are now in a position to summarize this account in the form of MRs. In DS, (14), repeated below, has an MR as in Fig. 7.1.

(14)   If John talks to some partygoers, the children will laugh at him.

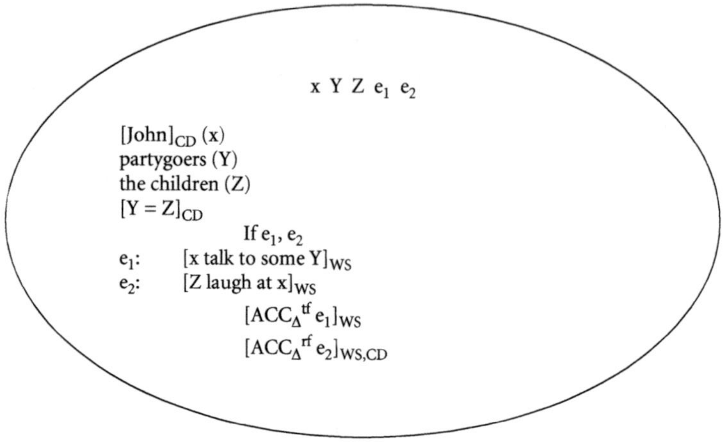

$$x \ Y \ Z \ e_1 \ e_2$$

$\text{[John]}_{CD} \ (x)$
partygoers (Y)
the children (Z)
$[Y = Z]_{CD}$

$$\text{If } e_1, e_2$$
$e_1: \quad [x \text{ talk to some } Y]_{WS}$
$e_2: \quad [Z \text{ laugh at } x]_{WS}$

$$[ACC_\Delta{}^{tf} \ e_1]_{WS}$$
$$[ACC_\Delta{}^{rf} \ e_2]_{WS,CD}$$

FIGURE 7.1. MR for sentence (14): the non-presupposing reading

Following the DRT notation, I am using capital letters for plural referents (sets taken collectively). I depart from the DRT ontology as far as the representation of anaphors is concerned. 'Partygoers' and 'the children' pick out two different discourse referents because they introduce distinct conceptual material. The resolution of the anaphoric link allows us in e_2 to substitute Y for Z. On the other hand, the proper name 'John' and the pronoun 'him' anaphoric on it pick out the same discourse referent: pronominal anaphora does not normally introduce the problem of identification of concepts but rather the matching of features such as person, gender, or number and hence, for the purpose of MRs, can be represented by the identity of the discourse referent. In Kamp and Reyle's (1993) version of DRT, there is a rule that specifies that one always takes new discourse referents when extending a DRS. So, for an anaphoric pronoun, we would have a new discourse referent and then represent the resolution of the anaphoric link by means of an equation, e.g. '$x = y$'. This rule, however, is subject to theoretical debates. The problem with this rule is that it requires a top-down resolution of presupposition, while in fact it has proven more adequate to resolve them by adding them to the main DRS ('justifying' them in the main DRS) as discourse interpretation progresses (van Eijck 2001; Kamp 2001). In DS, the problem does not arise, however. Compositionality is a property of an MR, not WS, and on this assumption we have considerably more freedom in representing the linguistic expressions and structures used in the act of communication. To be more precise, it seems that all we need be concerned about in making a decision on this matter is the information content of the conditions predicated of discourse referents. Hence, in Fig. 7.1, we have only one discourse referent *x* for 'John' and 'him', while we have *X* and *Y* for 'partygoers' and 'the children'.

I have also made some other assumptions in this formalism that require an explanation. First, I have assumed that the futurity of e_1 equals that of tenseless future and I represented it as $[ACC_\Delta{}^{tf} e_1]_{WS}$. In this work, I cannot investigate the issue as to whether this is exactly correct or not. All that matters is that it is an intuitively plausible, simple, and harmless move. The modality of the antecedent is rather weak and hence it is only plausible to use *tf* that is significantly 'less modal', judging by the scale we proposed in Fig. 6.9. 'Will' of e_2 is of the type $ACC_\Delta{}^{rf}$, which is arrived at by CD and WS. The accented counterpart in (14a) is represented as in Fig. 7.2.

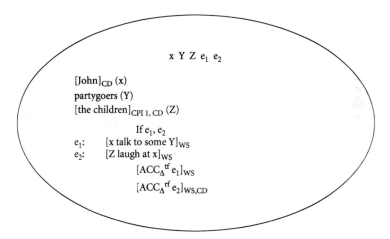

$$x\ Y\ Z\ e_1\ e_2$$

$$[\text{John}]_{CD}\ (x)$$
$$\text{partygoers}\ (Y)$$
$$[\text{the children}]_{CPI\,1,\,CD}\ (Z)$$

$$\text{If } e_1, e_2$$
$$e_1: \quad [x \text{ talk to some } Y]_{WS}$$
$$e_2: \quad [Z \text{ laugh at } x]_{WS}$$
$$[ACC_\Delta{}^{tf}\ e_1]_{WS}$$
$$[ACC_\Delta{}^{rf}\ e_2]_{WS,CD}$$

FIGURE 7.2. MR for sentence (14a): the presupposing reading

Let us consider '$[\text{the children}]_{CPI\,1,\,CD}\ (Z)$' of Fig. 7.2. The referent for 'the children' is accented in this example and this accenting triggers CPI 1 and produces disjoint referents *Y* and *Z* for 'partygoers' and 'the children'. Next, the reading of the definite description 'the children' is by CD taken to be the default referential one, as discussed in Chapter 4. Fig. 7.2 is then the MR of the presupposing reading. Example (10) acquires an analogous analysis.

It seems, therefore, that MRs, founded on the PoL, DI, and PI principles of DS, provide a uniform tool for explaining the behaviour of the alleged 'genuine ambiguities' of partial matches in presuppositional anaphora. The overarching principle of the degrees of salience/intentionality/intentions on which this analysis is founded gives DS an advantage over sets of rules such as those reviewed in Section 7.4.

The role of DI and PI has been discussed at length above. Now it is necessary to comment on the compatibility with PoL. The default and non-default degrees of salience in partial matches witness against the need for underspecified semantics in the following way. Although binding is essentially a semantic phenomenon, while accommodation is essentially pragmatic, they constitute a *continuum* in the search for antecedents along the projection line and they are both guided by a syntactic restriction on possible sites.[19] The output of intentionality, in the form of the informative intention and referential intention where applicable, interacts with the output of syntactic processing and produces a semantic representation, in accordance with PoL. Neither ambiguity nor underspecification need be postulated. Underspecified semantics is not questioned either by van der Sandt or by others working on presupposition and anaphora. However, the fact that there are scales of preferred binding/accommodation sites, that is scales of preferred interpretations, witnesses against the need to postulate an underspecified representation as a separate, theoretically interesting level of analysis. Perhaps it also acts in favour of abandoning the semantics/pragmatics boundary altogether. Binding is a 'mostly' semantic phenomenon, and binding sites are arrived at through a variety of sources which, in DS, are semantic: WS, CD, CPI 1, and SCD 1. Accommodation is a 'mostly' pragmatic phenomenon, but is led by a syntactic rule on preferred sites and, as before, by WS, CD, CPI 1, and SCD 1 of DS. Due to ascribing compositionality to the post-merger representation (MR), DS is a sufficiently flexible framework to incorporate all these sources of utterance meaning. The output of these sources is semanticized and where multiple representations are viable, they are ordered on the scale of preference. Neither ambiguity nor underspecification ensues. Syntax (WS) renders the first stage towards the semantic interpretation which is called underspecified semantics but this stage in utterance interpretation need no longer be stressed as separate in the analysis of utterance meaning.

7.6 Summary

In sum, binding is preferred to accommodation, and there are preferences both among binding sites and among accommodation sites. Partial matches do not seem to exhibit a 'genuine ambiguity' either. There are rules that tie, by default, topic (unstressed anaphor) with binding, and focus (stressed anaphor) with accommodation, for example in (10)–(10a), (14)–(14a), (23)–(23a), and (24)–(24a). One can explain these rules either in terms of van der Sandt's preference order, where discourse principles and non-linguistic knowledge are left as loose generic labels but binding and accommodation are carefully worked out, or in terms of some similar approaches discussed in this chapter. For example, Asher and Lascarides dispense with accommodation in favour of the overarching relation of binding presuppositions to the context through rhetorical links. I argue that there is no 'genuine ambiguity' as part of the semantic analysis in approaches of this type. In addition, as a more economical alternative, I have suggested ordering the interpretations on the scale of salience/intentionality/intentions, according to the general assumptions of DS.[20]

Notes

1 Non-monotonicity is also the case with the entailment of the negation of (5a).

2 See Chapter 1 and Jaszczolt 2002a: chs. 10–11 for an extensive discussion of the current views.

3 See Geurts 1998b, 1999 for a comparison of the approaches. Karttunen, Stalnaker, and Heim uphold the idea of contextual satisfaction according to which presuppositions of a sentence must be entailed by the context. Heim's account is problematic with respect to propositional attitude sentences: 'Tom believes that his brother is happy' presupposes that Tom believes that he has a brother rather than the intuitively correct 'Tom has a brother'. See Heim (1992) on the preference for *de re* readings and Geurts (1998b) on *exportation* and *importation* which bear some similarity to van der Sandt's original proposal of indexing presuppositions for the speaker or for the the the subject of the attitude (1988: 226–7).

4 My emphasis.

5 Van der Sandt (1988: 158) talks about a 'systematic ambiguity with respect to contextual parameters'.

6 I discuss the role of focus in Section 7.4.

7 Asher (1999) also provides rules for discourse focus in the form of the relations *Contrast* and *Parallel* which I shall not discuss in the present context.

8 See also van Deemter 1998; Asher and Lascarides 1998a.

9 It has to be borne in mind that accenting does not always equal focusing. See e.g. Lambrecht and Michaelis 1998 on *topic* accents.

10 See also Dekker 1998; Geurts 1998b.

11 This has been done, among others, by Blok and Eberle (1999); Büring (1999); Eckardt (1999); Jäger (1999); Partee (1999); and other contributions to Bosch and van der Sandt (1999).

12 A more detailed spelling out of this intuition is provided in Cohen's (1999) paper. According to Cohen, Rooth's alternatives that arise in the focusing of a phrase are induced by means of presupposition. The computation of alternatives and the projection of presupposition are governed by the same principles. Cohen gives convincing examples in which the disappearance of the presupposition also gives the wrong set of alternatives:

John always [agrees]$_F$ with Mary.

$^?$John always has a discussion with Mary and [agrees]$_F$ with her. (p. 62).
The presupposition has to be present and induce the same set of alternatives as focus. Cf. also:

> Assuming that there is some mechanism which derives the presuppositions of a sentence in context, we do not need any additional device in order to derive the set of alternatives induced by the sentence in that context. (Cohen 1999: 54)

See also Jaszczolt (2001) for further discussion and for a review of the core literature on focus.

13 The authors also stress the importance of the information value of anaphors: an antecedent with a non-specific interpretation cannot be less informative than the anaphor if there is an identity relation between them (see the Informative Anaphors Hypothesis; Krahmer and van Deemter (1998: 365)).

14 See also Chapter 2.

15 On types of anchoring see also Kamp 1996.

16 See also Zeevat 2002.

17 This is only one of several hierarchies of referring available in the literature. For a discussion see Jaszczolt 1999*b*: ch. 5. See also Walker et al. 1998 for Centering Theory. The degrees of salience are also compatible with von Heusinger's (2000*a*) argument that anaphoric expressions pick out the most accessible referent.

18 See also van der Sandt (1988: 158–60) on the role of context in establishing the factuality of the *if*-clause.

19 Van Eijck (2001: 333) accounts for this continuum by pointing out that if the context is not known, the anaphoric expression that is linked to such context simply carries the weakest possible information content. Chierchia (1995: 222) points out that definites carry 'anaphoric indices' that can be contextually supplied—there is no conceptual cut-off between sentential anaphora and contextual resolution. See also Spenander (2002: 179) on bridging as a category that employs both binding and accommodation.

20 This translation of discourse rules into intentions revives the spirit of Stalnaker's (1973) proposal that the presupposition relation has to be explained in terms of the speaker's beliefs and intentions, although it does not uphold its dispositional flavour: presupposing is not regarded here as a linguistic disposition to behave as if one had certain beliefs (cf. Stalnaker 1974: 202), neither are beliefs regarded as dispositions to act (cf. Stalnaker 1984: 15).

8

The Myth of Sentential Connectives?

8.1 The optimist's approach to sentential connectives and the Gricean legacy

Connectives of propositional calculus such as conjunction, disjunction, implication, equivalence, and negation are intuitively translatable as *and, or, if... then, if and only if,* and *not* (*it is not the case that*), respectively. The fact that they can constitute a self-contained class in propositional calculus gave rise to the supposition that they also have a special, privileged status in natural language and thus constitute a well-defined, 'natural' category that shares important semantic and pragmatic properties. The discussion stems directly out of Grice's (1975) proposal that sentential connectives in English have the semantics of their logical counterparts, while the additional meanings they may convey are a pragmatic overlay of conversational implicature. In this chapter I propose to reanalyse this class of expressions by discussing their meaning as it is arrived at in utterance interpretation and, subsequently, by representing the meaning of relevant utterances in terms of MRs. Let us begin with a very brief overview of the semantic problems posed by such connectives in English.

8.1.1 *Irregular* and

Sentential conjunction can easily be ascribed the property of being ambiguous. In (1), *and* seems to mean 'and then' as is evident from the difference caused by reversing the order of the conjuncts in (2). In (3), it conveys 'and as a result', as is evident from (4), while in (5) and (6) *and* remains an 'uncontaminated', so to speak, logical conjunction.

(1)   They got married and went to live in Australia.

(2)   They went to live in Australia and got married.

(3)   He started drinking and his wife left him.

(4)   His wife left him and he started drinking.

(5)   We listened to the music and looked at the beautiful violinist.

(6)   We looked at the beautiful violinist and listened to the music.

Arguments for the semantic contribution of these additional aspects of the meaning of *and* are ample.[1] While for Cohen (1971) these differences in the meaning of *and* signalled that the semantics of connectives may be richer than that of their logical counterparts, for post-Gricean pragmaticists the particular meaning of *and* is arrived at through pragmatic enrichment. The current orthodoxy is that *and* has a unary, unambiguous semantics.[2] The meaning enrichment is ascribed to nonce-inference, that is context-triggered pragmatic inference (e.g. Carston 1988, 2002a), or to presumed meanings, that is generalized conversational implicatures (e.g. Levinson 1995, 2000). It seems, however, that both orientations may be correct and the properties of the process of enrichment depend on the particular sentence, without sacrificing shortcuts in processing. Carston's account (e.g. 2002a: 227) comes close to DS in that she admits shortcuts in inference such as using 'frequently encountered and used scripts', for example a script for shooting and dying as a cause–consequence relation in example (7).

(7)   She shot him in the head and he died instantly. (from Carston 2002a: 223).

Proponents of GCIs cannot incorporate intermediate solutions: for Levinson (2000), GCIs are local, they can arise as soon as the potentially ambiguous expression is uttered, they need not be post-propositional. DS differs from either stance, albeit to different degrees. Let us take an utterance of sentence (8).

(8)   I dropped the glass and it broke.

It would be rather far-fetched to maintain that there is a cognitive default that governs our use of the collocation 'dropping a glass + glass's breaking'. Naturally, there is nothing to stop us from concocting an intention-based explanation according to which the informative intention of (8) is stronger if the speaker means causal *and* rather than a simple conjunction. By this token, whenever there is doubt, we would assign the causal reading by default. But such an intention-based explanation would heavily overgenerate and is not a hypothesis that is worth constructing. Let us now compare (8) with (9).

(9)   I looked up and it started snowing.

Unlikely as it might be, a causal explanation is also possible in (9): if the speaker is equipped with the supernatural powers, let us say, of Santa Claus who wishes to give children a white Christmas, a gaze up at the heavens may be the cause of a snowfall. How do we draw a boundary between utterances in which the default causal meaning ensues and the ones in which it does not? Sentence (10) seems to be situated somewhere in-between.

(10)   I smiled and John smiled too.

The only common-sense solution seems to be that the context of interpretation makes it clear as to whether an enrichment of *and* is the case. But this does not yet mean that there are no default enrichments. As was argued at length in Part I, the contributions to the merger representation that are not the result of conscious pragmatic inference can only be a result of unconscious, assumed meaning assignment by default. These defaults are of two types: those that have to do with the way our mental states are, and those that have to do with the ways society and culture operate. We have also established that CD is not an active source of meaning information for sentential conjunction *and*. But we still have SCD 1 to consider. In order to ascribe the particular enrichments in (8)–(10) (if any) to the particular source (SCD 1 or CPI 1), we need the situation in which the act of communication took place. This context-dependence does not mean that there are no social–cultural defaults: in the context provided by my writing this chapter and in particular writing examples (8)–(10) on the page, (8) conveys a causal conjunction by SCD 1 as I know and I assume the reader knows that when one drops a glass it *normally* breaks. Sentence (9) has a standard logical conjunction because I know, and I know that the reader knows, that I am not equipped with the power to cause a snowfall. The utterance of (10) cannot be judged, even approximately, on the basis of the sentence alone, although a pause after 'I smiled' is likely to result in a causal connection, while its lack may convey a standard logical conjunction.

To sum up, it seems plausible to assume, on the basis of conversational practice as well as the theory of DS as presented so far, that cognitive defaults and social–cultural defaults have very different characteristics from presumptive meanings of the type advocated by Levinson (2000).They are not default interpretations for words or expressions that arise as soon as the expression is produced and then readily submit to cancellation wherever the context requires it. Defaults of DS are not as 'strong', so to speak. First, they appear 'post-propositionally', after the utterance of the sentence has been completed. Secondly, while cognitive defaults are universal in that they are governed by the structure and operations of the human brain, social–cultural defaults are more ordinary 'shortcuts' in reasoning: where the inference pattern is active in the processor's knowledge base because it pertains to active social or cultural knowledge, there is no need for conscious pragmatic processing. It seems that if there are any default interpretations to do with sentential connectives, they are likely to be of this weaker, social–cultural kind.

This view is fully compatible with recent experimental findings with respect to the speed of semantic processing. In his experimental work, Sanford (2002) showed that words that are highly relevant for the discussed situation receive less semantic processing than less relevant ones. This is explained in terms of Sperber's (2000) hypothesis that the encyclopaedic knowledge that pertains to content words is retrieved over time and that this process of retrieval stops when enough information has been retrieved to process the intended meaning. In other words, when the situation of discourse makes the meaning of a word prominent for the context of this particular utterance, the semantic analysis of the lexical item is stopped as it would have been redundant. If, for example, 'breaking' occurs in the context of 'dropping a glass', we have a default scenario that imposes the sense of cause–consequence without the need for processing it separately. Although the experimental work analysed there is not directly related to connectives, the conclusions easily apply: breaking requires little processing because *and as a result* is already present in the default schema. It is worth noting that default schemata are widely accepted by advocates of nonce-inference (e.g. the relevance-theoretic approach by Carston 2002*a*), and that our social–cultural defaults may prove to be a middle solution in the 'GCI vs. nonce-inference' debate. This is, however, an issue for future research and will not be resolved swiftly.

Now, according to Gómez Txurruka (2003), there is no need to postulate temporal or other defaults for *and*. She has developed an SDRT account of *and*, based on Asher and Lascarides's discourse relations. Instead of defaults, *and* comes with the information that coordination is taking place, and world knowledge points the hearer towards the rhetorical structure rules such as *Narration, Result*, or *Parallel* that account for various readings. In DS, we have no discourse rules but we have world knowledge that triggers the SCD 1 and CPI 1 sources of information about meaning. In real terms, the similarity of the two explanations is diaphanous: *and* is simply a coordinating sentential conjunction, and some aspect of the situated act of communication allows the hearer to process it as simple coordination, cause–consequence link, or temporal conjunction.

All in all, the point I am making is this. The debates over the semantics and pragmatics of sentential conjunction *and* can be easily surpassed when we acknowledge the fact that conscious pragmatic inference or default enrichment are themselves the product of the act of communication situated in context. *Pace* Levinson (2000), context-dependence and nonce-inference are very different concepts and context-dependence does not preclude defaults when the latter are understood as CDs[3] and SCDs 1. In view of the above, the MR for (8) is likely to look as in Fig. 8.1. The representations are partial in that past tense verb forms are left unanalysed for the reasons discussed in Section 6.6, namely that it is still an open question whether 'pastness' is best regarded as tense or modality.

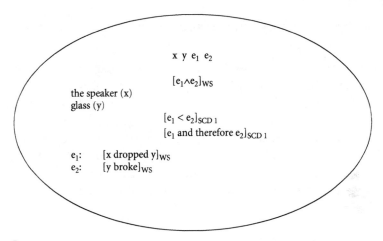

[P]FIGURE 8.1. MR for sentence (8): conjunction

The temporal and causal connections between e_1 and e_2 are due to SCD 1. Note that 'therefore' need not be a temporal cause–consequence link. That is, 'e_1 and therefore e_2' does not entail that e_1 precede e_2. Reasons can be simultaneous with what they are reasons for, as in (11):

(11)   Our first violinist played a solo recital and the rest of us played as a trio instead of a quartet last night.

That is why, in Fig. 8.1, we have both conditions '$e_1 < e_2$' and 'e_1 and therefore e_2'.

8.1.2 Or *and no more*

Disjunction in English is intuitively regarded as an expression of uncertainty as to which of the disjuncts is the case. In other words, the speaker utters (12) when he or she is not in a position to utter any of (13)–(15).

(12)   He drives a Ford or a Vauxhall.

(13)   He drives a Ford.

(14)   He drives a Vauxhall.

(15)   He drives a Ford and a Vauxhall.

This exclusive meaning of *or* is even more apparent in (16) and (17).

(16)   He likes either venison or lamb.

(17)   Tell me the secret password or you are dead.

On the other hand, in examples like (18) *or* is normally inclusive, meaning 'an accredited journalist, an Oxbridge graduate, or both': one can qualify for admission on both criteria.

(18)   You can attend the society debate if you are an Oxbridge graduate or an accredited journalist.

In virtue of the Gricean principle of cooperation, the speaker is expected to use disjunction when asserting both disjuncts would be inappropriate, that is the use of *or* is governed by the scale <and, or>. This scale does not, however, help with the choice between the inclusive and exclusive reading: '*a* or *b* or both' does not mean '*a* and *b*'. In fact, sometimes the choice between the two readings of *or* is not very important for the interpretation of the utterance and need not be borne in mind by the interlocutors. In example (19), it seems irrelevant that the subject can be both silly and misinformed.

(19)   You are either silly or misinformed.

In (18), the inclusive aspect of *or* is not very prominent either. As van der Auwera and Bultinck observe:

it is clear that there are contexts in which the difference between 'and' and 'or' gets neutralized, in the sense that the overall semantics can be arrived at with the meaning of 'and' as well as with the meaning of 'or' (...). (van der Auwera and Bultinck 2001: 180)

They also mention Maricopa, a Yuman language of a native American people in south-central Arizona, in which there is no expression for *and*, and the juxtaposition of two expressions can have either the conjunctive or disjunctive meaning. They conclude that any generalizations concerning the natural language *and* and *or* are difficult. However, there are still sufficiently strong reasons to adopt scalarity of <and, or>. English conjunction and disjunction easily fit in the Aristotelian square of oppositions in that (i) $\land$ has a contrary $\land\neg$, $\neg\lor$; (ii) $\lor$ has a subcontrary $\lor\neg$, $\neg\land$; and (iii) exclusive disjunction can be easily built into the square of oppositions between $\neg\land$ and $\lor$.[4] Naturally, this 'building into' the square of oppositions has to be understood in terms of *concepts* for conjunction and disjunction rather than words. This conceptual distinction can then be approached in terms of pragmatic or semantic scales. What is important, however, is the fact that languages do not lexicalize exclusive disjunction ('and not'). It is only natural to conclude with van der

Auwera and Bultinck (2001: 181), that this fact 'may well be situated at the cognitive level'. This would give strong reasons to doubt the possibility of any cognitive default interpretations to do with exclusive *or*. Social–cultural defaults, however, come out unharmed: in agreement with the discussion of their 'weak' default status in Section 8.1.1, we can see them as triggered by frequently encountered scenarios.

This is as far as we can proceed at present in rethinking disjunction.

What we end up with is a rather complex pattern of use of *or*. Analysed in terms of DS, the use of *or* would not yield to clearly discernible sources of information that govern the readings. In other words, we cannot truthfully say that, for example, *or* is mostly exclusive and this is its most salient meaning, arrived at through WS and CD. It seems that, just as is the case with conjunction, the processing of sentential disjunction gives rise to more and less salient interpretations but these interpretations are based on the content of the sentence. If there are defaults, they are not defaults for *or* but rather defaults for the *sentence*. In other words again, *or* in (20) is exclusive not because this is a default for *or* but because through WS and CPI 1 the hearer arrives at the exclusive interpretation: the lecture is either on Monday or on Tuesday. The inference from the premise that there is only one, continuous event of a lecture allows the hearer to conclude that it is not on both.

(20)   The lecture is on Monday or Tuesday.

The MR for (20) will now look as in Fig. 8.2. We are regarding 'the lecture being on Monday' and 'the lecture being on Tuesday' as events, in that the event of the lecture taking place on a certain day of the week is the meaning that is likely to be recovered by a model hearer as that intended by the speaker.

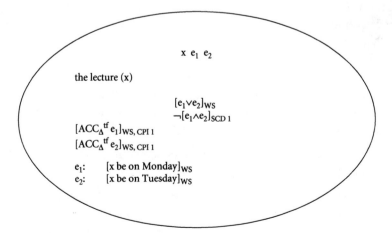

FIGURE 8.2. MR for sentence (20): disjunction

As can be seen from the MR, three sources of information are active in the interpretation of (20): WS, SCD 1, and CPI 1. The disjunction $e_1 \vee e_2$ is obtained through WS, while the exclusive meaning of 'or' is obtained via SCD 1. A tenseless future meaning of 'is' is obtained via the WS and CPI 1 because, as was argued in Chapter 6, the modal ACC_Δ e (where $\Delta = \vdash$) is obtained in this way. WS and the default scenario of talking about the day of the week of an eventuality by means of the present simple tense merge their resources to produce the *tf* value of Δ.[5]

The observations concerning the sentential *and* also apply to *or*: it seems that instead of the nonce-inference–default dilemma, it is more adequate to adopt a mid-way solution that consists of various sources of information such as WS, CD, SCD 1, and CPI 1, juggling their division of labour as the particular act of communication dictates it. What we gain in this way is the ability to account for the salience of some interpretations without sacrificing the plausibility of the interpretation, that is without postulating defaults that massively overgenerate.

8.1.3 *Freedom of denial*

According to the so-called Atlas–Kempson thesis, sentences of the type 'The A is not B' are not ambiguous. They are semantically general, non-specific, or vague.[6] The thesis of the lack of ambiguity is taken from Grice (1975) but the argumentation is developed further. Gricean reasoning, taken further, yields the result that the presupposition-preserving negation ('There is a unique A and it is not B') is derivable from the non-presupposing, wide-scope negation ('It is not the case that there is a unique A and it is B'). The reason for this is that the narrow-scope predicate negation entails the wide-scope sentence negation. For the supporters of general semantics, both readings are pragmatically inferable from a general, underdetermined representation.[7]

What will matter to us at present is what unifies the two standpoints, namely the view that there is no ambiguity of negation. Sentence (21) is supposed to support this view. It shows an application of Lakoff's (1970) test of conjunction reduction that substitutes 'and so did x', 'and the same goes for x' for the second occurrence of the same predication. According to Atlas, such a crossed reading is possible in the case of (21).

(21)   The King of France is not wise, and the same (thing) goes for the Queen of England. (from Atlas 1977: 326; 1989: 76).

If Atlas's intuitions are robust, then negation is not ambiguous between presupposition-preserving ('there is a Queen of England') and presupposition-denying ('there is no King of France').[8] But there are problems with this reasoning. First, Lakoff's test is not decisive. Secondly, the intuitions about the acceptability of (21) are not that strong, they are not widely shared. Next, as I discussed in Chapter 4 and at length elsewhere,[9] there is more to sentences 'The A is not B' than the scope of negation. The definite description has a very salient referential reading and hence, instead of the Russellian existential quantifier reading, it seems to trigger the interpretation akin to directly referring expressions. For example, (22) can trigger (22a):

(22) The president of the US is not a fool.
(22a) $\neg$ Fool (a)

In DS, PoL prevents us from assuming unwarranted sense-generality. To repeat, the sources of information, WS, CD, SCD 1, and CPI 1 jointly provide a semantic, compositional representation and hence any intermediate result of utterance processing that is prior to the merger is of no interest to us. In other words, compositionality ensues at a late, post-merger stage. So, all we want to know is the reading produced on a particular occasion of a production of a communicative act. It seems that just as in the case of *and* and *or*, so in the case of negation it would be rather implausible to look for uniform semantic properties. As a working hypothesis, I propose that negation is neither presupposition-preserving nor presupposition-denying. In fact, it can operate on any type of content. As was convincingly demonstrated by Carston (e.g. in 1996), negation can operate on different types of material. Negation is truth-functional but can operate on the result of the so-called 'echoic' use of language.[10] For example, the use of the polarity items in (23)– (23b) suggests that in (23b) the negated content is 'put in quotes', so to speak: the speaker's utterance in (23) is echoed there.

(23) Mary is sometimes late.
(23a) She isn't *ever* late; she's always punctual.
(23b) She isn't *sometimes* late; she's always punctual. (from Carston 1996: 324).[11]

We endorse this proposal of truth-functional negation that operates on various types of material.[12] At the same time, presuppositions are already accounted for in DS: they are anaphors, they are landing sites for binding or accommodation, provided respectively by the discourse or by the context.

All in all, negation ends up as a common-sense concept of denial, conceptualized as absence or lack, and it operates at various stages of MR construction. It frequently operates after presuppositional anaphora resolution. On some occasions, however, it operates before the presuppositional anaphora resolution has a chance to set off and then the anaphoric link is denied. In standard terms, we have a presupposition denial as in (24).

(24)   Tom's wife is not in New York—Tom doesn't have a wife.

The MR for the first clause of (24), repeated as (24a), where 'not' is unaccented, is likely to look as in Fig. 8.3. 'Is' is left unanalysed.

(24a)   Tom's wife is not in New York.

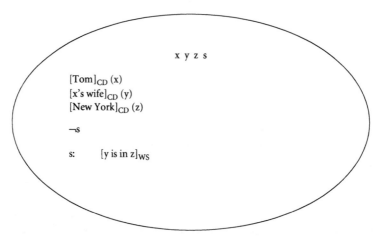

^PFIGURE 8.3. MR for sentence (24a): negation

By force of default accommodation discussed in Chapter 7, on this reading 'Tom's wife' acquires a discourse referent. In other words, the presupposition that Tom has a wife is globally accommodated. This means that in the following clause there has to be a process of cancellation of this CD. This cancellation is possible because CPI 1 triggers the interpretation of the entire sequence in (24) according to which ¬s obtains the non-presupposing, wide-scope reading. The final MR for (24) is likely to be as in Fig. 8.4. As before, the representation of temporality is left out.

But this MR does not seem a very probable representation: the discourse referent y is introduced and then the condition [x's wife]$_{CD}$ (y) is cancelled by ¬s$_2$. The reason for this is that (24) is not a very probable sequence when 'not' is unaccented. The narrow-scope reading of negation, triggered by the default, presupposing, referential reading of the description 'Tom's wife', would have to produce backtracking and presupposition cancelling once the second clause of (24) is produced. This is costly and unlikely, unless some special effect is intended. The topic has been widely discussed in the literature[13] and

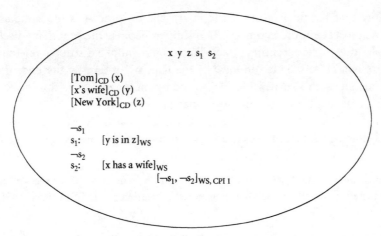

^PFIGURE 8.4. MR for sentence (24): presupposition cancelling

I shall have nothing new to add to it. Let us move on to (24) with accented *not*, repeated below as (24b).

(24b)   Tom's wife is NOT in New York—Tom doesn't have a wife.

The focusing of negation in the first clause produces the effect that the material on which negation operates is not specified until more information is obtained. In terms of processing, it means that the speaker signals that caution is required as there is some unusual interpretation of *not* involved. The MR will be as in Fig. 8.5.

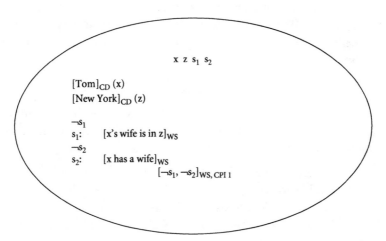

^PFIGURE 8.5. MR for sentence (24b): non-presupposing reading

Note that the final result of the interpretation process is the same as in Fig. 8.4, just the route is simpler. It is simpler because the processing itself is simpler due to the accenting of *not*. The assignment of a discourse referent to 'Tom's wife' is suspended in view of the flagging of *not*. By the end of the second clause, this suspension is resolved by means of CPI 1: Tom does not have a wife and hence negation on s_1 has the wide scope.

Now, in DS, truth-conditional content is the post-merger content. Hence, the following problem pointed out by Horn does not arise in DS—just as it does not arise on Carston's account:

> when we bear in mind what a truth function must be a function of, we recognize the implausibility in the view that negation is invariably truth-functional. (Horn 1989: 434)

The speaker can negate the entire post-merger representation (MR). This option is provided by the underlying tenet of DS, namely that compositionality is to be sought on the level of MR rather than WS. Questioning this view of negation would mean questioning DS and this is an entirely different, cross-paradigm debate.

The DS view is also compatible with that of Geurts (1998*a*: 293), who suggests that negation is aimed both at linguistic objects and objects in the world. His rephrasing of the Carston–Horn debate is too programmatic at present to be assessed, but it is clear that it does away with some unwarranted representations in the analysis of negation. Instead of finding the culprit of ambiguities of reading, namely the operator or the content operated on, Geurts accepts what seems like a natural merger of WS and context: the speaker negates whatever representation is intended to be negated, without regard to its provenance. If I am correct, this is very close to the DS view on which negation operates freely at various stages of the MR construction.

8.1.4 *The imperfect conditional perfection*

Conditional perfection is the name of the process by which the conditional *if . . . (then)* is taken to mean a biconditional *if and only if*, as exemplified in the oft repeated sentence in (25), read as (25a) or (25b).

(25)   If you mow the lawn, I'll give you five dollars.
(25a)   If and only if you mow the lawn will I give you five dollars.
(25b)   I'll give you five dollars just in case/only if you mow the lawn.
(25c)   If you don't mow the lawn, I won't give you five dollars. (from van der Auwera 1997: 169, after Geis and Zwicky 1971).

Conditional perfection is the case of an 'invited inference' to (25c), triggered by Grice's cooperative principle, and is possibly governed by the scale $<$(if p, q and if r, q and if s, q, ...), ..., (if p, q)$>$ (van der Auwera 1997: 172). Naturally, this account applies to conditionals that refer to states of affairs rather than to epistemic (26) or speech act (27) conditionals.

(26)   If she's divorced, [then] she's been married.

(27)   John has left, in case you haven't heard. (from van der Auwera 1997: 170).

In spite of ample research on conditional perfection, the very intuition behind it has remained largely unshaken for over thirty years. But this intuition is not as steadfast as it is taken to be. Let us consider example (25) again. The speaker wants his/her lawn to be mowed and offers the addressee five dollars for doing it. But it does not seem to follow that the only possible way of obtaining five dollars from the speaker is mowing his or her lawn. What does follow, however, is a restriction of the domain of discourse, or, alternatively, a restriction (specification) of the topic of discourse. Mowing the lawn is the topic of this discourse and issuing a conditional request is the purpose of the act of communication. Perhaps, then, we should end at this restriction and not take it any further, that is not make it look like a strengthening to an equivalence. In other words, it is at least contentious whether mowing the lawn and obtaining five dollars are bi-uniquely linked. Naturally, earning five dollars has to be understood by the addressee as a strong incentive for mowing the lawn. But this incentive is not the same as perfection to a biconditional or an inference to 'if not p then not q'. Conditional perfection is just too strong a tool to account for the restriction of the domain of discourse that takes place when the conditional is used.

Let us attempt to reconstruct the process of interpretation of (25) as it would look on the domain restriction/topic specification view, and in particular in the DS framework that endorses it. The addressee hears (25). WS yields an 'if p, q' structure in which there are concepts pertaining to the speaker's giving five dollars and the addressee's mowing the lawn. The addressee knows that the conditional construction is used for a purpose: an action of mowing the lawn is a way of obtaining five dollars. This knowledge is part of the knowledge of language, and thus we ascribe it to WS. What other components of processing are discernible there? Perhaps by CPI 1 the addressee infers that there are no other obvious ways of earning five dollars from the speaker. Perhaps, even, this seems the *only* way. But the addressee cannot be sure that this is the only way: what is uttered is a conditional and what is processed is a constraint on the accessible situations that strengthens this conditional to the plausible, salient scenario for obtaining five dollars: just mow the lawn and you will get it. No *default perfection* to a biconditional through CD or SCD 1 need ensue. The MR for (25) is likely to look as shown in Fig. 8.6.

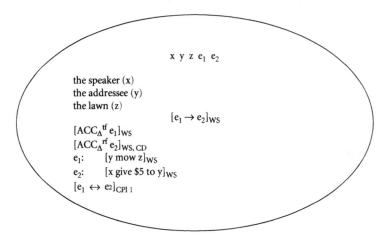

$$x\ y\ z\ e_1\ e_2$$

the speaker (x)
the addressee (y)
the lawn (z)

$$[e_1 \rightarrow e_2]_{WS}$$

$$[ACC_\Delta^{tf}\ e_1]_{WS}$$
$$[ACC_\Delta^{rf}\ e_2]_{WS,\ CD}$$
$$e_1: \quad [y\ mow\ z]_{WS}$$
$$e_2: \quad [x\ give\ \$5\ to\ y]_{WS}$$
$$[e_1 \leftrightarrow e_2]_{CPI\ 1}$$

FIGURE 8.6. MR for sentence (25): conditional perfection

This MR reflects our earlier argument that conditional perfection, if at all present, is consciously pragmatically inferred in the particular discourse situation. Futurity is analysed with reference to the values of ACC_Δ proposed in Chapter 6: Δ^{tf} is the result of the processing of the form of the antecedent, and Δ^{rf} is the default reading of *will* obtained via CD, in agreement with the argument for degrees of strength of *will* from Chapter 6.

8.2 Summary: the unitary DS account

It is apparent even from this preliminary investigation that, if we follow the assumptions of DS, the processing of English *and, or, not,* and *if* is less interesting and problematic than it is made out to be. There is no conclusive evidence that would preclude us from treating these sentential connectives in English as if they were analogous to the truth-functional operators of propositional logic. Some other aspects of their meaning can be easily attributed to pragmatic inference or defaults, especially on the assumption that WS on its own does not produce a level of representation. In other words, it is not the case that, for example, negation is wide-scope or sense-general by WS, and 'later on' in processing becomes narrow-scope or echoic through CD, SCD 1, or CPI 1. There is no interesting 'earlier–later' distinction here; there is a merger, MR, to which WS, CD, SCD 1, and CPI 1 contribute. They all produce the reading of the utterance with a connective that is taken to be the one intended by the speaker. What is evident from the MRs in Figs 8.1–8.6 is that there are no stable patterns for connectives: both CPI 1 and SCD 1 are triggered by the particular content in the particular context.

8.3 Future projections

Chapter 8 should bear the subtitle *Digression* or *Innuendo*, as it has never been intended as one of the core, interesting applications of DS. The aim of this chapter has been to point out that sentential connectives in natural language—or, at least, in English—do not constitute a self-contained, interesting category. Their 'enriched' meaning is in fact a 'post-propositional' enrichment arrived at in MR through quite ordinary processes of application of pragmatic inference or 'shortcuts' through inference in the form of SCDs. As the MRs for sentences with *and, or, if,* and negation demonstrate, nothing peculiar to sentential connectives is taking place there. Just as 'nanny' becomes processed as 'female nanny' in (28), by SCD 1, so 'and' becomes processed as 'and as a result' in (29) by CPI 1. The only difference is that the class of sentential connectives selected here is founded on the class of truth-functional connectives of propositional logic and, in fact (and predictably), retains a strong trace of their truth-functionality.[14]

(28) By the fountain stood a little boy with his nanny.

(29) I inserted a ticket in the slot and the barrier opened.

The readings for (28) and (29) proposed above are both quite standard. They are not, however, *default* in any interesting sense. Namely, they are not Levinson's (2000) GCIs arrived at though the I-principle. Neither are they cognitive defaults arrived at through DI of DS. Sentence (28) is a result of applying cultural knowledge to the act of communication. This application is likely to be unconscious, effortless, founded on previously encountered stereotypes, and hence is likely to fall under an SCD 1. Inserting a ticket in a slot in order to release a barrier at, for example, a car park is much less likely to be a cultural default than a result of CPI 1: it requires some conscious processing, conscious pragmatic inference. So, just as in Chapter 2, we end up with a rather vague, intuitive explanation of what is going on in utterance processing. However, vague as it is, it seems to get the sources of meaning information right. The ascription of the sources to the instances of utterance interpretation, that is, for example, classification of the inference from 'nanny' to 'female nanny' as conscious (CPI 1) or unconscious (SCD 1), has to be left, in the end, to experimental confirmation. This is a positive result, however: MRs of DS provide a theoretical structure that is flexible enough to accommodate experimental findings. At the same time, they are not immune to falsification: it is not difficult to agree what in a particular experimental design would falsify the CD, SCD 1, or even CPI 1 account and bring us back full circle to the compositionality of WS sought by analytic philosophers of the early (and not so early) twentieth century. And, as I discussed in Section 8.1.1, social–cultural defaults seem to lie half-way between 'strong', local GCIs of Levinson (2000) and relevance-theoretic nonce-inference that uses frequently encountered scripts (e.g. Carston 2002*a*). Since in DS the level at which compositional semantics is sought is different from that adopted in the above post-Gricean orientations, such 'weak' defaults are perfectly acceptable. Debate on this issue seems an obvious topic for further work on comparing the three theories.

Notes

1   Cohen 1971; Carston 1988, 1998*a*, 2002*a*; Wilson and Sperber 1998; Recanati 1989*a*, to mention a few.

2   See Carston 1988 on the functional independence principle, and Recanati 1989*a* on the availability principle and the scope principle as tests for the contribution of pragmatically inferred aspects of meaning to *what is said*.

3   Cf. the condition for Z in Fig. 7.2.

4   See van der Auwera and Bultinck (2001) for a three-layered scalar square for modals, quantifiers, and connectives.

5   This is not to say that Δ^{tf} is the only possible interpretation of (20). We can also have: 'The lecture is [normally] on Monday or Tuesday'.

6   Atlas 1977, 1989. See also Jaszczolt (1999*b*: 13–17) for further discussion and references.

7   See Atlas 1977, 1989; Carston 2002*a* (mainly the diagram on p. 290).

8   See e.g. Carston (2002*a*: 271–2) for a brief summary of the core standpoints in this debate.

9   E.g. Jaszczolt 1999*a*, 1999*b*.

10   'A representation is used echoically when it attributes some aspect of its form or content to someone other than the speaker herself at that moment and expresses an attitude to that aspect; Carston (2002*a*: 298).

11   My emphasis. NB Carston upholds the Gricean line on negation: negation has a wide scope, and presupposition-preserving, narrow-scope negation is pragmatically derived from it.

12   The compatibility with Horn's (1985, 1989) proposal of metalinguistic negation will not be taken up here. See Jaszczolt 1999*b*: section 1.2.4. Metalinguistic and descriptive negation reflect the 'built-in duality of use' (Horn 1985: 132), which is to be

understood as a pragmatic ambiguity. Instead of pragmatic ambiguity, we opt for different roles of (unitary) negation in MRs, which is not very far removed from Carston's proposal of differences in the material on which negation operates.

13 E.g. Horn 1985, 1989; Carston 1996, 1999; Burton-Roberts 1989, 1999. See Jaszczolt 2002a: ch.8 for the overview of presupposition and focus, as well as for further references.

14 Even this latter class is not a 'natural' class; propositional calculus can be built with only a proper subset of them.

9

Default Semantics for Number Terms

9.1 Number terms and number concepts

At first sight, during the past three decades or so, the semantics of number terms has been made more complicated and contentious than such terms seem to require. The problem is this. Utterance (1), for example, can convey the meaning that the speaker has exactly, approximately, or, occasionally, at least five pounds in his/her pocket.

(1) I have five pounds in my pocket.

Number terms are, then, potentially good candidates for semantic ambiguity. 'Five' in (1) can mean 'exactly five', 'approximately five', 'at least five', and even further unspecified just 'five'. In the context as in (2), it is likely to convey 'at least five'.

(2) A: If only I had five pounds in my pocket we could get a beer.
     B: I have five pounds in my pocket.

I shall use the expression 'number term' to refer to numeral expressions of a natural language, such as 'five', 'sixteen', 'one hundred and twenty-two'. Number terms correspond to those numeral expressions that are also known in the literature as *numerals proper* (Greenberg 1978). They are distinguished from expressions which also belong to the language numeral system of a language but are not numerals proper, such as 'the square root of four'. Since the 1970s, it has been popular to think of number terms such as *five* as being logically bound to mean 'at least five', leaving other meanings such as 'exactly five' to pragmatic inference.[1] Horn (1976: 33) proposes that a sentence containing cardinal number term *n* asserts lower-boundedness ('at least *n*') and may, in a particular context of discourse, implicate upper-boundedness ('at most *n*'), to result in the 'exactly *n*' reading. Number terms are not ambiguous; rather, 'what is *said* is systematically underdetermined by what is *uttered*' (Horn 1992: 172). Alternatively, *five* has also been taken to have semantically underdetermined meaning. In other words, on this view, *five* has a semantics that is underdetermined among 'exactly five', 'at least five', and, in some types of contexts, 'at most five' (see Carston 1998*b*). This move allows one to account for (3) where 'five' seems to convey the meaning of 'at most five'.

(3)   I can lend you five pounds.

Semantic underdetermination also accounts for the 'exactly five' meaning of the number term 'five' as in (4) and (5):

(4)   I have more than five pounds in my pocket.

(5)   I have less than five pounds in my pocket.

Sentences (4) and (5) would be ill-formed if the semantic content of *five* were 'at least five'.[2] Be that as it may, both on the 'at least' and the underspecified semantics account, number terms are scalar. They build up sequences based on the general scale $<\ldots,$ five, four, three, two, one$>$.[3]

   More recently, this way of cutting the semantics/pragmatics pie has been questioned. Instead, some linguists reverted to the traditional, common-sense 'exactly *n*' meaning as the semantic meaning of number terms. Apart from the most obvious reason for this, namely reflecting common intuitions, the reasons are ample. If *n* was semantically 'at least *n*', then 'at least' and 'at most' would not be symmetrical: the role of 'at least' would be just to prevent an implicature from arising. For example, in (1a), the implicature that the speaker has exactly five pounds, or at most five pounds, would not arise.[4]

(1a)   I have at least five pounds in my pocket.

The 'exactly' semantics is also preferable for collective readings, as (6) demonstrates.

(6)   Five men pushed the lorry out of a snow-drift.

Sentence (6) does not entail that one, two, three, or four men pushed the lorry out of a snow-drift, neither does it mean that at least five men did it. Exactly five men pushed the lorry together. In fact, downward entailment need not be present in distributive readings either, as (7) demonstrates.

(7)   If you fail three times, you are excluded. (from Koenig 1993: 143).

Furthermore, intuitions seem to be strong that terms expressing measurements have no downward or upward entailments and so they testify to punctual, 'exactly' semantics. Sentence (1) seems to mean that the speaker has exactly five pounds in his/her pocket. In sentences (8)–(10), this intuition of the punctual semantics is even stronger.

(8)   The ticket costs £5.

(9)   My cat weighs 10lbs.

(10)   The petrol station is 2km from here. (adapted from Koenig 1993: 144).

This, of course, holds with the proviso that in conversation it is often more appropriate to round the measurements up or down, and so (8) is not incompatible with, say, (8a), (9) with (9a), and (10) with (10a).

(8a)   The ticket costs £4.99.

(9a)   My cat weighs 10lbs 2oz.

(10a) The petrol station is 2.2 km from here.

Punctual semantics ('no more, no less' = 'exactly') is compatible with the 'approximately' meaning. The way to think about it is that in asserting (8)–(10), a margin of error is allowed, and, as I argue later in Section 9.3, the approximation is even assumed. So, (8a)–(10a) conform to the 'exactly' semantics, although, at the same time, they make use of the approximation, the margin of error.

Koenig's argument for the punctual semantics of number terms is this. By Horn's Q-principle (or the first part of Grice's Quantity maxim),[5] a number term that pertains to a proper subset A of a set B carries greater informativeness than a number term that pertains to the set B when both are predicated of the same situation. So, (1) is more informative than (11) when predicated of the same situation and is the optimal way of describing the situation in which the speaker has (approximately) five, but not six or nearly six, pounds in his/her pocket. Sentence (1) implicates (12) without having to resort to semantic underdetermination or the 'at least' semantics.

(1)   I have five pounds in my pocket.

(11)   I have four pounds in my pocket.

(12)   I don't have six pounds in my pocket.

Examples with two number terms that allow for different scoping relations also seem to point towards the punctual semantics. Example (13) is attested to have four salient readings (Kempson and Cormack 1981: 267).[6] The most salient one seems to be the 'doubly-collective' in (13a) where a set of exactly two examiners marks a set of exactly six papers.[7]

(13)   Two examiners marked six scripts.

(13a) Two examiners marked a set of six scripts between them.

In fact, 'between them' seems redundant, while in order to achieve the distributive reading, 'each' seems to be required, unless the context directs the addressee to the interpretation that, say, only two among the examiners managed to mark as many as six scripts (each) in, for example, three hours.

It has to be noted that Kempson and Cormack (1981: 270) combine the resources of the 'at least' semantics of number terms and underspecified semantics of scope relations to account for the possible readings. When one cuts the semantics/pragmatics pie in this way, the salience, or possibly the default status of some readings, remains, so to speak, the decoration on the pie that does not affect the way it is cut. Punctual semantics is diametrically different. Spelled out in this useful metaphor, it cuts the semantics/pragmatics pie much more generously for the semantics: semantics, with the salience of the 'exactly' reading, is the cake, while pragmatics, understood as implicatures, is the decoration.

9.2 Exact value, 'absolute value', and default use

With the help of the analysis of intonation patterns in Norwegian, Fretheim (1992) argues that Horn's pragmatic upper bound on number terms can only be inferred as a conversational implicature if the cardinal is salient in the discourse. Otherwise, cardinals have the 'exactly *n*' meaning. In Norwegian, the 'at least' interpretation of cardinal number terms is only possible when the term refers to an entity that is salient in discourse. Leaving aside the discussion of the semantic status of the pragmatic inference to 'exactly *n*', that is leaving aside the question as to whether it is Horn's implicature or, say, Carston's enrichment, let us focus on the evidence that some prosodic or other prominence on 'three' is required in order to produce (14). This prominence can be signalled by intonational contour or by a cleft construction, as in (14a) and (14b) respectively—or by a combination of the two as in (14c).

(14)   Lizzie doesn't have three sisters—she has four.
(14a)   Lizzie doesn't have THREE sisters—she has FOUR.
(14b)   It is not three sisters that Lizzie has but four.
(14c)   It is not THREE sisters that Lizzie has but FOUR.

The meaning of *three*, by this argument, is likely to be 'exactly three'. This 'exactly three' can be arrived at through different means though. One way to do it is to say that cardinal number terms are indeed scalar but their meaning is not unilateral, lower-bounded, as in the case of other scalars. Instead, it is bilateral. This direction is taken by Geurts (1998*a*, 1998*c*). Scalars have different interpretations in that *some* can mean 'some and possibly all' or 'some but not all'. Number terms are different. They are either exceptional, bilaterally bounded scalars, or, alternatively, they are not scalars at all, which, on Geurt's argument (1998c: fn 9), is just a terminological matter. What he argues against is that the upper bound of number terms is a GCI, as Levinson, Gazdar, Horn, and others have it. He also argues that GCI is a dubious category; instead, we should simply talk of default inferences. For number terms, this would seem to mean that the 'exactly' meaning is semantic. It is not a GCI, although, judging by the fact that Geurts is happy to classify number terms as scalars (albeit exceptional ones), it is arrived at through a pragmatic, strong, possibly default inference.

Geurts sides here with nonce-inferentialists. On the other hand, he is happy to accept the intuitions of default inference. If I understand him correctly, this is not far removed from the DS account. DS goes further in attributing the default 'exactly' meaning of cardinal number terms to the interaction of the WS and CD sources of meaning information, while arriving at other possible meanings through WS and CPI 1,WS and SCD 1, or WS alone. Section 9.3 demonstrates how these readings are represented in MRs.

Another way to account for the salience of the 'exactly' interpretation is to weaken it somewhat conceptually. Bultinck (2002, 2003) distinguishes the following *values* of *two*: at least two, at most two, exactly two, and two-absolute value. *Value* is understood as *use*, while the *meaning* of *two* comprises all of the enumerated values. Absolute value is an interesting proposal. It essentially means 'just two', without any commitment to there being more, less, or exactly two:

'absolute value' uses do not involve any explicit commitment with respect to the possibility of there being more or less than n elements in the set denoted by the NP. Naturally, being part of an NP, an 'absolute value' use of a numeral asserts the existence of n elements, which implies that the speaker asserts that the cardinality of the set will not be less than 'n'. However, this fact is not emphasized by the speaker: the possibility that there are less than n elements is excluded by virtue of the assertion of existence through the use of the NP containing the numeral, but this possibility is not excluded explicitly. ... Unlike 'at most n', 'at least n' or 'exactly n' uses, 'absolute value' uses do not focus on the epistemic stance of the speaker towards his or her expression of cardinality. (Bultinck 2003: 19)

Such non-committal uses of cardinal number terms are quite common, as was attested in Bultinck's (2002) empirical study. In particular, they are common in phrases that introduce new topics, such as direct object NPs.[8]

Now, Bultinck claims that the absolute value interpretation of number terms is their coded, literal meaning. It is their *default meaning* (Bultinck

2002: 287), in the sense that denoting cardinality is the default meaning of cardinal number terms. But denoting cardinality is not the same as having absolute value: 'exactly *n*' denotes cardinality in a much simpler and better way. In fact, Bultinck seems to say, if I understand him correctly, that the 'absolute value' and 'exactly' interpretations do not differ in truth conditions but in modality: the 'absolute value' use conveys an expression of the attitude of the speaker towards the possibility of there being more, or less, members of the set denoted by *n*.[9] This attitude can be stronger or weaker, culminating in the use of the number term in which it acquires a clearly 'exactly *n*' interpretation. He examines these senses of number terms with respect to the type of grammatical and conceptual context in which they occur, concentrating on the simple number term *two*, and concludes that the majority of utterances containing this number term use it in the 'absolute value' or the 'exactly' sense. So, the default is either 'exactly' or 'absolute value'. But, Bultinck's argument goes, the 'exactly' use is decomposable into the more general, non-committal 'absolute value' use, plus pragmatic factors that combine with it and render the 'exactly' use. Hence the absolute value is the semantics of number terms. This argument requires a closer scrutiny though. The strongest evidence for 'absolute value' is the empirical fact that, alongside the 'exactly' value, it is a very common use of cardinal number terms, at least of simple ones like *two*. This shows that speakers use *two* either without commitment to the cardinality of the set, or with a strong commitment. Now, the fact that it is theoretically possible to decompose the 'strong-commitment' use into the 'no-commitment plus pragmatic enrichment' is not yet evidence that the semantics of *two* is 'absolute value' *two*. This move is correct only on the assumption that it rests on the particular notion of the semantics/pragmatics interface, namely that of underspecified, 'impoverished', so to speak, semantics supplemented with a rich overlay of pragmatic processes. The move also requires a particular notion of default: if the absolute value is to be the default use, then it can only be such *qua* being 'closer to the semantics' than the 'exactly' use: the 'exactly' is arrived at through the 'absolute'. In other words, all uses of *two* would have to have the 'default', semantic, absolute value stage in their processing.

So far so good, but this is not the sense of default or of semantic meaning that we adopted in the theory of DS. Therefore, some transposition is required before we can use Bultinck's insights. The terms that require translating before exporting Bultinck's ideas to DS are: the expression 'absolute value', 'default', and 'semantic meaning'. Now, stressing the fact that speakers use number terms without commitment is certainly a move in the right direction. But can absolute value, so understood, be regarded as a default in the sense of DS?

Before we answer this question, we must reanalyse 'absolute value' in terms of DS. This is necessary because we want to know what the absolute value reading means in the theory where there is no underspecified semantics. In earlier sections of this chapter I used the term 'just *n*'. 'Absolute value' seems to mean precisely that: just *n*, without clear commitment to the cardinality of the set. Absolute value is not just an underdetermined value which stops short of requiring pragmatic enrichment. It is simply 'just *n*, whatever it means'. Moreover, 'just *n*' is probably a more accurate term as it does not run the risk of confusion with the well established term *absolute use* of numerals which, in Greenberg's (1978) study of universals for cardinal numerals, means the use of number terms for counting.[10] Neither does it run the risk of being understood as a species of underspecification: it is 'just *n*', no more to be said. So, in my DS analysis in the following section, I shall speak of *just n.*

Let us assume then that Bultinck's 'absolute value' reading is equivalent to our non-committal 'just *n*'. I shall now substitute the term 'just *n*' for 'absolute value'. The first question to ask is whether it is indeed a reading that is separate from the ones standardly distinguished, namely 'exactly', 'at least', and 'at most'. According to Bultinck's empirical findings, and also in agreement with my strong intuitions, speakers frequently use *two* to mean 'just two', without any further commitments as to the cardinality of the set. But then, the 'exactly two' interpretation of *two* is also very common and, on Bultinck's analysis, the two are not unrelated: *exactly two* entails *just two*. In fact, *at least two* and *at most two* also entail *just two*. So, perhaps *just two* is a component in the processing of cardinal number terms, at least of simple ones like *two*, that sometimes ends up being the final component: nothing beyond 'just two' is then intended. Translating this into a stage-by-stage processing of *two*, we obtain ('two' > 'just two' > (optional) 'exactly two'). But in DS, there are no stages; there are mergers. In the DS-theoretic process of forming an MR, we obtain 'just two' as the output of one source of meaning information: WS. What for Bultinck was the first stage in the processing of the number term, for a DS-theorist is the output of one of the sources, WS, that contribute to the merger representation.

In DS, default interpretations are interpretations that arise without conscious pragmatic inference. They arise through the interaction of (i) word meaning and sentence structure, and optionally (ii) the default strength of intentionality of the corresponding mental state, or (iii) the default scenario reached by the hearer without conscious processing, that is as a social or cultural schema (scenario, script, etc.). On the strength of the argument produced in Chapter 2, defaults are not local; they arise after the utterance has been completed. In Recanati's (2003) terminology, they arise 'globally', 'post-propositionally'. In DS, default is not restricted to the output of grammatical processing: it cannot be so restricted because grammatical processing is not given a privileged role over other sources of meaning information but rather is treated on a par with them. In other words, to repeat, MRs draw on WS, CD, SCD 1, and CPI 1 and merge information from these four sources. An interpretation is a default one when WS combines with CD or SCD 1 as sources of meaning information for the particular utterance. Absolute value is the output of WS. The 'exactly' interpretation carries more informational content, it is the output of WS and CD: the informative intention is stronger than in the case of the absolute value interpretation. Suffice it to say that default in DS is, so to speak, one-step removed from Bultinck's default. While for Bultinck defaults seem to arise on the level of logical form, as the output of syntax (our WS), in DS defaults are interpretations that arise as the output of WS, and CD or SCD 1—that is, any sources of information except for CPI 1.[11]

To sum up, the problem is this. How do 'just *n*' uses of number terms fit in the types of defaults distinguished in DS, that is CD and SCD 1? We have just said that 'just *n*' uses involve only WS. They are neither of a CD nor of an SCD 1 type. They are not defaults on the DS understanding of the term. They are just common uses of number terms *in some circumstances*. In other words, the answer may lie in the specificity of contexts in which the high frequency of 'just *n*' uses is attested. Bultinck (2002) observes that the absolute value use is common when a new referent is introduced:

the principal factor influencing the value interpretation of a numeral [our number term, KJ] is not so much the nature of the syntactic construction in which the numeral occurs, but the tendency of the NP in this construction to introduce new topics, with more or less emphasis (due to focalization). The preponderance of 'absolute value' uses of *two* in direct object phrases, e.g., is caused by the tendency of direct object phrases to introduce new referents, as new referents typically do not co-occur with definiteness markers. In general, *the absence of definiteness markers leaves the 'absolute value' interpretation of numerals intact.* (Bultinck 2002: 265)[12]

This indicates that 'just *n*' ('absolute value') is not a dominant use *tout court*; it is common in restricted types of contexts and is triggered by semantic consideration of information structure. In the DS-theoretic analysis, it fits under the output of WS. We can conclude that it is not the default use on the DS sense of 'default'. It is only default in Bultinck's sense of (i) being the output of grammatical processing and, in this sense, temporally prior, preceding pragmatic processing, and (ii) being common in some types of contexts.

The difference between Bultinck's and my account in understanding semantic meaning follows from the above discussion. In DS, 'semantic' means the level of merger representations, hence includes the output of WS, CD, SCD 1, and CPI 1. It is thus 'semantic meaning' in the wide sense: in DS, any representation of the meaning of the utterance (or discourse, or act of communication) that is not an implicature (result of SCD 2 or/and CPI 2) belongs to semantic meaning.

9.3 Merger representations for CD and CPI 1 readings of cardinal number terms

All in all, it seems that number terms are not as problematic as the last three decades of theorizing make them out to be. The intuitions of the 'exactly' or 'absolute' semantics are strong and, I believe, they can be further supported by the DS analysis. Let us start with an example that is simpler than (1), namely an example in which the approximative readings can be excluded. In (15), the speaker conveys the information that Lizzie has four sisters, rather than five, six, seven, or more.

(15)   Lizzie has four sisters.

The speaker means that Lizzie has exactly four sisters. The informative intention is clearly stronger on this reading than on the one, say, in which Lizzie has at least four sisters. The Q-principle invoked by Koenig[13] also holds. It is perhaps worth pointing out that PI, the principle of primary intention, is not applicable here. By definition, quantifying expressions such as number terms do not exhibit a primary intention as a rule. We obtain the default 'exactly' reading via PoL and DI. The 'at least' meaning in (15b) is less informative; it carries a weaker informative intention. By DI, it also signals that the corresponding mental state of the speaker has weaker intentionality than that pertaining to (15a).

(15a)   Lizzie has exactly four sisters.
(15b)   Lizzie has at least four sisters.

An additional argument comes from referential intention. As I argued at greater length elsewhere,[14] the fact that PI does not apply to number terms by default does not mean that utterances with number terms are *never* understood referentially. Utterance (15), on the standard (15a) reading, can easily trigger further conversation which demonstrates that the addressee takes the phrase 'four sisters' to be referential, as for example in (16). In example (17) this referential intention is even more salient due to the first-person predication.

(16)   A: Lizzie has four sisters.
        B: Really? What are their names?

(17)   A: I have four sisters.
        B: Really? What are their names?

This diversified salience of different readings of utterances with number terms strongly suggests that the DS-theoretic analysis is on the right track. In DS, (15) has a default interpretation as in (15a) and also gives rise to departures from the default such as (15b) achieved by means of employing conscious pragmatic inference. Reading (15a) is more informative than its alternatives, where informativeness is defined as directly proportional to the property of being a proper subset of a truth set, after Koenig (1993), as discussed in Section 9.1. Reading (15a) carries a stronger informative intention; it is also more likely to come with a referential intention than its counterpart in (15b). This is evident from the rather unlikely reading in (16a): if speaker A is not conveying the exact number, then the speaker is unlikely to 'think referentially', so to speak, of every sister of Lizzie's. Square brackets contain the reading that would, on this unlikely scenario, be intended by A and recovered by B.

?(16a)   A: Lizzie has [at least] four sisters.
          B: Really? What are their names?

The 'at most four', 'approximately four', and 'just (absolute) four' readings can also be obtained in context, albeit with varying degrees of difficulty.

    In sum, on the DS analysis, number terms seem to have the default 'exactly' semantics and non-default 'at least', 'approximately', 'just *n*', 'at most' readings. The 'exactly' sense comes with stronger intentionality of the corresponding mental state and with a stronger referential intention. We obtain the default (15a) by WS and CD, and (15b), both repeated below, by WS and CPI 1.

(15a)   Lizzie has exactly four sisters.
(15b)   Lizzie has at least four sisters.

Readings (10b)–(10c) of (10) are also obtained by CPI 1.

(10)   The petrol station is 2km from here.
(10b)   The petrol station is approximately 2km from here.
(10c)   The petrol station is at least 2km from here.

The 'approximately' reading is qualitatively different from 'at least' and 'at most': it is triggered by contexts such as units of measurement ('km'), but it is also compatible with the 'at least', 'at most', and 'just *n*' readings. It is also compatible with the 'exactly' reading in the sense that 'exactly' means 'neither more nor less, within some margin of error'. In other words, it is a looser use (Carston 2002*a*) of 'exactly'. In (10b), the petrol station is, say, neither 1, nor 3 km away, it is *exactly* 2km away, but within, say, a margin of error of 200m.

It is not difficult to envisage scenarios in which (10c) obtains. For example, (10c) can ensue in conversation (10′):

(10′)   A: We are out of petrol. Shall we push the car?
        B: The petrol station is 2km from here.

Sentence (10b) is slightly different. To repeat, the fact that the number term 'two' is followed by a measure term 'km' triggers the inference to the 'approximately' reading, just as was the case in (8) and (9) in Section 9.1. 'Approximately' is compatible with other uses of number terms. Now, the 'at most' reading is different again. It seems to ensue in contexts where permission, restriction, allowance is conveyed (see Carston 1998*b*), as in (3) repeated below, or in (18).

(3)   I can lend you five pounds.

(18)   She can have three small bars of chocolate a week without putting on weight.

This reading is triggered by WS, and arrived at by CPI 1: the words 'can', 'allowed', 'permitted', and so forth point to the interpretation on which the upper limit of what is permitted is salient for the purpose of the conversation.

Finally, the 'just *n*' reading is the WS reading. It obtains when no commitment is made on the part of the speaker to the cardinality of the set to which the number term corresponds. Examples are ample. In (3), on a particular scenario, the speaker may not indeed consider the possibilities of lending exactly £5, lending £4.90, or lending £5.10. The precisification may not enter the mental state and may not enter the intended content of the utterance.[15]

It is obvious from this summary how these uses of cardinal number terms can be represented in DS. As an illustration, let us take (15) on its (15a) reading, and (10) on its (10b) reading, both repeated below. Sentence (15) obtains the MR as in Fig. 9.1, and (10) as in Fig. 9.2.

(15)   Lizzie has four sisters.
(15a) Lizzie has exactly four sisters.

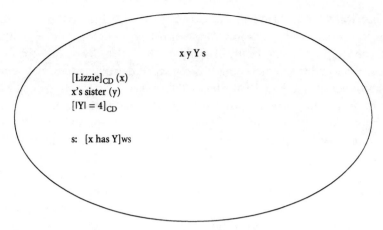

^PFIGURE 9.1. MR for sentence (15): 'exactly four'

Y stands for a plural discourse referent ('sisters'), a set of ys, and the cardinality of this set is 4, stated as a condition $|Y| = 4$. This condition is arrived at via CD: 'exactly four' was independently argued to be the cognitive default reading of 'four'.

(10)   The petrol station is 2km from here.
(10b)   The petrol station is approximately 2km from here.

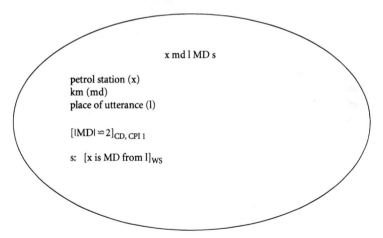

^PFIGURE 9.2. MR for sentence (10): 'approximately 2km'

l stands for the discourse referent for location (in this case, 'here' is taken to be the place of utterance), *md* for the discourse referent for the measure of distance, |MD| for the cardinality of the set of units specified as the measure of distance (km), and '$\simeq$' for 'approximately equals'. The condition $[|MD| \simeq 2]_{CD,\ CPI\ 1}$ is the result of applying the CD to 'two' and obtaining 'exactly two', and then combining this punctual, default sense of two with a pragmatic loosening, by CPI 1, of 'exactly' triggered by the presence of the term for measuring distance (km). As I argued earlier in this section, 'exactly' and 'approximately' are compatible modalities in that 'approximately' adds a margin of error for the 'no more no less' (that is, 'exactly') interpretation. In this sense, the 'approximately' meaning is the 'default', salient reading for simple number terms used with units of measure: it is likely that such phrases as 'two kilometres' and 'five pounds' are *rounded* rather than *exact*. However, this is not an interesting sense of 'default': the interesting aspect of it is that it is founded on CD and loosened by CPI 1.

Note that although DS subscribes to the default 'exactly' semantics of number terms, the DS solution differs qualitatively from the punctual semantics proposed in the literature, for example by Koenig and (tentatively) Geurts. In DS, CPI 1 does not result in implicatures. It produces a semantic representation. To repeat, on the DS account, semantics has as its object acts of communication. Semantic representation is a truth-conditional merger representation to which WS, CD, SCD 1, and CPI 1 all contribute. As a result, we have semantic representations of *utterances* with number terms, in the form of MRs, that can be default MRs when they utilize the CD source of information, or non-default MRs when they utilize CPI 1, where the output of CD and CPI 1 is in both cases merged with the output of WS.

9.4 Summary and further directions

Geurts (1998a: 296) stipulates that different types of expressions allow for different degrees of underdetermination in semantics. This seems to be an intuitively plausible and theoretically promising proposal. Number terms and determiners such as 'a few' have the 'exactly' sense, while for adjectives such as 'warm', 'bad', 'intelligent', the 'at least' sense is basic (primary).[16] While 'warm' and 'bad' are scalar, 'three' and 'four' are not. I argued in Section 9.3 that instead of the rigid solution as to what enters into the semantics of number terms, we are better off recognizing *what* enters *when* into their semantics. I suggested that WS, CD, and CPI 1 interact as sources of meaning information to render 'exactly *n*', 'approximately *n*', 'at least *n*', 'at most *n*', or 'just *n*', as the situation of the act of communication requires.

I have largely confined the discussion to cardinal number terms, having had little to say about the corresponding numbers themselves. But an argument from numbers can be built that supports, albeit weakly, the default 'exactly' semantics of number terms. The 'at least' semantics or the under-determined semantics make it difficult to account for the truth conditions of mathematical statements such as '$2 + 2 = 4$', unless we propose that numbers and number terms have significantly different properties. By downward entailment, $2 + 2$ should also equal 1, 2, and 3. Other related difficulties with mathematical statements go without saying. Pursuing this path, it would seem necessary to assume that number terms and numbers (numerical values) are semantically distinct in that number terms have either 'at least' semantics or are unspecified between 'exactly', 'at least', 'just', and 'at most' n.[17] On the other hand, it has been demonstrated in recent experimental work that humans can compare numbers across auditory and visual modalities virtually effortlessly, which leads to the conclusion that humans use an abstract representation of number both for hearing and seeing numerosities (Barth et al. 2003). And if they use an abstract representation of number, they are not likely to use an abstract representation of number term that has different properties from this concept of numerical value. Hypothetical as these links may be, it is intuitively correct to surmise that numerical value as a cross-modal conceptualization of number has a strong impact on talking about numbers.

Experimental evidence in favour of the 'exactly' semantics of number terms is still inconclusive. However, it has been noted (Papafragou and Musolino 2003) that, while in the case of the scales <all, some>, <finish, start> children overwhelmingly accept a lower scalar term for a description of a situation compatible with a stronger term, they do not do so for numerical scales such as <three, two>.[18] Papafragou and Musolino tentatively conclude that at least children—but possibly also adults—do not have the 'at least' semantics for cardinal number terms. The semantics is either 'exact' or unspecified. They also note that the 'exact' semantics, both for children and adults, is assumed in the developmental literature on children's acquisition of number terms.[19] A great amount of experimental work is to be done before we find satisfactory evidence, one way or another, for the theories of number terms that are currently on offer. However, it is justified to sum up that the punctual, 'exactly' semantics has considerable cognitive support, at least in the sense of semantics proposed in the theory of DS.

Next, I have not said much about the various possibilities of interpretation associated with collective versus distributive readings and with different scoping of number quantifiers. It goes without saying that there are preferred interpretations there. For example, (6), repeated below, carries a strong sense of a collective action.

(6)   Five men pushed the lorry out of a snow-drift.

Similarly, (19) carries a strong sense of a collective action of five men carrying two pianos, one by one, up the stairs.

(19)   Five men carried two pianos upstairs.

I will have little to add to the common intuitions concerning such examples. The salient interpretations are the result of CPI 1. Salient collective interpretation can also be a result of just WS alone. For example, in (20), it is the lexical item 'quartet' that, arguably, gives the collective reading of 'four'.

(20)   Four very talented musicians played a Mozart string quartet.

Arguably, on some occasions, they could also be a result of SCD 1. In (21), it is cultural knowledge to the effect that a string quartet consists of two violinists (and a cellist and a viola player) that gives rise to the collective reading of 'two'.

(21)   Two very talented violinists played a Mozart string quartet.

The distributive reading is, of course, also possible in (21) but is much less salient.

Kamp and Reyle (1993: 321) note that a satisfactory paraphrase of a collective reading would have to signal the fact that the effort of the individuals is in some sense combined—as physical effort or as acting towards a common goal. They provide examples in which the collective reading is very strong or even obligatory and the distributive reading, if at all possible, has to be derived through an additional step after the collective reading has been produced and discarded. As I pointed out in Jaszczolt (1999*b*: 69), in DS we could employ *collective intentions* (Searle 1990*b*) to explain this salience of collective readings. Collective intentions are not reducible to individual intentions and, on the DS account, they come with a primary referential intention attributed to a *set*. As a result, the collective reading could be regarded as the default. This solution is too strong though. It can be classified in the same category as our earlier stipulation in Chapter 8 that the connective *and* is by default temporal or causal. Although it is possible to construe such an analysis using the resources of DS, this is not a correct analysis: DS would violently overgenerate. In the preceding chapters, in order to remain true to the facts, we have only employed referential intention and the PI principle where there was sufficiently incontrovertible reason to assume that referential intention is intrinsically connected with the use of a particular type of expression. So, just as in the case of sentential conjunction *and*, so in the case of collective predications do we stand by the WS + CPI 1, WS + SCD 1, and occasionally WS alone as sources of meaning information.

Finally, I had nothing to say in this chapter about the cross-linguistic diversification of numeral systems. The issue is largely tangential to the present concern. For example, Guana, an Arawakan language, has only five proper cardinal numerals: 1, 2, 3, 4, 'many' (see Greenberg 1978: 256). The DS account of number terms should also apply to this system, namely it should apply to concepts for 1, 2, 3, and 4. 'Many' is, normally, given an indefinite value, here as more than four (Greenberg 1978) and hence belongs to a different sub-class of quantifying expressions.

Notes

1 Cf. e.g. Horn 1976, 1985, 1992; Levinson 1988, 2000; Kempson and Cormack 1981. For criticism see e.g. Sadock 1984; Carston 1998*b*.

2 See also Carston 1998*b*.

3 The numerical value zero is often included in the scale but this is clearly a mistake: zero is never expressed as part of the numeral system of any language. This is one of Greenberg's (1978) universals about numeral systems of the languages of the world. When reference is made to an empty class, this is rendered by a negative construction, not a number term.

4 See Jaszczolt 1999*b*: section 1.2.6 for a discussion.

5 Roughly: 'say as much as you can', given that the following also holds: 'don't say more than you must'.

6 Further permutations of scope and type of reading (distributive, collective) result in other, more context-dependent readings.

7 This raises the problem as to the kind of objects that a set of examiners and a set of scripts make: are they plural objects, or sets of objects? Do we need higher-order logic to talk about plurals? For a discussion see Higginbotham 1998 and Bostock 1998.

8 See Bultinck (2002: 265).

9 Bultinck (2002: 287–9).

10 Greenberg (1978) distinguishes discourse and non-discourse use of cardinal numerals. Non-discourse uses are called absolute, and consist of the use for abstract counting ('one, two, three,...') and counting of concrete objects ('one banana, two bananas,...'). This latter distinction is particularly important because some languages use classifiers that interact with number terms. See Greenberg (1978: 286–7).The term 'absolute' is used for languages which distinguish non-discourse (absolute) forms of numerals, such as the above, used for counting, and separate discourse forms, called contextual. The dichotomy is then *absolute versus contextual forms*.

11 Alternatively, it is not inconceivable that number terms just have a punctual, 'exactly *n*' semantics by force of WS. Then there would be no defaults but the unique lexical 'exactly *n*' meaning of a number term. This option, attractive as it may seem for its simplicity, runs into obvious problems in 'at least', 'at most', and 'just *n*' uses. Examples such as ?(i) would have to be regarded as self-correction:

?(i) I can lend you £5. In fact, I could lend you less if you want.

12 My emphasis.

13 See Section 9.1 above.

14 In Jaszczolt 1999*b*: section 2.6.3.

15 Note that 'just *n*' is not the same as 'approximately *n*'. In the case of 'just *n*' there is no commitment as to the range of numerical values that *n* can take but 'just *n*' may involve approximation: 'whatever is meant by *n* is meant approximately'. In this sense the two are compatible.

16 Terms 'basic sense' and 'primary sense' are Geurts's own expressions. I take them to mean that the basic, primary sense can be either 'exactly' semantics or 'at least' semantics.

17 See Horn (1992: 173), discussing Atlas.

18 See Papafragou and Musolino (2003) on their experiments with scales in Greek. See also Noveck and Sperber 2004.

19 See Papafragou and Musolino (2003: 279) for references.

10

Concluding Remarks and Future Prospects

10.1 'Pragmatic' truth conditions and dynamic 'semantics'

At a cursory glance, it may seem that Default Semantics mixes together two quite distinct orientations: dynamic, truth-conditional semantics and truth-conditional pragmatics. On closer inspection, though, it is not an ad hoc mixture. The combination is perfectly coherent. Let us briefly compare its main tenets with its first parent theory, namely DRT, and then with its second parent theory, namely truth-conditional pragmatics. Like DRT, it is a semantic theory, it is dynamic in its account of context change, and it is truth-conditional. But unlike DRT, it is not a theory of linguistic competence. It is a theory of the processing of acts of communication. In other words, the 'semantics' becomes a semantics of acts of communication. Such acts are only partly based on the sentence; they also rely on other sources of meaning information such as conscious pragmatic processes and various shortcuts through this processing in the form of defaults. In other words, the mechanism of DRT is applied, so to speak, 'one level up', to the output of the merger of meaning information that comes from all the sources available in the situation of communication. To formalize such a merger is not a simple matter. In order to do that, DS does not go *beyond* truth conditions but instead conceives of the truth-conditional content in a different manner. Instead, truth conditions are predicated of a 'pragmatics-rich' content. This is where truth-conditional pragmatics fits in. Like truth-conditional pragmatics, DS allows the contribution of the output of pragmatic processes to the truth-conditional representation of meaning. As a result, it yields a programme for discourse interpretation that has potentially the degree of formalization of dynamic semantics, but the object to which this formalism is applied is a merger construct that is akin to thoughts: it is a generalization over the speaker's thought, as (re)constructed by the model hearer, that is fine-grained only to such an extent as is necessitated for representing the truth-conditional content. In other words, DS is a dynamic theory of meaning that has only those aspects of thought as its object that have to be processed by the interlocutors in utterance interpretation. The granularity of merger representations is dictated by the purpose of the situation at hand.

The advantages of such a programme should now be obvious. It is a proposal of formalizing the process of communication, in which sentences are processed alongside other sources of information. We are not restricted to syntactic configuration or word meaning: meaning information that comes from this source (our WS) can be overridden by the output of the other three sources of the MR (our CPI 1, CD, and SCD 1). In this way we can handle referential mistakes, as well as speaker's main communicated meaning such as that of the mother in (1) (adapted from Bach 1994a).

(1)   Peter: Mummy, I cut my finger.
       Mother: Oh, you are not going to die!
                  [communicated meaning: it's not a big deal, there is no need to worry, and so forth]

We can account for the centrality of this communicated meaning by placing it *in* the merger representation as the post-merger effect of the interaction of the four sources of meaning information distinguished in DS. We thus obtain *abstracts over thoughts*, merger representations that pertain to those constituents and aspects of thought that contribute to the truth-conditional, communicated content.

Default Semantics is not in direct competition with either dynamic semantics or various post-Gricean accounts that fall within the orientation of truth-conditional pragmatics. It addresses the process of discourse interpretation at the 'post-merger' stage, having little to say about what happens before the merger is completed. It takes the formal devices of dynamic representational semantics 'one level up' to such post-merger representations. The price to pay, at least at the current stage of the development of DS, is that the account of the separate outputs of WS, CD, SCD 1, and CPI 1 is not sufficiently well worked out. The theory is much less advanced in accounting for what happens prior to the merger than in working out the compositional post-merger output.

A lot still has to be done to make the programme more refined, to improve on the adjustments of the DRT language used here. Also, a lot can be done as far as the scope of applications is concerned: the handful of applications presented in Part II is only an example of what the theory can do. But the cognitive foundations, I hope, are in place. The formalization of other types of expressions and other linguistic phenomena will undoubtedly require new amendments and extensions of the starting language which is the language of DRSs. That is why I alternate between calling Default Semantics a 'programme' and a 'theory': the theoretical cognitive foundations are worked out, while the language of MRs is not yet complete. I say more about future applications in Section 10.2.

Now, many syntactic theories of natural language propagate the view that the semantics of natural language and of formal languages are diametrically different.[1] This question cannot be constructively solved at the present state of theorizing about meaning. However, what we can say with confidence is that our use of language is governed by principles of some or other mental logic: meaning is at the same time a prerequisite and an outcome of valid arguments of some kind, be it deductive or defeasible.[2] In other words, the correlation between meaning and reasoning is unquestionable, and so seems to be the rationale for a formal account of discourse. DS is an attempt to construe such a formal account of an informal phenomenon. In order to make sense of this 'semanticization' of 'pragmatic truth-conditions', let us put DS in the context of Blutner and van der Sandt's apt summary of the changing semantics/ pragmatics boundary. They say:

> From a methodological perspective work on underspecification forces us to rethink the traditional way in which the semantics/pragmatics boundary has been drawn. In recent years (and under the influence of the 'dynamic turn') there has been a shift in emphasis from pragmatics to semantics. Many phenomena which had been labeled pragmatic in earlier theories turned out to be amenable to a semantic treatment in dynamic theories ('intonational' focus, 'pragmatic' presupposition, connotations of temporal succession, etc.). Recent work in underspecification seems to push us in the opposite direction. Once we allow 'flat' underspecified representations we shift much of the burden of determining the information that a sentence conveys back to pragmatics again. The point is more than just a matter of terminology and brings us to questions of lexical representation, abduction, defeasible reasoning and the role of contextual accommodation in linguistic processing. (Blutner and van der Sandt 1998: 1)

In DS, while some of the sources of meaning representation are 'pushed into pragmatics', the model of reasoning in discourse processing is semantic, formal, and dynamic. Since the objective of the whole project is representing discourse meaning, we can 'push it into semantics' on the common-sense, naive understanding of what semantics is supposed to do, namely *to provide a cognitively adequate theory for representing meaning of discourses in natural language by a model hearer.*[3]

10.2 The scope of Default Semantics

To sum up, it is fair to say, I think, that while the cognitive foundations are worked out in the form of a self-contained theory, the application to natural language expressions and various semantic phenomena and problems are still open to future research. This is a positive note though. The formalization adapted and extended from DRT and transposed onto the level of abstracts over thoughts is being worked out as new applications of Default Semantics are being worked out. In Part II I have exemplified applications to extensional and intensional contexts, and at the same time to contexts that do and do not make use of the referential intention and the PI principle in the process of discourse interpretation. I have also looked at anaphora understood as a context-based phenomenon that includes making up, 'accommodating' the antecedent when the discourse requires it. Finally, I have looked at the equivalents of 'logical words' in natural language such as sentential connectives and some quantifiers. Therefore, the spectrum is broad enough, across various scales of measurement (reference–no reference, extensional–intensional, existing context–made up context, and so forth) to conjecture that further applications are possible. As I remarked before, the language of the MRs may have to be further amended and extended to account for the new phenomena. But the foundations of the dynamic semantic theory of acts of communication are in place. I shall thus conclude with an apt quotation from a rationalist of a very different camp but which is equally applicable across the board:

all of this is part of what you might call the 'Galilean style': the dedication to finding understanding, not just coverage. Coverage of phenomena itself is insignificant and in fact the kinds of data that, say, physicists use are extremely exotic. If you took a videotape of things happening out the window, it would be of no interest to physical scientists.   (Chomsky 2002: 102)

It is the thought, and the truth-conditionally pertinent abstract over thought, that count.[4]

Notes

1 See e.g. Chomsky (2002: 110).
2 See Geurts (2003) who reaches a similar conclusion in his experimental study of syllogistic reasoning.
3 The rationale for this objective was discussed throughout Part I.
4 I owe thanks to Thorstein Fretheim for pointing out to me the need to discuss the possible scope of application of Default Semantics.

References

ABUSCH, D. 1988. 'Sequence of tense, intensionality and scope'. In: H. Borer (ed.), *Proceedings of the Seventh West Coast Conference on Formal Linguistics*. Stanford: CSLI. 1–14.

ALLAN, K. 2001. *Natural Language Semantics*. Oxford: Blackwell.

ARISTOTLE. 1928. *De Interpretatione*. Transl. by E. M. Edghill. In: *The Works of Aristotle*. Vol. 1. Oxford: Clarendon Press. 16a–23b.

ASHER, N. 1986. 'Belief in Discourse Representation Theory'. *Journal of Philosophical Logic* 15, 127–89.

——. 1999. 'Discourse and the focus/background distinction'. In: P. Bosch and R. van der Sandt (eds.), *Focus: Linguistic, Cognitive, and Computational Perspectives*. Cambridge: Cambridge University Press. 247–67.

ASHER, N. and A. LASCARIDES. 1995. 'Lexical disambiguation in a discourse context'. *Journal of Semantics* 12, 69–108.

——. and ——. 1998a. 'The semantics and pragmatics of presupposition'. *Journal of Semantics* 15, 239–300.

——. and ——. 1998b. 'Bridging'. *Journal of Semantics* 15, 83–113.

——. and ——. 2001. 'Indirect speech acts'. *Synthese* 128, 183–228.

——. and ——. 2003. *Logics of Conversation*. Cambridge: Cambridge University Press.

ATLAS, J. D. 1977. 'Negation, ambiguity, and presupposition'. *Linguistics and Philosophy* 1, 321–36.

——. 1979. 'How linguistics matters to philosophy: Presupposition, truth, and meaning'. In: C.-K. Oh and D. A. Dinneen (eds.), *Syntax and Semantics*. Vol. 11. New York: Academic Press. 265–81.

——. 1989. *Philosophy Without Ambiguity: A Logico-Linguistic Essay*. Oxford: Clarendon Press.

——. 2005. *Logic, Meaning, and Conversation: Semantical Underdeterminacy, Implicature, and Their Interface*. Oxford: Oxford University Press.

VAN DER AUWERA, J. 1985. *Language and Logic: A Speculative and Condition-Theoretic Study*. Amsterdam: J. Benjamins.

——. 1997. 'Conditional perfection'. In: A. Athanasiadou and R. Dirven (eds.), *On Conditionals Again*. Amsterdam: J. Benjamins. 169–90.

——. and B. BULTINCK. 2001. 'On the lexical typology of modals, quantifiers, and connectives'. In: I. Kenesei and R. M. Harnish (eds.), *Perspectives on Semantics, Pragmatics, and Discourse. A Festschrift for Ferenc Kiefer*. Amsterdam: J. Benjamins. 173–86.

——. and V. A. PLUNGIAN. 1998. 'Modality's semantic map'. *Linguistic Typology* 2, 79–124.

VAN DER AUWERA, J., N. DOBRUSHINA, and V. GOUSSEV. 2001. 'A semantic map for imperative-horatives'. Draft for *Proceedings from Contrastive Linguistics and Typology in Europe*. Unpublished paper.

BACH, K. 1984. 'Default reasoning: Jumping to conclusions and knowing when to think twice'. *Pacific Philosophical Quarterly* 65, 37–58.

——. 1987a. *Thought and Reference*. Oxford: Clarendon Press.

——. 1987b. 'On communicative intentions: A reply to Recanati'. *Mind and Language* 2, 141–54.

——. 1992. 'Intentions and demonstrations'. *Analysis* 52, 140–6.

——. 1994a. 'Semantic slack: What is said and more'. In: S. L. Tsohatzidis (ed.), *Foundations of Speech Act Theory: Philosophical and Linguistic Perspectives*. London: Routledge. 267–91.

——. 1994b. 'Conversational impliciture'. *Mind and Language* 9, 124–62.

——. 1995. 'Remark and reply. Standardization vs. conventionalization'. *Linguistics and Philosophy* 18, 677–86.

——. 1997. 'Do belief reports report beliefs?'. *Pacific Philosophical Quarterly* 78. Reprinted in: K. M. Jaszczolt (ed.), *The Pragmatics of Propositional Attitude Reports*. Oxford: Elsevier Science. 111–36.

——. 1998. 'Postscript (1995): Standardization revisited'. In: A. Kasher (ed.), *Pragmatics: Critical Concepts*. Vol. 4. London: Routledge. 712–22.

——. 2000. 'Quantification, qualification and context: A reply to Stanley and Szabó'. *Mind and Language* 15, 262–83.

——. 2001. 'You don't say?'. *Synthese* 128, 15–44.

——. and R. M. HARNISH. 1979. *Linguistic Communication and Speech Acts*. Cambridge, MA: MIT Press.

BARTH, H., N. KANWISHER, and E. SPELKE. 2003. 'The construction of large number representations in adults'. *Cognition* 86, 201–21.

BENNETT, M. and B. PARTEE. 1972. *Toward the Logic of Tense and Aspect in English*. Reproduced in 1978 by IULC.

BINNICK, R. I. 1991. *Time and the Verb: A Guide to Tense and Aspect*. Oxford: Oxford University Press.

BLAKEMORE, D. 1987. *Semantic Constraints on Relevance*. Oxford: B. Blackwell.

BLOK, P. I. and K. EBERLE. 1999. 'What is the alternative? The computation of focus alternatives from lexical and sortal information'. In: P. Bosch and R. van der Sandt (eds.), *Focus: Linguistic, Cognitive, and Computational Perspectives*. Cambridge: Cambridge University Press. 105–20.

BLOOM, P. 2002. 'Mindreading, communication and the learning of names for things'. *Mind and Language* 17, 37–54.

BLUTNER, R. 2000. 'Some aspects of optimality in natural language interpretation'. *Journal of Semantics* 17, 189–216.

——. and VAN DER SANDT. 1998. Editorial Preface. Special Issue on underspecification and interpretation. *Journal of Semantics* 15, 1–3.

——. and H. Zeevat. 2004. 'Editors' introduction: Pragmatics in Optimality Theory'. In: R. Blutner and H. Zeevat (eds.), *Optimality Theory and Pragmatics*. Basingstoke: Palgrave Macmillan. 1–24.

——. and ——. (eds). 2004. *Optimality Theory and Pragmatics*. Basingstoke: Palgrave Macmillan.

Bolzano, B. 1837. *Wissenschaftslehre*. Sulzbach. Reprinted in 1929–31. 2nd edn. Leipzig: Felix Meiner. Trans. as *Theory of Science* by B. Terrell in 1973. Dordrecht: D. Reidel.

Bosch, P. and R. van der Sandt (eds.) 1999. *Focus: Linguistic, Cognitive, and Computational Perspectives*. Cambridge: Cambridge University Press.

Bostock, D. 1998. 'On motivating higher-order logic'. *Proceedings of the British Academy* 95, 29–43.

Brandom, R. B. 1994. *Making it Explicit: Reasoning, Representing, and Discursive Commitment*. Cambridge, MA: Harvard University Press.

Brentano, F. 1874. *Psychologie vom empirischen Standpunkt*. Leipzig: Duncker and Humblot. Reprinted in 1924. Leipzig: Felix Meiner. 2nd edn. Trans. as *Psychology from an Empirical Standpoint* by A. C. Rancurello, D. B. Terrell, and L. L. McAlister in 1973. London: Routledge and Kegan Paul.

Brown, G. 1995. *Speakers, Listeners and Communication: Explorations in Discourse Analysis*. Cambridge: Cambridge University Press.

Bultinck, B. 2002. Numerous Meanings: The Meaning of English Cardinals and the Legacy of Paul Grice. Doctoral dissertation, University of Antwerp. Also forthcoming from Oxford: Elsevier.

——. 2003. 'Why Paul Grice should have been a corpus linguist: The meaning of English numerals'. Unpublished paper.

Büring, D. 1999. 'Topic'. In: P. Bosch and R. van der Sandt (eds.), *Focus: Linguistic, Cognitive, and Computational Perspectives*. Cambridge: Cambridge University Press. 142–65.

Burton-Roberts, N. 1989. *The Limits to Debate: A Revised Theory of Semantic Presupposition*. Cambridge: Cambridge University Press.

——. 1999. 'Presupposition-cancellation and metalinguistic negation: A reply to Carston'. *Journal of Linguistics* 35, 347–64.

Cappelen, H. and E. Lepore. 2002. 'Indexicality, binding, anaphora and a priori truth'. *Analysis* 62, 271–81.

Carston, R. 1988. 'Implicature, explicature, and truth-theoretic semantics'. In: R. M. Kempson (ed.), *Mental Representations: The Interface Between Language and Reality*. Cambridge: Cambridge University Press. 155–81.

——. 1994. 'Conjunction and pragmatic effects'. In: R. E. Asher (ed.), *The Encyclopedia of Language and Linguistics*. Oxford: Pergamon Press. Vol. 2. 692–8.

——. 1996. 'Metalinguistic negation and echoic use'. *Journal of Pragmatics* 25, 309–30.

——. 1998a. 'Postscript (1995)' to Carston 1988. In: A. Kasher (ed.), *Pragmatics: Critical Concepts*. Vol. 4. London: Routledge. 464–79.

CARSTON, R. 1998*b*. 'Informativeness, relevance and scalar implicature'. In: R. Carston and S. Uchida (eds.), *Relevance Theory: Applications and Implications*. Amsterdam: J. Benjamins. 179–236.

——. 1999. 'Negation, "presupposition" and metarepresentation: A response to Noel Burton-Roberts'. *Journal of Linguistics* 35, 365–89.

——. 2001. 'Relevance Theory and the saying/implicating distinction'. *UCL Working Papers in Linguistics* 13, 1–34.

——. 2002*a*. *Thoughts and Utterances: The Pragmatics of Explicit Communication*. Oxford: Blackwell.

——. 2002*b*. 'Linguistic meaning, communicated meaning and cognitive pragmatics'. *Mind and Language* 17, 127–48.

——. forthcoming. 'Truth-conditional content and conversational implicature'. In: C. Bianchi (ed.), *The Semantics/Pragmatics Distinction*. Stanford: CSLI.

CHIERCHIA, G. 1995. *Dynamics of Meaning: Anaphora, Presupposition, and the Theory of Grammar*. Chicago: University of Chicago Press.

CHOMSKY, N. 1995. *The Minimalist Program*. Cambridge, MA: MIT Press.

——. 2001. 'Derivation by phase'. In M. Kenstowicz (ed.), *Ken Hale: A Life in Language*. Cambridge, MA: MIT Press. 1–52.

——. 2002. *On Nature and Language*. Cambridge: Cambridge University Press.

——. 2004. 'Beyond explanatory adequacy'. In: A. Belletti (ed.), *Structures and Beyond: The Cartography of Syntactic Structures*, vol. 3. New York: Oxford University Press. 104–31.

CLAPP, L. 1995. 'How to be direct and innocent: A criticism of Crimmins and Perry's theory of attitude ascriptions'. *Linguistics and Philosophy* 18, 529–65.

CLAPP, L. 2000. 'Beyond sense and reference; An alternative response to the problem of opacity'. In: K. M. Jaszczolt (ed.), *The Pragmatics of Propositional Attitude Reports*. Oxford: Elsevier Science. 43–75.

——. 2002. 'Davidson's program and interpreted logical forms'. *Linguistics and Philosophy* 25, 261–97.

COHEN, A. 1999. 'How are alternatives computed?'. *Journal of Semantics* 16, 43–65.

COHEN, L. J. 1971. 'Some remarks on Grice's views about the logical particles of natural language'. In: Y. Bar-Hillel (ed.), *Pragmatics of Natural Languages*. Dordrecht: D. Reidel. 50–68.

COMRIE, B. 1985. *Tense*. Cambridge: Cambridge University Press.

CONDORAVDI, C. 2002. 'Temporal interpretation of modals: Modals for the present and for the past'. In: D. Beaver et al. (eds.), *The Construction of Meaning*. Stanford: CSLI. 59–88.

CRESSWELL, M. J. 1985. *Structured Meanings: The Semantics of Propositional Attitudes*. Cambridge, MA: MIT Press.

CRIMMINS, M. 1992. *Talk about Beliefs*. Cambridge, MA: MIT Press.

——. and J. PERRY. 1989. 'The prince and the phone booth: Reporting puzzling beliefs'. *Journal of Philosophy* 86, 685–711.

CROUCH, R. S. and S. G. PULMAN. 1993. 'Time and modality in a natural language interface to a planning system'. *Artificial Intelligence* 63. Reprined in: F. C. N. Pereira and B. J. Grosz (eds.). 1994. *Natural Language Processing*. Cambridge, MA: MIT Press. 265–304.

DAHL, Ö. 1985. *Tense and Aspect Systems*. Oxford: B. Blackwell.

DAMASIO, A. R. 1999. 'How the brain creates the mind'. *Scientific American*, December, 74–9.

DAVIDSON, D. 1967. 'The logical form of action sentences'. In: N. Rescher (ed.), *The Logic of Decision and Action*. Pittsburgh: University of Pittsburgh Press. Reprinted in: D. Davidson. 1980. *Essays on Actions and Events*. Oxford: Clarendon Press. 105–22.

——. 1968–9. 'On saying that'. *Synthese* 19, 130–46.

——. 1969. 'The individuation of events'. In: N. Rescher (ed.), *Essays in Honor of Carl G. Hempel*. Dordrecht: D. Reidel. Reprinted in: D. Davidson. 1980. *Essays on Actions and Events*. Oxford: Clarendon Press. 163–80.

VAN DEEMTER, K. 1998. 'Ambiguity and idiosyncratic interpretation'. *Journal of Semantics* 15, 5–36.

——. and S. PETERS (eds.) 1996. *Semantic Ambiguity and Underspecification*. Stanford: CSLI.

DEKKER, P. 1998. 'Speaker's reference, descriptions and information structure'. *Journal of Semantics* 15, 305–34.

——. 2000. 'Coreference and representationalism'. In: K. von Heusinger and U. Egli (eds.), *Reference and Anaphoric Relations*. Dordrecht: Kluwer. 287–310.

DONNELLAN, K. S. 1989. 'Belief and the identity of reference'. In: P. A. French, T. E. Uehling, and H. K. Wettstein (eds.), *Contemporary Perspectives in the Philosophy of Language* 2 (*Midwest Studies in Philosophy* 14). Minneapolis: University of Minnesota Press. Reprinted in: C. A. Anderson and J. Owens (eds.). *Propositional Attitudes: The Role of Content in Logic, Language, and Mind*. Stanford: CSLI. 201–14.

DOWTY, D. R. 1979. *Word Meaning and Montague Grammar: The Semantics of Verbs and Times in Generative Semantics and in Montague's PTQ*. Dordrecht: D. Reidel.

——. 1986. 'The effects of aspectual class on the temporal structure of discourse: Semantics or pragmatics?'. *Linguistics and Philosophy* 9, 37–61.

——., WALL, R. E., and S. PETERS. 1981. *Introduction to Montague Semantics*. Dordrecht: D. Reidel.

DUMMETT, M. 1969. 'The reality of the past'. *Proceedings of the Aristotelian Society* 69, 239–58.

ECKARDT, R. 1999. 'Focus with nominal quantifiers'. In: P. Bosch and R. van der Sandt (eds.), *Focus: Linguistic, Cognitive, and Computational Perspectives*. Cambridge: Cambridge University Press. 166–86.

VAN EIJCK, J. 2001. 'Incremental dynamics'. *Journal of Logic, Language and Information* 10, 319–51.

VAN EIJCK, J. and H. KAMP. 1997. 'Representing discourse in context'. In: J. van Benthem and A. ter Meulen (eds.), *Handbook of Logic and Language*. Amsterdam: Elsevier Science. 179–237.

ENÇ, M. 1987. 'Anchoring conditions for tense'. *Linguistic Inquiry* 18, 633–57.

——. 1996. 'Tense and modality'. In: S. Lappin (ed.), *The Handbook of Contemporary Semantic Theory*. Oxford: Blackwell. 345–58.

FLEISCHMAN, S. 1982. *The Future in Thought and Language: Diachronic Evidence from Romance*. Cambridge: Cambridge University Press.

FODOR, J. A. 1994. *The Elm and the Expert: Mentalese and Its Semantics*. Cambridge, MA: MIT Press.

——. 1998. *Concepts: Where Cognitive Science Went Wrong*. Oxford: Clarendon Press.

——. 2001. 'Language, thought and compositionality'. *Mind & Language* 16, 1–15.

——. and E. LEPORE. 2001. 'Why compositionality won't go away: Reflections on Horwich's "deflationary" theory'. *Ratio* 14. Reprinted in J. A. Fodor and E. Lepore. 2002. *The Compositionality Papers*. Oxford: Clarendon Press. 43–62.

——. and ——. 2002. *The Compositionality Papers*. Oxford: Clarendon Press.

FORBES, G. 1990. 'The indispensability of *Sinn*'. *Philosophical Review* 99, 535–63.

——. 1997. 'How much substitutivity?'. *Analysis* 57, 109–113.

FREGE, G. 1892. 'Über Sinn und Bedeutung'. *Zeitschrift für Philosophie und Philosophische Kritik* 100, 25–50. Trans. as 'On sense and reference' in P. T. Geach and M. Black (eds.). 1952. *Translations from the Philosophical Writings of Gottlob Frege*. Oxford: B. Blackwell. Reprinted in 1960. 2nd edn. 56–78.

FRETHEIM, T. 1992. 'The effect of intonation on a type of scalar implicature'. *Journal of Pragmatics* 18. Reprinted (with Postscript) in A. Kasher (ed.), 1998. *Pragmatics: Critical Concepts*. Vol. 4: *Presupposition, Implicature and Indirect Speech Acts*. London: Routledge. 480–511.

GEIS, M. L. and A. M. ZWICKY. 1971. 'On invited inferences'. *Linguistic Inquiry* 2, 561–6.

GENNARI, S. P. 2003. 'Tense meanings and temporal interpretation'. *Journal of Semantics* 20, 35–71.

GEURTS, B. 1998a. 'The mechanisms of denial'. *Language* 74, 274–307.

——. 1998b. 'Presuppositions and anaphors in attitude contexts'. *Linguistics and Philosophy* 21, 545–601.

——. 1998c. 'Scalars'. In: P. Ludewig and B. Geurts (eds.), *Lexikalische Semantik aus kognitiver Sicht*. Tübingen: Gunter Narr. 95–117.

——. 1999. *Presuppositions and Pronouns*. Oxford: Elsevier Science.

——. 2000. 'Buoyancy and strength'. *Journal of Semantics* 17, 315–33.

——. 2002. 'Donkey business'. *Linguistics and Philosophy* 25, 129–56.

——. 2003. 'Reasoning with quantifiers'. *Cognition* 86, 223–51.

——. and R. van der SANDT. 1999. 'Domain restriction'. In: P. Bosch and R. van der Sandt (eds.), *Focus: Linguistic, Cognitive, and Computational Perspectives*. Cambridge: Cambridge University Press. 268–92.

GIBBS, R. W. and J. F. MOISE. 1997. 'Pragmatics in understanding what is said'. *Cognition* 62, 51–74.

GINZBURG, J. and I. A. SAG. 2000. *Interrogative Investigation: The Form, Meaning, and Use of English Interrogatives.* Stanford: CSLI.

GÓMEZ TXURRUKA, I. 2003. 'The natural language conjunction *and*'. *Linguistics and Philosophy* 26, 255–85.

GREENBERG, J. H. 1978. 'Generalizations about numeral systems'. In: J. H. Greenberg (ed.), *Universals of Human Language.* Vol. 3: *Word Structure.* Stanford: Stanford University Press. 249–95.

GRICE, H. P. 1975. 'Logic and conversation'. In: P. Cole and J. L. Morgan (eds.), *Syntax and Semantics.* Vol. 3. New York: Academic Press. Reprinted in: H. P. Grice. 1989. *Studies in the Way of Words.* Cambridge, MA: Harvard University Press. 22–40.

——. 1978. 'Further notes on logic and conversation'. In: P. Cole (ed.), *Syntax and Semantics.* Vol. 9. New York: Academic Press. Reprinted in: H. P. Grice. 1989. *Studies in the Way of Words.* Cambridge, MA: Harvard University Press. 41–57.

GRICE, P. 2001. *Aspects of Reason.* Ed. by R. Warner. Oxford: Clarendon Press.

GROENENDIJK, P. and M. STOKHOF. 1991. 'Dynamic Predicate Logic'. *Linguistics and Philosophy* 14, 39–100.

——. and ——. 2000. 'Meaning in motion'. In: K. von Heusinger and U. Egli (eds.), *Reference and Anaphoric Relations.* Dordrecht: Kluwer. 47–76.

GUNDEL, J. K. 1999. 'On different kinds of focus'. In: P. Bosch and R. van der Sandt (eds.), *Focus: Linguistic, Cognitive, and Computational Perspectives.* Cambridge: Cambridge University Press. 293–305.

——., N. HEDBERG, and R. ZACHARSKI. 1993. 'Cognitive status and the form of referring expressions in discourse'. *Language* 69, 274–307.

——., K. BORTHEN, and T. FRETHEIM. 1999. 'The role of context in pronominal reference to higher order entities in English and Norwegian'. In: P. Bouquet L. Serafini, P. Brezillon, M. Benerecetti, and F. Castellani (eds.), *Modeling and Using Context.* Proceedings of the conference Context 99, Trento, Italy. Berlin: Springer Verlag. 475–8.

HAJIČOVA, E., PARTEE, B. H., and P. SGALL. 1998. *Topic–Focus Articulation, Tripartite Structures, and Semantic Content.* Dordrecht: Kluwer.

HAPPÉ, F. and E. LOTH. 2002. ' "Theory of mind" and tracking speakers' intentions'. *Mind and Language* 17, 24–36.

HEIDEGGER, M. 1953. *Sein und Zeit.* Tübingen: Max Niemeyer. Trans. J. Stambaugh as *Being and Time.* 1996. Albany: State University of New York Press.

HEIM, I. 1992. 'Presupposition projection and the semantics of attitude verbs'. *Journal of Semantics* 9, 183–221.

VON HEUSINGER, K. 2000a. 'Anaphora, antecedents, and accessibility'. *Theoretical Linguistics* 26, 75–93.

——. 2000b. 'The reference of indefinites'. In: K. von Heusinger and U. Egli (eds.), *Reference and Anaphoric Relations.* Dordrecht: Kluwer. 247–65.

——. 2002. 'Choice functions and the anaphoric semantics of definite NPs'. In: K. von Heusinger, R. Kempson, and W. Meyer-Viol (eds.), Proceedings of the Workshop

'Choice Functions and Natural Language Semantics'. Arbeitspapier 110. Universität Konstanz. 63–83.

——. and U. EGLI. 2000. 'Introduction: Reference and the semantics of anaphora'. In: K. von Heusinger and U. Egli (eds.), *Reference and Anaphoric Relations*. Dordrecht: Kluwer. 1–13.

HIGGINBOTHAM, J. 1998. 'On higher-order logic and natural language'. *Proceedings of the British Academy* 95, 1–27.

——. 2001. 'Why is Sequence of Tense obligatory?'. *Oxford University Working Papers in Linguistics, Philology, and Phonetics* 6, 67–90.

HINTIKKA, J. 1962. *Knowledge and Belief: An Introduction to the Logic of the Two Notions*. Ithaca: Cornell University Press.

——. 1969. 'Semantics for propositional attitudes'. In: J. W. Davis, D. J. Hockney, and W. K. Wilson (eds.), *Philosophical Logic*. Dordrecht: D. Reidel. Reprinted in A. Marras (ed.), 1972. *Intentionality, Mind and Language*. Urbana: University of Illinois Press. 429–57.

HINZEN, W. 2001. 'The pragmatics of inferential content'. *Synthese* 128, 157–81.

HORN, L. R. 1976. *On the Semantic Properties of Logical Operators in English*. Bloomington: Indiana University Linguistics Club.

——. 1984. 'Toward a new taxonomy for pragmatic inference: Q-based and R-based implicature'. In: *Georgetown University Round Table on Languages and Linguistics* Ed. by D. Schffrin. Washington, DC: Georgetown University Press. 11–42.

——. 1985. 'Metalinguistic negation and pragmatic ambiguity'. *Language* 61, 121–74.

——. 1988. 'Pragmatic theory'. In: F. J. Newmeyer (ed.), *Linguistics: The Cambridge Survey*. Vol. 1. Cambridge: Cambridge University Press. 113–45.

——. 1989. *A Natural History of Negation*. Chicago: University of Chicago Press.

——. 1992. 'The said and the unsaid'. *Ohio State University Working Papers in Linguistics* 40 (SALT II Proceedings). 163–92.

HORNSTEIN, N. 1990. *As Time Goes By: Tense and Universal Grammar*. Cambridge, MA: MIT Press.

HORWICH, P. 1990. *Truth*. Oxford: Clarendon Press. Reprinted in 1998. 2nd edn.

——. 1998. *Meaning*. Oxford: Clarendon Press.

HUSSERL, E. 1900–01. *Logische Untersuchungen*. Vol. 2. Halle: Max Niemeyer. Reprinted in 1984 after the 2nd edn. (1913–21). The Hague: Martinus Nijhoff. *Husserliana* 19/1. Trans. as *Logical Investigations* by J. N. Findlay in 1970. London: Routledge and Kegan Paul.

JACKENDOFF, R. 1983. *Semantics and Cognition*. Cambridge, MA: MIT Press.

——. 1990. *Semantic Structures*. Cambridge, MA: MIT Press.

——. 1991. 'Parts and boundaries'. *Cognition* 41. Reprinted in: B. Levin and S. Pinker (eds.), *Lexical and Conceptual Semantics*. Oxford: Blackwell. 9–45.

——. 2003. *Foundations of Language: Brain, Meaning, Grammar, Evolution*. Oxford: Oxford University Press.

JÄGER, G. 1999. 'Topic, focus, and weak quantifiers'. In: P. Bosch and R. van der Sandt (eds.), *Focus: Linguistic, Cognitive, and Computational Perspectives.* Cambridge: Cambridge University Press. 187–212.

JASZCZOLT, K. M. 1997. 'The Default *De Re* Principle for the interpretation of belief utterances'. *Journal of Pragmatics* 28, 315–36.

——. 1998. 'Reports on beliefs: Default interpretations and default intentions'. *Journal of Literary Semantics* 27, 31–42.

——. 1999a. 'Default semantics, pragmatics, and intentions'. In: K. Turner (ed.), *The Semantics/Pragmatics Interface from Different Points of View.* Oxford: Elsevier Science. 199–232.

——. 1999b. *Discourse, Beliefs, and Intentions: Semantic Defaults and Propositional Attitude Ascription.* Oxford: Elsevier Science.

——. 2000a. 'The default-based context-dependence of belief reports'. In: K. M. Jaszczolt (ed.), *The Pragmatics of Propositional Attitude Reports.* Oxford: Elsevier Science. 169–185.

——. 2000b. 'Belief reports and pragmatic theory: the state of the art'. Introduction to: K. M. Jaszczolt (ed.), *The Pragmatics of Propositional Attitude Reports.* Oxford: Elsevier Science. 1–12.

——. 2001. Review of Bosch and van der Sandt, '*Focus: Linguistic, Cognitive and Computational Perspectives*'. *Journal of Pragmatics* 33, 1651–63.

——. 2002a. *Semantics and Pragmatics: Meaning in Language and Discourse.* London: Longman.

——. 2002b. 'Against ambiguity and underspecification: Evidence from presupposition as anaphora'. *Journal of Pragmatics* 34, 829–49.

——. 2003a. 'The modality. of the future: A Default-Semantics account'. In: P. Dekker and R. van Rooy (eds.), *Proceedings of the 14th Amsterdam Colloquium.* ILLC, University of Amsterdam. 43–8.

——. 2003b. Review of Nuyts *Epistemic Modality, Language, and Conceptualization: A Cognitive–Pragmatic Perspective. Journal of Pragmatics* 35, 657–63.

——. 2004. 'Prolegomena to Default Semantics'. *Research in Language* 2, 7–31. Also in: S. Marmaridou, K. Nikiforidou, and E. Antonopoulou (eds.), forthcoming. *Reviewing Linguistic Thought: Converging Trends for the 21st Century.* Berlin: Mouton.

JOKIĆ, A. and Q. SMITH (eds.) 2003. *Time, Tense, and Reference.* Cambridge, MA: MIT Press.

KAMP, H. 1979. 'Events, instants and temporal reference'. In: R. Bäuerle, U. Egli, and A. von Stechow (eds.), *Semantics from Different Points of View.* Berlin: Springer. 376–417.

——. 1981. 'A theory of truth and semantic representation'. In: J. Groenendijk, T. M. V. Janssen, and M. Stokhof (eds.), *Formal Methods in the Study of Language,* Mathematical Centre Tract 135, Amsterdam, 277–322. Reprinted in: J. Groenendijk, T. M. V. Janssen, and M. Stokhof (eds.), *Truth, Interpretation and Information. Selected Papers from the Third Amsterdam Colloquium.* Dordrecht: FORIS. 1–41. Also in:

P. Portner and B. H. Partee (eds.), *Formal Semantics: The Essential Readings*. Oxford: Blackwell. 189–222.

KAMP, H. 1990. 'Prolegomena to a structural account of belief and other attitudes'. In: C. A. Anderson and J. Owens (eds.), *Propositional Attitudes: The Role of Content in Logic, Language, and Mind*. Stanford: CSLI. 27–90.

——. 1996. 'Some elements of a DRT-based theory of the representation of mental states and verbal communication.' Forthcoming as chapter 3 of H. Kamp and U. Reyle, *From Discourse to Logic II*.

——. 2001. 'Presupposition computation and presupposition justification: One aspect of the interpretation of multi-sentence discourse'. In: M. Bras and L. Vieu (eds.), *Semantic and Pragmatic Issues in Discourse and Dialogue: Experimenting with Current Dynamic Theories*. Oxford: Elsevier. 57–84.

——. 2003. 'Temporal relations inside and outside attitudinal contexts'. Handout of the paper presented at the workshop 'Where Semantics Meets Pragmatics', LSA Summer School, University of Michigan, July.

——. and U. REYLE. 1993. *From Discourse to Logic: Introduction to Modeltheoretic Semantics of Natural Language, Formal Logic and Discourse Representation Theory*. Dordrecht: Kluwer.

KAPLAN, D. 1989. 'Demonstratives: An essay on the semantics, logic, metaphysics, and epistemology of demonstratives and other indexicals'. In J. Almog, J. Perry, and H. Wettstein (eds.), *Themes from Kaplan*. New York: Oxford University Press. 481–563.

KEARNS, K. 2000. *Semantics*. London: Macmillan.

KEMPSON, R. M. 1975. *Presupposition and the Delimitation of Semantics*. Cambridge: Cambridge University Press.

——. 1977. *Semantic Theory*. Cambridge: Cambridge University Press.

——. 1979. 'Presupposition, opacity, and ambiguity'. In: C.-K. Oh and D. A. Dinneen (eds.), *Syntax and Semantics*. Vol. 11. New York: Academic Press. 283–97.

——. 1986. 'Ambiguity and the semantics–pragmatics distinction'. In: C. Travis (ed.), *Meaning and Interpretation*. Oxford: B. Blackwell. 77–103.

——. and A. CORMACK. 1981. 'Ambiguity and quantification'. *Linguistics and Philosophy* 4, 259–309.

KEMPSON, R., MEYER-VIOL, W., and D. GABBAY. 2001. *Dynamic Syntax: The Flow of Language Understanding*. Oxford: Blackwell.

KING, J. C. 2001. *Complex Demonstratives: A Quantificational Account*. Cambridge, MA: MIT Press.

——. and J. STANLEY. 2005. 'Semantics, pragmatics, and the role of semantic content'. In: Z. G. Szabó (ed.). *Semantics vs. Pragmatics*. Oxford: Oxford University Press. 111–164.

KOENIG, J.-P. 1993. 'Scalar predicates and negation: Punctual semantics and interval interpretations'. *Chicago Linguistic Society* 27. Part 2: The Parasession on Negation. 140–55.

KRAHMER, E. and K. VAN DEEMTER. 1998. 'On the interpretation of anaphoric noun phrases: Towards a full understanding of partial matches'. *Journal of Semantics* 15, 355–92.

KRIPKE, S. A. 1977. 'Speaker's reference and semantic reference'. *Midwest Studies in Philosophy* 2. Reprinted in: P. A. French, T. E. Uehling, and H. K. Wettstein (eds.), 1979. *Contemporary Perspectives in the Philosophy of Language*. Minneapolis: University of Minnesota Press. 6–27.

——. 1979. 'A puzzle about belief'. In: A. Margalit (ed.), *Meaning and Use*. Dordrecht: D. Reidel. Reprinted in: N. Salmon and S. Soames (eds.), 1988. *Propositions and Attitudes*. Oxford: Oxford University Press. 102–48.

LADUSAW, W. 1977. 'Some problems with tense in PTQ'. *Texas Linguistic Forum* 6, 89–102.

LAKOFF, G. 1970. 'A note on vagueness and ambiguity'. *Linguistic Inquiry* 1, 357–9.

LAMBRECHT, K. 1994. *Information Structure and Sentence Form*. Cambridge: Cambridge University Press.

——. and L. A. MICHAELIS. 1998. 'Sentence accent in information questions: Default and projection'. *Linguistics and Philosophy* 21, 477–544.

LARSON, R. K. and P. LUDLOW. 1993. 'Interpreted Logical Forms'. *Synthese* 95, 305–55.

LARSON, R. and G. SEGAL. 1995. *Knowledge of Meaning: An Introduction to Semantic Theory*. Cambridge, MA: MIT Press.

LASCARIDES, A. and N. ASHER. 1993. 'Temporal interpretation, discourse relations and commonsense entailment'. *Linguistics and Philosophy* 16, 437–93.

——. and A. COPESTAKE. 1998. 'Pragmatics and word meaning'. *Journal of Linguistics* 34, 387–414.

——. and J. OBERLANDER. 1993. 'Temporal coherence and defeasible knowledge'. *Theoretical Linguistics* 19, 1–37.

——., A. COPESTAKE, and E. J. BRISCOE. 1996. 'Ambiguity and coherence'. *Journal of Semantics* 13, 41–65.

——., E. J. BRISCOE, N. ASHER, and A. COPESTAKE. 1996. 'Order independent and persistent typed default unification'. *Linguistics and Philosophy* 19, 1–89.

LEITH, M. and J. CUNNINGHAM. 2001. 'Aspect and interval logic'. *Linguistics and Philosophy* 24, 331–81.

LEPORE, E. and K. LUDWIG. 2000. 'The semantics and pragmatics of complex demonstratives'. *Mind* 109, 199–240.

——. and ——. 2002. 'What is logical form?'. In: G. Preyer and G. Peter (eds.), *Logical Form and Language*. Oxford: Clarendon Press. 54–90.

LEVINSON, S. C. 1983. *Pragmatics*. Cambridge: Cambridge University Press.

——. 1987. 'Minimization and conversational inference'. In: J. Verschueren and M. Bertuccelli-Papi (eds.), *The Pragmatic Perspective. Selected Papers from the 1985 International Pragmatics Conference*. Amsterdam: J. Benjamins. 61–129.

——. 1988. 'Generalized conversational implicature and the semantics/pragmatics interface'. Unpublished paper.

LEVINSON, S. C. 1995. 'Three levels of meaning'. In: F. R. Palmer (ed.), *Grammar and Meaning. Essays in Honour of Sir John Lyons.* Cambridge: Cambridge University Press. 90–115.

——. 2000. *Presumptive Meanings: The Theory of Generalized Conversational Implicature.* Cambridge, MA: MIT Press.

——. 2003. *Space in Language and Cognition: Explorations in Cognitive Diversity.* Cambridge: Cambridge University Press.

——., S. KITA, D. B. M. HAUN, and B. H. RASCH. 2002. 'Returning the tables: Language affects spatial reasoning'. *Cognition* 84, 155–88.

——., MEIRA, S., and The Language and Cognition Group. 2003. ' "Natural concepts" in the spatial topological domain—adpositional meanings in cross-linguistic perspective: An exercise in semantic typology'. *Language* 79, 485–516.

LEWIS, D. 1973. *Counterfactuals.* Oxford: B. Blackwell.

——. 1986. *On the Plurality of Worlds.* Oxford: Blackwell.

LI, P. and L. GLEITMAN. 2002. 'Turning the tables: Language and spatial reasoning'. *Cognition* 83, 265–94.

LUDLOW, P. 1995. 'Logical form and the hidden-indexical theory: A reply to Schiffer'. *Journal of Philosophy* 92, 102–7.

——. 1996. 'The adicity of "believes" and the hidden indexical theory'. *Analysis* 56, 97–101.

——. 1999. *Semantics, Tense, and Time: An Essay in the Metaphysics of Natural Language.* Cambridge, MA: MIT Press.

——. 2000. 'Interpreted Logical Forms, belief attribution, and the dynamic lexicon'. In: K. M. Jaszczolt (ed.), *The Pragmatics of Propositional Attitude Reports.* Oxford: Elsevier Science. 31–42.

——. 2002. 'LF and natural logic'. In: G. Preyer and G. Peter (eds.), *Logical Form and Language.* Oxford: Clarendon Press. 132–68.

——. and S. NEALE. 1991. 'Indefinite descriptions: In defense of Russell'. *Linguistics and Philosophy* 14, 171–202.

LYONS, J. 1977. *Semantics* (2 volumes). Cambridge: Cambridge University Press.

LYONS, W. 1995. *Approaches to Intentionality.* Oxford: Clarendon Press.

McTAGGART, J. E. 1908. 'The unreality of time'. *Mind* 17. Reprinted in: J. E. McTaggart. 1934. *Philosophical Studies.* London: E. Arnold. 110–31.

MELLOR, D. H. 1993. 'The unreality of tense'. In: R. Le Poidevin and M. MacBeath (eds.), *The Philosophy of Time.* Oxford: Oxford University Press. 47–59.

——. 1998. *Real Time II.* London: Routledge.

MOLTMANN, F. 2003. 'Propositional attitudes without propositions'. *Synthese* 135, 77–118.

MONTAGUE, R. 1970. 'Universal Grammar'. *Theoria* 36. Reprinted in: R. Thomason (ed.). 1974. *Formal Philosophy: Selected Papers of Richard Montague.* New Haven: Yale University Press. 222–46.

——. 1973. 'The proper treatment of quantification in ordinary English'. In: K. J. J. Hintikka, J. M. E. Moravcsik, and P. Suppes (eds.), *Approaches to Natural Language: Proceedings of the 1970 Stanford Workshop on Grammar and Semantics.* Dordrecht:

D. Reidel. Reprinted in: *Formal Philosophy: Selected Papers of Richard Montague*, ed. by R. H. Thomason. 1974, New Haven: Yale University Press. 247–70.

MOZERSKY, J. M. 2001. 'Smith on times and tokens'. *Synthese* 129, 405–11.

MULKERN, A. E. 1996. 'The game of the name'. In: T. Fretheim and J. K. Gundel (eds.), *Reference and Referent Accessibility*. Amsterdam: J. Benjamins. 235–50.

MUSKENS, R. 2000. 'Underspecified semantics'. In: K. von Heusinger and U. Egli (eds.), *Reference and Anaphoric Relations*. Dordrecht: Kluwer. 311–38.

NEALE, S. 1990. *Descriptions*. Cambridge, MA: MIT Press.

——. 2001. *Facing Facts*. Oxford: Clarendon Press.

NICOLLE, S. and B. CLARK. 1999. 'Experimental pragmatics and what is said: A response to Gibbs and Moise'. *Cognition* 69, 337–354.

NOVECK, I. A. 2001. 'When children are more logical than adults: Experimental investigations of scalar implicature'. *Cognition* 78, 165–188.

——. and D. SPERBER (eds.). 2004. *Experimental Pragmatics*. Basingstoke: Palgrave Macmillan.

NUYTS, J. 2001. *Epistemic Modality, Language, and Conceptualization: A Cognitive–Pragmatic Perspective*. Amsterdam: J. Benjamins.

OGIHARA, T. 1996. *Tense, Attitudes, and Scope*. Dordrecht: Kluwer.

PALMER, F. R. 1979. *Modality and the English Modals*. London: Longman.

——. 1986. *Mood and Modality*. Cambridge: Cambridge University Press.

PAPAFRAGOU, A. 2000. *Modality: Issues in the Semantics–Pragmatics Interface*. Amsterdam: Elsevier Science.

——. 2002. 'Mindreading and verbal communication'. *Mind and Language* 17, 55–67.

——. and J. MUSOLINO. 2003. 'Scalar implicatures: Experiments at the semantics–pragmatics interface'. *Cognition* 86, 253–82.

——., C. MASSEY, and L. GLEITMAN. 2002. 'Shake, rattle,' n' roll: The representation of motion in language and cognition'. *Cognition* 84, 189–219.

PARSONS, T. 1990. *Events in the Semantics of English: A Study in Subatomic Semantics*. Cambridge, MA: MIT Press.

PARSONS, J. 2002. 'A-theory for B-theorists'. *Philosophical Quarterly* 52, 1–20.

——. 2003. 'A-theory for tense logicians'. *Analysis* 63, 4–6.

PARTEE, B. H. 1984. 'Compositionality'. In: F. Landman and F. Veltman (eds.), *Varieties of Formal Semantics*. Dordrecht: Foris. Reprinted in: B. H. Partee (ed.). 2004. *Compositionality in Formal Semantics: Selected Papers by Barbara H. Partee*. Oxford: Blackwell. 153–81.

——. 1999. 'Focus, quantification, and semantics–pragmatics issues'. In: P. Bosch and R. van der Sandt (eds.), *Focus: Linguistic, Cognitive, and Computational Perspectives*. Cambridge: Cambridge University Press. 213–231.

PEDERSON, E., E. DANZIGER, D. WILKINS, S. LEVINSON, S. KITA, and G. SENFT. 1998. 'Semantic typology and spatial conceptualization'. *Language* 74, 557–89.

PEREGRIN, J. 2000. 'Reference and inference: The case of anaphora'. In: K. von Heusinger and U. Egli (eds.), *Reference and Anaphoric Relations*. Dordrecht: Kluwer. 269–86.

Powell, G. 2001. 'Complex demonstratives'. *UCL Working Papers in Linguistics* 13, 43–71.

Pratt, I. and N. Francez. 2001. 'Temporal prepositions and temporal generalized quantifiers'. *Linguistics and Philosophy* 24, 187–222.

Prior, A. N. 1957. *Time and Modality*. Oxford: Clarendon Press.

Prior, A. N. 1967. *Past, Present and Future*. Oxford: Clarendon Press.

——. 1968. *Papers on Time and Tense*. Oxford: Clarendon Press.

——. 2003. *Papers on Time and Tense: New Edition*. Oxford: Oxford University Press.

Pustejovsky, J. 1995. *The Generative Lexicon*. Cambridge, MA: MIT Press.

Quine, W. V. O. 1956. 'Quantifiers and propositional attitudes'. *Journal of Philosophy* 53. Reprinted in: A. Marras (ed.), 1972. *Intentionality, Mind and Language*. Urbana: University of Illinois Press. 402–14.

Recanati, F. 1989a. 'The pragmatics of what is said'. *Mind and Language* 4. Reprinted in: S. Davis (ed.), 1991. *Pragmatics: A Reader*. Oxford: Oxford University Press. 97–120.

——. 1989b. 'Referential/attributive: A contextualist proposal'. *Philosophical Studies* 56, 217–49.

——. 1993. *Direct Reference: From Language to Thought*. Oxford: Blackwell.

——. 1994. 'Contextualism and anti-contextualism in the philosophy of language'. In: S. L. Tsohatzidis (ed.), *Foundations of Speech Act Theory: Philosophical and Linguistic Perspectives*. London: Routledge. 156–66.

——. 2000. *Oratio Obliqua, Oratio Recta: An Essay on Metarepresentation*. Cambridge, MA: MIT Press.

——. 2001. 'What is said'. *Synthese* 128, 75–91.

——. 2002a. 'Does linguistic communication rest on inference?'. *Mind and Language* 17, 105–26.

——. 2002b. 'The Fodorian fallacy'. *Analysis* 62, 285–9.

——. 2002c. 'Unarticulated constituents'. *Linguistics and Philosophy* 25, 299–345.

——. 2003. 'Embedded implicatures'. http://jeannicod.ccsd.cnrs.fr/documents.

——. 2004. *Literal Meaning*. Cambridge: Cambridge University Press.

Reichenbach, H. 1948. *Elements of Symbolic Logic*. New York: Macmillan.

Richard, M. 1990. *Propositional Attitudes: An Essay on Thoughts and How We Ascribe Them*. Cambridge: Cambridge University Press.

——. 1995. 'Defective contexts, accommodation, and normalization'. *Canadian Journal of Philosophy* 25, 551–70.

Rooth, M. 1996. 'Focus'. In: S. Lappin (ed.), *The Handbook of Contemporary Semantic Theory*. Oxford: Blackwell. 271–97.

van Rooy, R. 2001. 'Exhaustivity in dynamic semantics; Referential and descriptive pronouns'. *Linguistics and Philosophy* 24, 621–57.

Russell, B. 1905. 'On denoting'. *Mind* 14. Reprinted in 1956 in: *Logic and Knowledge. Essays 1901–1950*. London: George Allen and Unwin. 49–56.

——. 1919. 'Descriptions'. From *Introduction to Mathematical Philosophy*. London: George Allen and Unwin. 167–180. Reprinted in: A. P. Martinich (ed.), 1996. *The Philosophy of Language*. Oxford: Oxford University Press. 3 edn. 208–14.

SADOCK, J. M. 1984. 'Whither radical pragmatics?'. In: *Georgetown University Round Table on Languages and Linguistics 1984*. Ed. by D. Schiffrin. Washington, DC: Georgetown University Press. 139–49.

SALMON, N. 1986. *Frege's Puzzle*. Cambridge, MA: MIT Press.

VAN DER SANDT, R. A. 1988. *Context and Presupposition*. London: Croom Helm.

——. 1992. 'Presupposition projection as anaphora resolution'. *Journal of Semantics* 9, 333–77.

SANFORD, A. J. 2002. 'Context, attention and depth of processing during interpretation'. *Mind and Language* 17, 188–206.

SAUL, J. M. 2002. 'What is said and psychological reality; Grice's project and relevance theorists' criticisms'. *Linguistics and Philosophy* 25, 347–72.

SAURER, W. 1984. *A Formal Semantics of Tense, Aspect and Aktionsarten*. Reproduced by IULC.

SCHIFFER, S. 1977. 'Naming and knowing'. *Midwest Studies in Philosophy* 2. Reprinted in: P. A. French, T. E. Uehling, and H. K. Wettstein (eds.), 1979. *Contemporary Perspectives in the Philosophy of Language*. Minneapolis: University of Minnesota Press. 61–74.

——. 1982. 'Intention-based semantics'. *Notre Dame Journal of Formal Logic* 23, 119–56.

——. 1991. 'Does Mentalese have a compositional semantics?'. In: B. Loewer and G. Rey (eds.), *Meaning in Mind: Fodor and his Critics*. Oxford: Blackwell. 181–99.

——. 1992. 'Belief ascription'. *Journal of Philosophy* 89, 499–521.

——. 1994. 'A paradox of meaning'. *Noûs* 28, 279–324.

——. 1996. 'The Hidden-Indexical Theory's logical-form problem: A rejoinder'. *Analysis* 56, 92–7.

——. 2003. *The Things We Mean*. Oxford: Clarendon Press.

SEARLE, J. R. 1983. *Intentionality: An Essay in the Philosophy of Mind*. Cambridge: Cambridge University Press.

——. 1984. 'Intentionality and its place in nature'. *Synthese* 61. Reprinted in J. R. Searle, 2002. *Consciousness and Language*. Cambridge: Cambridge University Press. 77–89.

——. 1990a. 'Consciousness, unconsciousness and intentionality'. In: C. A. Anderson and J. Owens (eds.), *Propositional Attitudes: The Role of Content in Logic, Language, and Mind*. Stanford: CSLI. 269–84.

——. 1990b. 'Collective intentions and actions'. In: P. R. Cohen, J. Morgan, and M. E. Pollack (eds.), *Intentions in Communication*. Cambridge, MA: MIT Press. 401–15.

SEGAL, G. 2001. 'Two theories of names'. *Mind and Language* 16, 547–63.

SEGAL, G. M. A. 2000. *A Slim Book about Narrow Content*. Cambridge, MA: MIT Press.

SLOBIN, D. I. 1996. 'From "thought and language" to "thinking for speaking"'. In: J. J. Gumperz and S. C. Levinson (eds.), *Rethinking Linguistic Relativity*. Cambridge: Cambridge University Press. 70–96.

SOAMES, S. 1987. 'Direct reference, propositional attitudes, and semantic content'. *Philosophical Topics* 15. Reprinted in: N. Salmon and S. Soames (eds.), 1988. *Propositions and Attitudes*. Oxford: Oxford University Press. 197–239.

——. 1995. 'Beyond singular propositions?' *Canadian Journal of Philosophy* 25, 515–49.

——. 2002. *Beyond Rigidity: The Unfinished Semantic Agenda of Naming and Necessity*. Oxford: Oxford University Press.

SPENANDER, J. 2002. Presuppositions in Spoken Discourse. Doctoral dissertation, Stockholm University.

SPENCER, C. 2001. 'Belief and the principle of identity'. *Synthese* 129, 297–318.

SPERBER, D. 1985. 'Apparently irrational beliefs'. In: *On Anthropological Knowledge*. Cambridge: Cambridge University Press. 35–63.

——. 1997. 'Intuitive and reflective beliefs'. *Mind and Language* 12, 67–83.

——. 2000. 'Metarepresentations in an evolutionary perspective'. In: D. Sperber (ed.), *Metarepresentations: A Multidisciplinary Perspective*. Oxford: Oxford University Press. 117–38.

——. and D. WILSON. 1986. *Relevance: Communication and Cognition*. Oxford: Blackwell. Reprinted in 1995. 2nd edn.

——. and ——. 2002. 'Pragmatics, modularity and mind-reading'. *Mind and Language* 17, 2–23.

SRIOUTAI, J. in progress. *Time Conceptualization in Thai with Special Reference to dıai ıII, kh3oe:y, kıaml3ang, y3u:I, and cıa*. PhD dissertation, University of Cambridge.

STALNAKER, R. C. 1973. 'Presuppositions'. *Journal of Philosophical Logic* 2, 447–57.

——. 1974. 'Pragmatic presuppositions'. In: M. K. Munitz and P. K. Unger (eds.), *Semantics and Philosophy*. New York: New York University Press. 197–213.

——. 1975. 'Indicative conditionals'. *Philosophia* 5. Reprinted in A. Kasher (ed.), 1976. *Language in Focus*. Dordrecht: D. Reidel. 179–196.

——. 1976. 'Possible worlds'. *Noûs* 10, 65–75.

——. 1978. 'Assertion'. *Syntax and Semantics* 9. New York: Academic Press. Reprinted in: R. C. Stalnaker, 1999. *Context and Content*. Oxford: Oxford University Press. 78–95.

——. 1984. *Inquiry*. Cambridge, MA: MIT Press.

STANLEY, J. 2000. 'Context and logical form'. *Linguistics and Philosophy* 23, 391–434.

——. 2002. 'Making it articulated'. *Mind and Language* 17, 149–68.

——. and Z. G. SZABÓ. 2000. 'On quantifier domain restriction'. *Mind and Language* 15, 219–61.

VON STECHOW, A. 2000. 'Some remarks on choice functions and LF-movement'. In: K. von Heusinger and U. Egli (eds.), *Reference and Anaphoric Relations*. Dordrecht: Kluwer. 193–228.

STEEDMAN, M. 1997. 'Temporality'. In: J. van Benthem and A. ter Meulen (eds.), *Handbook of Logic and Language*. Amsterdam: Elsevier Science. 895–938.

DE SWART, H. 1998. *Introduction to Natural Language Semantics*. Stanford: CSLI.

SZABOLCSI, A. 1997. 'Strategies for scope taking'. In: A. Szabolcsi (ed.), *Ways of Scope Taking*. Dordrecht: Kluwer. 109–54.

TALMY, L. 1985. 'Lexicalization patterns: Semantic structure in lexical forms'. In: T. Shopen (ed.), *Language Typology and Syntactic Description*. Vol. 3. Grammatical Categories and the Lexicon. Cambridge: Cambridge University Press. 57–149.

——. 2000. *Toward a Cognitive Semantics* (2 volumes). Cambridge, MA: MIT Press.

THORNTON, A. 1987. *Maori Oral Literature as Seen by a Classicist.* Dunedin: University of Otago Press.

TRAUGOTT, E. C. 1989. 'On the rise of epistemic meanings in English: An example of subjectification in semantic change'. *Language* 65, 31–55.

——. and R. B. DASHER. 2002. *Regularity in Semantic Change*. Cambridge: Cambridge University Press.

ULTAN, R. 1972. 'The nature of future tenses'. *Working Papers on Language Universals* 8. Reprinted in: J. H. Greenberg (ed.), 1978. *Universals of Human Language*. Vol. 3, *Word Structure*. Stanford, CA: Stanford University Press. 83–123.

VELTMAN, F. 1996. 'Defaults in update semantics'. *Journal of Philosophical Logic* 25, 221–61.

VENDLER, Z. 1967. *Linguistics in Philosophy*. Ithaca: Cornell University Press.

VICENTE, B. 2002. 'What pragmatics can tell us about (literal) meaning: A critical note on Bach's theory of impliciture'. *Journal of Pragmatics* 34, 403–21.

WALKER, M. A., A. K. JOSHI, and E. F. PRINCE (eds.). 1998. *Centering Theory in Discourse*. Oxford: Clarendon Press.

WEKKER, H. C. 1976. *The Expression of Future Time in Contemporary British English*. Amsterdam: North-Holland.

WERTH, P. 1997. 'Remote worlds: The conceptual representation of linguistic *would*'. In: J. Nuyts and E. Pederson (eds.), *Language and Conceptualization*. Cambridge: Cambridge University Press. 84–115.

WHORF, B. L. 1956. 'Science and linguistics'. In: *Language, Thought and Reality: Selected Writings of Benjamin Lee Whorf*. Ed. by J. B. Carroll. Cambridge, MA: MIT Press. 207–19.

WILSON, D. 1975. *Presuppositions and Non-Truth-Conditional Semantics*. London: Academic Press.

——. 2000. 'Metarepresentation in linguistic communication'. In: D. Sperber (ed.), *Metarepresentations: A Multidisciplinary Perspective*. Oxford: Oxford University Press. 411–48.

WILSON, D. and D. SPERBER. 1993. 'Linguistic form and relevance'. *Lingua* 90, 1–25.

——. and ——. 1998. 'Pragmatics and time'. In: R. Carston and S. Uchida (eds.), *Relevance Theory: Applications and Implications*. Amsterdam: J. Benjamins. 1–22.

——. and ——. 2000. 'Truthfulness and Relevance'. *UCL Working Papers in Linguistics* 12, 215–54.

WOODS, M. 1997. *Conditionals*. Ed. by D. Wiggins. Oxford: Clarendon Press.

ZEEVAT, H. 1989. 'A compositional approach to Discourse Representation Theory'. *Linguistics and Philosophy* 12, 95–131.

——. 2000. 'Demonstratives in discourse'. *Journal of Semantics* 16, 279–313.

ZEEVAT, H. 2002. 'Explaining presupposition triggers'. In: K. van Deemter and R. Kibble (eds.), *Information Sharing: Reference and Presupposition in Language Generation and Interpretation.* Stanford: CSLI. 61–87.

ZWICKY, A. and J. SADOCK. 1975. 'Ambiguity tests and how to fail them'. In: J. P. Kimball (ed.), *Syntax and Semantics.* Vol. 4. New York: Academic Press. 1–36.

Index

Phrases such as "what is said", where analyzed in the text, are indexed in italics. Items appearing as notes are indexed as **n**, tables as **t**, and figures as **f**. In cases of abbreviations such as "WS", consult the list at the beginning of the book.